INSIDE
THE NRA

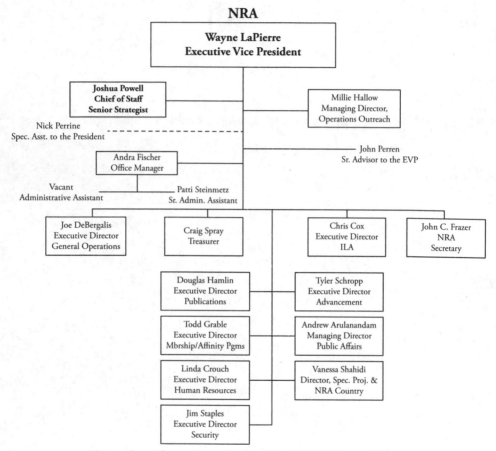

NRA

Wayne LaPierre
Executive Vice President

Joshua Powell
Chief of Staff
Senior Strategist

Millie Hallow
Managing Director,
Operations Outreach

Nick Perrine
Spec. Asst. to the President

John Perren
Sr. Advisor to the EVP

Andra Fischer
Office Manager

Vacant
Administrative Assistant

Patti Steinmetz
Sr. Admin. Assistant

Joe DeBergalis
Executive Director
General Operations

Craig Spray
Treasurer

Chris Cox
Executive Director
ILA

John C. Frazer
NRA
Secretary

Douglas Hamlin
Executive Director
Publications

Tyler Schropp
Executive Director
Advancement

Todd Grable
Executive Director
Mbrship/Affinity Pgms

Andrew Arulanandam
Managing Director
Public Affairs

Linda Crouch
Executive Director
Human Resources

Vanessa Shahidi
Director, Spec. Proj. &
NRA Country

Jim Staples
Executive Director
Security

This org chart reflects reality at the time of the 2019 NRA Annual Meeting.

INSIDE
THE NRA

*A Tell-All Account of Corruption, Greed, and
Paranoia Within the Most Powerful
Political Group in America*

Joshua L. Powell

Former Chief of Staff to Wayne LaPierre and
Senior Strategist for the National Rifle Association

TWELVE

New York Boston

Twelve
Hachette Book Group
1290 Avenue of the Americas, New York, NY 10104
twelvebooks.com
twitter.com/twelvebooks

First Edition: September 2020

Twelve is an imprint of Grand Central Publishing. The Twelve name and logo are trademarks of Hachette Book Group, Inc.

The publisher is not responsible for websites (or their content) that are not owned by the publisher.

The Hachette Speakers Bureau provides a wide range of authors for speaking events. To find out more, go to www.hachettespeakersbureau.com or call (866) 376-6591.

Unless otherwise noted, all photos courtesy of the author.

Library of Congress Cataloging-in-Publication Data has been applied for.

ISBNs: 978-1-5387-3725-5 (hardcover), 978-1-5387-3739-2 (large print), 978-1-5387-2059-2 (ebook)

Printed in the United States of America

LSC-C

10 9 8 7 6 5 4 3 2 1

This book is dedicated to the more than one hundred million gun owners, and the millions of other Americans, whatever their convictions about the Second Amendment, who deserve better.

Contents

"We must learn to live together as brothers or perish together as fools."

—Dr. Martin Luther King Jr., March 1964, St. Louis, Missouri

INSIDE
THE NRA

Fallen Angels

Friday, December 14, 2012, 9:30 a.m.
New York City—Bleecker and Broadway

After a raucous evening of too much drinking too late into the night in SoHo, I was nursing a bad hangover. I was in New York to meet with a team from Cerberus, the giant private equity firm. They had formed a fund called the Freedom Group to "roll up," or invest in, a number of gun companies, including Remington Arms and Bushmaster, in order to grow their portfolio. As somebody in the private equity retail business, a gun guy, and a fan of Remington, I was brought in in an advisory role. I had met with Bob Nardelli, the former CEO of Chrysler and now CEO of the Freedom Group, and a number of other execs at an off-site meeting in Savannah to hear their vision. I had a couple of calls planned with the guys from Remington to finalize some details from the meeting.

I had first gotten to know the group through my friend Tony

Makris, the head of the Mercury Group, a subsidiary of the marketing firm Ackerman McQueen. Through Tony I had met the Cerberus people and Wayne LaPierre, a hero of mine and the longtime executive director of the National Rifle Association. I had always been a gun rights advocate; Tony and I had met at the Safari Club in Reno, and Wayne and others had become aware of me through my efforts to pass Chicago's concealed weapons law. Since then I had become a part of the close-knit gun rights lobby, one of the gang.

9:34 a.m. Newtown, Connecticut—Sandy Hook Elementary School

"Stay put!" shouted the principal, Dawn Hochsprung, emerging from Room 9 with school psychologist Mary Sherlach. Moments later, 65-grain bullets from .223 cartridges, traveling at 3,200 feet per second, tore through their bodies and killed them both. Two shots, two kills. And with those shots, Adam Lanza had begun his killing spree.

9:34 a.m., New York City

I grabbed another coffee and a blueberry muffin at Dean & DeLuca and walked back to the apartment I was staying in.

9:35 a.m., Newtown

A caller from Sandy Hook Elementary was on the line with 911 dispatch, frantically screaming, "I hear shooting in the school. The police need to come…He's at the door, please Jesus, please Jesus." Dispatch, trying to keep the caller calm, told her to "take a deep breath, it will be okay. What's happening now?" A minute later the dispatcher delivered the message to the Newtown police officers: "Sandy Hook School caller is indicating she thinks there is someone shooting in the building."

9:37 a.m.

Police were dispatched immediately to the scene. None were prepared for what they encountered that day. Lanza had become a hunter, stalking his prey—but his targets were innocent, defenseless six- and seven-year-old elementary school children.

9:34–9:40 a.m., Sandy Hook Elementary

It is unclear whether Adam Lanza entered Classroom 8 or 10 first. In the span of six minutes he would fire 154 rounds from an AR-15. In Classroom 8, the police would find fourteen children dead, and a fifteenth would be pronounced dead after being taken to Danbury Hospital. One child survived, exiting after the officers arrived. Two other adults—substitute teacher Lauren Rousseau, thirty, and behavioral therapist Rachel D'Avino, twenty-nine—were also killed. The gunshots came from the same .223-caliber ammunition of an AR-15 rifle. At some point Lanza entered the other classroom and began targeting more victims.

9:40 a.m.

At this point, for reasons we will never know, Adam Lanza decided to stop the killing. He dropped his AR-15 rifle, with its Magpul thirty-round high-capacity magazine, to the linoleum floor in Classroom 10. He then pressed his Glock 20SF barrel against his head, just under his chin, and pulled the trigger. The 10mm hollow-point round did what it was designed to do, penetrating his skull and tearing through his cerebral cortex, killing him instantly.

In less than six minutes, Lanza had killed twenty-six children and adults, in an atrocity unparalleled in American history. He had meticulously planned and written about his intentions in the hours, days, and months preceding the day's horror. Lanza studied Sandy Hook's website and the school's security procedures, and had mapped out the massacre with obsessive detail. Investigators would later note that "he had long been on a path headed toward a deteriorating life of dysfunction and isolation." The report on the shootings went on to say that "his severe and deteriorating internalized mental health problems...combined with an atypical preoccupation with violence...[and] access to deadly weapons...proved a recipe for mass murder." In other words, this was no random event. He had been preparing and planning this unspeakable tragedy for years.

Lanza was found dressed in a "pale green pocket vest" over a black polo shirt. Everything else he wore that day was black—his T-shirt, sneakers, gloves, socks. All but two of his victims had been shot multiple times, execution style; six- and seven-year-old boys and girls were shot point-blank. The only explanation I would have later is that it was an act of pure evil.

9:57 a.m., New York City

I was with Wally McLallan, the guy who originally set up the Freedom Group with Cerberus CEO Steve Feinberg, and my girlfriend, Coco, at Wally's flat, about to jump on a call. Wally suddenly signaled to me. "Hey, man, I just saw there was a shooting up in Connecticut."

I responded, "I hope it's not a bad one. That's all we need." I spent the next few minutes flipping through the media "rundown": Drudge, CNN, Breitbart, MSNBC.

"This is not good. Turn on CNN. I hope he didn't use an AR." That was always the first question on the "checklist" we worked through when one of these shootings happened. Given my job working with Cerberus, it was the first thought on my mind, the first thought on all of our minds, something that would haunt me for years to come.

The next forty-five minutes was a flurry of phone calls. And the calls confirmed just how bad the news was. The Sandy Hook shooting was the one we all dreaded at Cerberus and at the NRA. Wally had spoken with Chris Cox—chief lobbyist at the NRA—and he was already gearing up for battle. "Just got off with Cox. It looks like the gun was possibly an AR. He and David Lehman figure mag bans, background checks, maybe even an assault weapons ban will be on the table. A total shit show."

The intensity, the rush of going into crisis mode, was oddly intoxicating. The day would be a slurry of death, politics, guns, and money, and like it or not, I had a front-row seat.

I called Tony Makris, who was Wayne LaPierre's longtime adviser. He told me, "Get ready. This is going to be the mother of all gunfights. It's really bad. There are still dead kids on the floor. Watch and learn. If we do this right the members will go nuts. Cats and dogs. I know exactly what to do."

He was completely focused on the reactions of the NRA members. That was a big part of the job. Honestly, the reality of what had taken place at the school hadn't sunk in yet, certainly for me.

The first responders to Sandy Hook described the scene as a river of red. Many have since quit the profession; human beings can only process so much. A number of the police officers on the scene that day will not discuss what they saw, for a multitude of good reasons. "Some things just shouldn't be talked or written about," one said. Seeing twenty dead young children was overload for just about anyone. The death toll would rise to twenty-seven that day, including Lanza's mother, whom he killed before coming to the school, after he took her guns for the shooting. It was a staggering amount of carnage, almost unimaginable. These were little children, innocent angels, the darlings of their parents. How does someone decide to pick up an AR-15 and shoot defenseless elementary school kids? And not just shoot them randomly, but with laser precision, putting multiple rounds in their small bodies like a terrorist militant?

I couldn't picture the fact that less than seventy miles from the apartment I was staying in, the bodies of two dozen six- and seven-year-olds were still bleeding on the floors of Sandy Hook Elementary School. Cerberus and the NRA quickly moved into fighting mode, working the checklist to figure out how to respond to the tsunami of bad publicity. *Was it an AR or a handgun? How many are dead? Did the shooter go through a background check? Did he steal the gun? What's the media saying?* We didn't miss a beat. The adrenaline and seductive intensity of the fight was palpable. It was all I could focus on. At the time, I believed we were fighting a righteous fight, on behalf of law-abiding gun owners everywhere.

That afternoon, Wally, Coco, and I settled in for a steak lunch at Peter Luger in Brooklyn, where we were joined by the owner of Crye Precision, a Brooklyn-based company that sells equipment and apparel for the U.S. armed forces, the Navy SEALS, and law enforcement officers. Conversation meandered from talk of the "war on terror" to the new film *Zero Dark Thirty*, all the while checking our phones.

"CNN says the body count will be north of twenty."

"Drudge saying two shooters but not confirmed."

"Still no indication of the gun used."

While we young "Merchants of Death" attacked our steaks and sipped glasses of French Cabernet, intoxicated with our own thoughts of defending gun rights, the country was in a state of utter shock at what had happened. But the reaction from gun owners was very different. They were sure the government would try to take away their guns. This was it. This was the time. Remington Arms, one of the companies owned by Cerberus, as well as Brownell's, the largest seller of assault rifle parts, and every gun store in America, saw their sales explode in the days that followed, as demand for the AR-15 went through the roof out of fear of a ban. Within days, lines formed at gun stores, and stores put limits on how many magazines customers could buy. It was unlike anything gun retailers and manufacturers had ever seen. On eBay a thirty-round Magpul magazine was trading at many multiples of the normal price.

We didn't talk much about the dead children over lunch, or the actual shooting. In truth, it just hadn't registered yet. At the end of lunch, someone said, "Shit. CNN just broke he used a Bushmaster AR, but it hasn't been confirmed..."

We all fell silent. Wally managed to get out "Jesus, this is not good. This is going to be bad." Bushmaster was one of the original investments in the Cerberus portfolio.

Wally stepped out to take a call, and when he came back, he said, "Feinberg is freaking out over the shooting and wants to dump Remington," referring to Steve Feinberg, the CEO of Cerberus.

"We're all getting on a call tomorrow. I called Pete Brownell [the second generation to own Brownell's in Iowa] to have him pull us a couple hundred mags, and a bunch of lowers [a gun's lower assembly]. I told him to grab half Magpul and half pressed metal. The call center in Montezuma is in meltdown mode. It's insane. He just ordered as many mags as he can get. At least if Congress bans ARs we've got the lowers..."

I still wasn't thinking about the children who died. I was completely caught up in this surreal crisis mode, trying to figure out what we needed to do and how we needed to respond.

Later that afternoon, I broke out of the bubble I was enveloped in and spoke with my ex-wife. She told me our kids—we had two young daughters—were very shaken up by the shooting. The police were going to be at school next week. Some parents were discussing pulling their kids from school. We talked about how tragic and frightening the shootings at Sandy Hook were, as I'm sure parents across the country did.

I talked to my youngest, who was six at the time, and she said, "Daddy, did you see all those kids who were killed?"

And with that, the grim reality of what had happened was beginning to set in. Finally. She was scared, and I could feel it. An awful feeling in my stomach that only a parent can know washed over me. I felt sick.

By late afternoon, images had spilled all over the media as the Newtown massacre led on every network—images of bloodstained white sheets, bodies being pushed out on gurneys, police cars, helicopters circling. Sandy Hook Elementary School looked like a war zone rather than an American school. An entire nation seemed to be asking, *How could this happen? How could twenty young children get gunned down in an elementary school?*

President Barack Obama gave a televised address on the day of the shootings. He was visibly shaken and seemed to fight to hold back his tears. "We're going to have to come together and take meaningful action to prevent more tragedies like this, regardless of the politics." His anger and sadness were palpable. "In the words of scripture, heal the brokenhearted and bind up their wounds." He would later say it was the hardest day of his presidency.

What I didn't understand yet, on that day as we leapt into panic mode to respond to the concern from our members, is that Sandy Hook marked a turning point for the NRA, and America, in terms of gun violence. The tragedy was so unimaginable—the brutal slaughtering of young children—that it scarred the nation in ways that would continue to be visible for years. I was part of a message machine that helped to perpetuate the problem and exacerbate the extremism of the gun debate, something I wouldn't fully appreciate for a long time. I would become lost. And my experience would ultimately convince me that the NRA itself had lost its mission, and lost its way too.

★

Six years later, in February 2018, Nikolas Cruz, a nineteen-year-old troubled ex-student, broke into Marjory Stoneman Douglas High School in Parkland, Florida, thirty miles northwest of Miami, and opened fire indiscriminately on classmates and teachers. Twelve students were killed inside the high school, and three more outside it. Two more died of their injuries in nearby hospitals. This killing spree sparked a national outrage. And for the first time, parents and politicians began to fight back in a bigger, more organized way. Survivors of Parkland, fellow students who had witnessed their friends die, took to the airwaves. Florida lawmakers, three weeks after the shootings in Parkland, passed the first gun control legislation in the state in twenty years, raising the age that people could buy guns from eighteen to twenty-one, and restricting those who were legally deemed mentally challenged from being able to purchase a gun.

And once again, the NRA was in the public's and the media's crosshairs. Six years had gone by, and yet Wayne LaPierre's response, first unveiled in a speech at CPAC, the Conservative Political Action Conference, was defiant. Instead of working to find solutions, Wayne went on the attack, blaming Democrats, the FBI, and socialism for the tragic shootings. He claimed that the real goal of people who advocated for gun control was to eliminate the Second Amendment and eradicate all individual freedom. And he finished his speech repeating the words he had uttered in the aftermath of Sandy Hook—that the only way to stop a bad guy with a gun was with a good guy with a gun.

Six years after Sandy Hook, it felt like we had done nothing to stop the violence and prevent shootings like Parkland from happening. And now the frustration boiled over, as the survivors of Parkland took to the airwaves to plead for an end to the violence, to plead on behalf of their slain classmates. We needed Wayne LaPierre to step up and offer genuine leadership and a way forward. And instead the NRA offered its standard playbook and the party line. It was a lost opportunity. With Parkland, all the anger over school shootings and mass murders seemed to converge, and the NRA itself was under attack once again. And I could see that the NRA needed to be fixed. I believed deeply in the Second Amendment but saw the increasingly extremist rhetoric from the NRA as a real problem that would have long-term consequences, in spite of recent wins.

A year and half before, in the summer of 2016, I had joined the association as Wayne LaPierre's chief of staff. My relationship with the NRA had continued in the years after Sandy Hook, and in 2014 I joined its board of directors, serving on the board's finance committee. Wayne desperately wanted someone to come in and help modernize the organization, and he turned to me. We had remained friends, catching up at NRA board meetings and during duck hunting trips with Tony Makris. Wayne had brought me in to streamline the organization. As he said to me on my first day at "the Building"—the name that was commonly used to refer to the NRA headquarters in the northern Virginia suburbs—"Well, it will be great if we can do this, but I don't know." Prophetic, if not exactly inspiring.

But as I quickly came to see, the waste and dysfunction at the NRA was staggering, costing the organization and its members hundreds of millions of dollars over the years. After poring though all of our vendor expenses, consulting agreements, and people on the dole for God knew what, it was apparent just how big the problem was, and how long it had gone on. It was a job doomed from the start. Ackerman McQueen, the organization's longtime marketing and media company, treated the association as its personal piggy bank, billing the NRA by 2018 almost $50 million, when you included the online streaming service NRATV, which they created and funded. Former Breitbart editor and TheBlaze television host Dana Loesch and Oliver North, who was wooed away from Fox News, received seven-figure salaries. And yet despite millions in production costs, the number of unique viewers per month was under fifty thousand. In other words, no one watched it.

And Wayne, I discovered, was personally in on the hustle. In 2019, Ackerman leaked documents showing that Wayne had billed over $275,000 in personal expenses—custom suits at a Beverly Hills Zegna—to Ackerman, which the NRA reimbursed him for, as well as hundreds of thousands of dollars for private jets and limousines to the Bahamas, Palm Beach, Reno, and Lake Como in Italy.[1] In the wake of the Parkland shootings, concerned about his personal security, Wayne and his wife, Susan, had Ackerman and the NRA explore purchasing a $6 million, eleven-thousand-square-foot mansion in a gated community beside a lake and a golf course in the Dallas area.

As I'll reveal, there are so many ways that membership money went up in smoke, due to mismanagement or incompetence or even possible corruption. The NRA's finances were so glaringly out of control that in 2019 the New York attorney general, Letitia James, opened an inquiry into the NRA's tax-exempt status.

But graft at the NRA was only part of our problem.

In hindsight, this is a sad story of a group of guys who thought they were doing the right thing, and then they weren't. Those of us at the top all had our moments of clarity, questioning what was going on. It felt like we had coined the phrase "What are we talking about?" as a kind of code to the insanity. "What are we talking about?" was applied to an array of topics during my time at the NRA. At one point or another we all had our personal meltdowns. But we forged on, like soldiers marching into a battle that they knew they couldn't win. By the fall of 2019, I'd come to believe I'd failed the team. I'd failed in my service to the membership. I'd lost the larger plot and was overtaken with just winning the fight at all costs. I became skilled at the art of giving the benefit of the doubt to NRA expense items, trying to defend what was clearly becoming obvious, years of mismanagement, often without all the facts at hand. I'd *become* the cover-up, or at least an accomplice.

This is my attempt to set the record straight. To tear back the curtain. People are going to attack me, malign me; they will be upset with the portrait I paint of the NRA. But I feel that the only way to create an organization that can genuinely better serve gun owners, and all Americans, is to show what the association has become, over the years with the current leadership. And to suggest the crucial role it *can* play in helping unite a country that today is too often divided.

The truth is, so many of the stories that I'll describe that came out in the media over the summer of 2019 were a sideshow, just as the story of Maria Butina, the Russian spy who supposedly connected oligarchs with the NRA and helped to steer Russian dark money to the Trump campaign in 2016, was a mere sideshow. There was no Russian dark money. Just a sad bunch of naïve old men seduced by a Russian agent's flattery and attention, who went on a junket to Russia when they should have stayed home.

Fake news circuses aside, I think the biggest transgression of the NRA under Wayne was that he turned the NRA into an organization of "No," in response to any effort to quell gun violence. He helped to create and fuel the toxicity of the gun debate over the years, until it became outright explosive. In the 1980s and 1990s, Wayne steered the NRA away from its roots as an organization focused on gun safety and education into a lobbying Death Star. His approach and messaging, and the NRA's, was deeply divisive, the brainchild of the angry and unrepentant Angus McQueen, head of the NRA's outside marketing firm, and the puppet master who constantly stirred up the most radical element of the association's five-million-strong membership. Any attempt to pass gun control legislation was seen as a slippery slope to overturning the Second Amendment. So Wayne, catalyzed by the messaging from Ackerman McQueen, fought fiercely against closing gun show sales loopholes and defeating universal background checks—things that the majority of gun owners are in favor of. Personally, I don't know of a single gun owner who hasn't bought a gun without having a background check.

The NRA's approach really came under fire with the rise of school shootings and mass murders. Before Columbine, in 1999, there had been no school shootings. Now there seem to be two or more a year. And parents, educators, and the public understandably would do anything to rein them in and safeguard our kids. People are angry and desperate for solutions, both to school shootings and gun violence.

They think that background checks and banning assault rifles—AR-15s—and high-capacity magazines are the solution, even if the data suggest that such measures wouldn't actually do much to curb gun violence or protect lives.

But the real point is that Wayne, and the ad agency that stood by his side for thirty-five years crafting the NRA's message, became infamous to the public for their no-holds-barred antagonism. The NRA become the doomful voice of "No." No to any gun-related suggestion if it would infringe in any way on gun rights.

To me, the NRA has completely shirked its obligations to gun owners, citizens, and the children of our country. The answer to twenty-six dead children and teachers in Sandy Hook Elementary School, thirty-two killed at Virginia Tech, twenty-six killed in Sutherland Springs, fifty-eight killed in Las Vegas, forty-nine killed in the Pulse nightclub in Orlando simply cannot be "No." No is not a solution.

Was the NRA responsible for Adam Lanza? Of course not. But they ought to help to find a solution. If not the NRA, then who? They are America's experts when it comes to guns and their use. Gun violence is an epidemic. Instead the NRA fueled a toxic debate by appealing to the paranoia and darkest side of our members, in a way that has torn at the very fabric of America. Rather than offering solutions, Wayne led a media approach that poured gas on the fire and sowed discord. He knew it would set the stage to drive more membership dollars. A tactic I was reminded of regularly. Rather than being part of the solution, working with the government and the public to find answers to gun violence, the NRA bullied and beat back any effort to find answers, or even to allow research on the subject.

This is not to say the NRA didn't have incredible impact and success on defending gun rights, but I believe it was an approach that divided the nation unnecessarily. The NRA helped craft and pass important pieces of legislation to bolster Second Amendment rights. But it also helped to pass legislation that banned research into gun violence. And it managed to get federal legislation through that protected gun manufacturers from being sued. Yes, the NRA had reasons for its positions—reasons I understand. Because the issue of gun rights is complex and nuanced; you can't reduce it to a 280-character tweet. But the only message to the public, to the grieving parents and classmates, that the NRA could offer was: more guns.

Egged on constantly by Angus McQueen, the real firebrand behind this rhetoric, Wayne in essence bowed to the most militant and extreme faction of the NRA's five million members. Whenever the organization fell short in its funding drives, Wayne would "pour gasoline on the fire" to ignite donations. And that strategy worked, time and again.

What Wayne didn't do was broaden the membership and reach out to the hundred million gun owners in the United States.[2] The NRA, I felt strongly, should be speaking for *all* gun owners, and all law-abiding citizens, not just the militant few. Polls show that most gun owners are in favor of universal background checks, banning bump stocks, and other solutions. Most gun owners are mothers, fathers, sons, daughters, construction workers, librarians, scientists, teachers—part of the fabric of America. They are as eager and determined to solve the issue of school shootings as anyone. But the NRA continues to focus its messaging and advertising toward the extreme fringe, continually stoking a toxic debate, hell-bent on keeping those donation dollars coming.

In my three and half years as the number two figure in the NRA, working side by side with Wayne, I saw incredible incompetence, a culture of political backbiting, and a *Game of Thrones* atmosphere that people outside our Merchants of Death bubble would never believe. Rather than being a well-oiled, data-driven lobbying machine, we were stuck back in the Dark Ages. There was no war room at the NRA, no coordinated effort between our lobbyists. There was no data machine that kicked out metrics the way a top-notch political lobbying shop would have.

As Wayne said to me on many occasions, "Josh, come on, you know it's all smoke and mirrors. The Wizard of Oz. Just pull back the green curtain."

He said it with a smile, and laughed! But I felt like I'd been punched in the gut. Smoke and fucking mirrors.

What I expected was a modern political machine, with computers flickering with algorithms, analysis, and messaging data. The truth is, Wayne abandoned the advocacy of the Second Amendment years ago and became exactly what he himself had once railed against in countless speeches and commercials—the elite, the Establishment, lost in a made-up dystopian world that he had created and sold to our members. Frankly, gun owners and everyday American citizens deserve a better advocate.

One time, after a *Hannity* segment on Fox, Wayne said candidly to me, "Josh, you know it's all an act. It's all show." An act and delusion the media bought, the members paid for, and we all believed.

Perhaps the crowning achievement of the National Rifle Association as a lobbying organization was the election of Donald Trump in 2016. But do the math, and the effect the NRA had on the 2016 presidential election was not what you might think. It wasn't the money or election hocus-pocus as we claimed, and believed, or that the media spun. The NRA political budget, even at $55 million—$30 million of which went to supporting Donald Trump—was a drop in the bucket.[3] To win an election you need votes. The simple truth was a whole bunch of gun-toting "deplorables" did just that. They voted. To them it was a choice between Lord Don or Lucifer Hillary. It was an easy choice for them. Our membership believed deep in their bones that Hillary would come for their guns, take away their right to protect themselves. Wayne and the senior leadership of the NRA had beat that response into them like Pavlov's dogs for twenty years.

Did Trump evolve into a Second Amendment guy? Sure, no question. The groundwork had been laid with his two older sons, who were NRA members; they hunted, shot, collected, the whole thing. They even got themselves in trouble for hunting lions!

On election night, as NBC called the race for Trump, Chuck Todd announced, "The NRA just bought themselves a Supreme Court justice."

I told Wayne at the time with all sincerity, "Congratulations, you just saved the Second Amendment."

Wayne, as always, said, "We all did it together."

The entire NRA felt vindicated. We had put all of our chips on Trump and the bet had paid off.

Little did we know how the years after would unfold for us.

While the NRA had been an early supporter of Donald Trump's campaign, having a pro-gun president ironically hurt the organization in terms of membership and donations. The association's fundraising efforts ran on fear, and the fear of gun rights being eroded disappeared with a Republican president and Congress.

And then came the lawsuits, the legal bills, and the infighting, leading to the quagmire the NRA finds itself in now. The state of New York started investigating where the NRA's money went. And when we tried, for the first time in our history, to get accurate billing records from Ackerman McQueen, whom we were paying untold millions, we were stonewalled. In 2019, lawsuits between the NRA and Ackerman McQueen flew back and forth. And then NRA president Oliver North, whose $2 million salary was paid by Ackerman McQueen, attempted to force Wayne to resign at the 2019 annual convention in Indianapolis, in order to keep the Ackerman spigot of graft flowing. The convention was a total shit show, with leaked letters to the media about an extortion attempt by North on the eve of a convention that was to be keynoted by—that's right—President Donald J. Trump. Wayne and I prevailed in this attempted coup, and North resigned on the eve of the board meeting, which became the number one news story in the world that day. Ultimately we fired Ackerman McQueen, severing our thirty-five-year relationship with the firm. In the wake of the attempted coup, NRA chief lobbyist Chris Cox, who had allied himself with North, was let go. In the end, eight board members resigned, longtime counsels Charles Cooper and Steve Hart were ushered out, and I departed in January 2020 myself. They assumed I'd be bought off in exchange for my silence and cooperation. They were wrong. In many ways it was a relief; I had lost my moral compass and come too close to the edge. Or to put it another way, I was an expendable pawn in a game that had become primarily about protecting the king.

As I'll spell out in this book, the finances of the NRA are in shambles; it has operated in the red for the past three years, despite annual revenues of roughly $350 million a year. An organization whose primary mission was originally devoted to gun safety, training, and education now spends only a small percentage of its budget on those things. The NRA had begun to mimic the "grifter" culture of Conservative Inc. It devolved into "how do I get mine?"—the same Establishment culture that had been robbing the conservative movement for decades and led to the rise of the Tea Party. And it derailed the NRA's mission. In spite of Wayne's attempts to paint the other side as the "Elites," he himself was the epitome of elitism, robbing every $45-dues-paying member to cover the costs of his own extravagance and his shameful mismanagement of a multi-hundred-million-dollar association.

And the New York investigation into the NRA and its tax-exempt status continues to pose an existential threat to NRA leadership and the nonprofit's very existence.

As I experienced firsthand every day, the NRA is closer in its politics and intrigue to the Vatican, and Wayne LaPierre was our pope. That last year I was there, rather than serving the membership, or advancing Second Amendment rights (which I firmly believe in), or attempting to appeal to the broader audience of gun owners in America, I found myself in a desperate battle to save the pope, to save Wayne, at any cost. Despite my zeal to reform the NRA, I had turned into the Establishment. I had been led to the dark side, and spent every hour of every day doing whatever was necessary to advance that goal. Our loyalties lay only with Wayne, rather than with the association or the members. There is nothing principled about that. And that was not what I had signed up for.

★

When I was a kid growing up on the shores of a small lake in Plainwell, Michigan, near Kalamazoo, the NRA meant something to me and to our community. Folks placed the round NRA sticker on the back of their truck with pride. They were members of a nationwide organization that supported gun rights and firearms training. In my small town in rural Michigan, all my classmates had guns. We all grew up shooting and fishing like so many boys do in the middle of the country. Back then, school shootings like Columbine didn't happen. During deer season some of us kept our rifles in our lockers on Fridays. It was a bucolic, almost Tom Sawyer–like upbringing. I wouldn't have recognized the adult Josh, working at the NRA, operating in the political vortex of Washington, where loyalty is traded like the baseball cards of my youth.

In what was to be my last summer at the NRA, in August 2019, I drove home to Plainwell for a visit. A few miles from my dad's place, I stopped at the Doster Country Store, not because I really needed anything but because in my mind that signaled I was home. Doster's is a local landmark. I bought a Diet Coke and a Slim Jim, and there I was, back in the town I grew up in, among the people who knew me as a boy. I don't even drink Diet Coke anymore. But I do there. And I ran straight into one of my father's friends, Jack, sporting denim overalls, with a few pencils, a ruler, and a small folding knife in his front pockets. "Your old man tells me you're working at the NRA! Cool." He pulled out his wallet. "I just got my new card!

"Hey, what was all that hubbub down in Indy about Ollie North?" he asked, referring to the NRA Annual Meeting in April.

"Just some family feud," I responded. "You know how that goes."

And as he stuck out a callused hand and said, "Great seeing you," it hit me so hard it nearly took my breath away.

What the fuck are you doing? I asked myself. *Jack is the beating heart of the National Rifle Association. A law-abiding, honest American who believes in God and country. And here I am, Mr. Chief of Staff, after taking the $45 he sent in last week, trying to explain away to the* New York Times *why it was okay that Wayne had expensed a private jet to the Bahamas to meet with some donor.*

I was caught in a position of trying to say that was all right. That the only answer to school shootings was to say: more guns. And that sums up my fault and the principal failure of the NRA. Its utter moral failure to serve the 100 million gun owners of America, the

5 million NRA members, and the 330 million citizens of our nation. It was a Wizard of Oz routine—it was all an act and a show—one that had ended badly.

Josh, I said to myself, *you have lost your way.*

What follows is a story of the money, greed, and incompetence that has brought the NRA to its knees. A story that will expose the inherent weakness of what the country sees as the most powerful lobbying group in history. It's a story of loyalties that shift with the wind. Of a paranoid, terrified CEO who went from being a puppet of his longtime ad agency to a puppet of a slick New York lawyer whom I helped hire. A story about an entirely screwed-up organization and CEO whose only answer to the gun debate was to push the fear button. But I tell it not just to pull back the curtain on the Wizard and show you how misguided and lost I found the NRA to be. I do it not to sell out—I am writing this book because I have to take you on a journey through the messy parts to show you what an organization like the NRA could be under better leadership. I do it out of a sense of hope for the future, for a better organization that can more effectively serve both gun owners and America.

Wayne's absence of leadership in the face of those gunned-down children in the schoolrooms of Sandy Hook and Parkland was unforgivable. Didn't he have a duty to show up, express empathy, and find a way forward? But that takes courage, and a commitment to something greater and bigger than yourself. As I would discover, Wayne LaPierre was only loyal to one thing: himself and his own survival. As his right-hand man, I witnessed what I saw as a stunning display of lies, petty politics, and a desperate effort to save himself at any cost. Wayne thought he *was* the NRA. His real loyalty was not to the Second Amendment, or to the NRA, or to the national debate on guns and gun violence, but to saving his own skin.

And I had bought into it all. I sold it, stirred it, drank it every day. I had protected and defended Wayne LaPierre, at all costs, for over three years. I was a true believer. I continue to hold our country's Second Amendment rights close to my heart. It is a uniquely American freedom, the birthright of every citizen. But my actions and speaking out for what's right will no longer be held hostage by the NRA or Wayne LaPierre.

There has to a better way for all Americans. I truly believe that, and I'm not going to give up on that belief quite yet.

That's why I'm writing this book. I'm going to find my way. To atone for my own failures, and present a better path forward for the membership of the NRA, for the hundred million gun owners who are not members, and for every American who wants their children to feel safer in our land of liberty and opportunity.

CHAPTER 1

I Am the NRA

I was born in Kalamazoo, Michigan, on May 8, 1973, and grew up in Plainwell, to the northwest, on the shores of a small lake in the neighborhood, Pine Lake, with my mom, dad, and younger brother, Noah. We moved there when I was in second grade. My parents found me an old fourteen-foot flat-bottomed boat that became my best friend. It had a four-horsepower Johnson engine, and leaked just enough that I carried around a bailer made out of a milk carton to keep the water out. I would spend the summers exploring the lake with my dog, fishing, hunting for turtles, camping on various islands. As I said, it was very much a Tom Sawyer–like existence. My friends and I would run around in the woods and the gravel pit with BB guns, shooting at chipmunks. Later, when I was older, my friends and I graduated to .22 Remingtons and then shotguns.

My dad was a professional photographer. We fished together, but he wasn't a hunter or a gun guy. But he had a very good friend, Carl, who had a German shorthaired pointer, and he would take me out sometimes to go bird hunting. I'll never forget when Carl first flipped open his gun case and put together his over-and-under shotgun. As a ten-year-old, I was intoxicated with all the trappings and gear of bird hunting: the dogs, the vests, the guns. Most summers Dad and Carl would go up north to the Au Sable River and fish the big hatch, which to brown trout fishermen was like the Super Bowl. Big flies and big fish. I'd wait until my dad got back to hear the stories. I longed to go, and finally got my shot as a young teenager. It was a place that prided itself on doing things "the way they had been done." I just fell in love with all of it—watching the old guys work thread at the fly-tying bench was incredibly alluring. Every time they went out fishing, they would record their catches in a book and make notes on the size, species, and location: *17" Brown Trout caught 2:00 am July 15th, brown hex, 50 yards beyond the landing.*

The first time I fired a shotgun was with a grade school pal of mine. Shane and I basically walked out his back door and shot at some cans. Not exactly with parental oversight. I'll never forget that sound of racking a shell in an 870. Very cool to my ears. I truly believe that a lot of boys are born with this hunter-gatherer gene, and when exposed to the right situation it can switch on and take off. I'll never forget being in Chicago on an elevator with a woman and her young son. He was smiling and holding his hand up like a gun: *bang, bang.* His mother was mortified. "I'm so sorry. He saw some show where they were shooting animals and he won't stop." I told her, "No, no, it's fine, really. It's just something boys have in their DNA." As we got out she said, "Thanks. I think you're right, it's just, you know." To me, that quick conversation was the epitome of the push-pull argument and allure of guns—it's often a debate about human nature.

When I was twelve a friend took me out duck hunting, and I was hooked immediately. Talk about cool stuff! Decoys, duck calls, shotguns. You get to call these birds, watch them decoy in, and all hell erupts when you start shooting. The dogs are running to retrieve birds; it all happens in seconds. I was hooked, and it remains my passion to this day.

The lake I grew up on had a couple good spots where you could hunt ducks, so my mom and I decided to give it try. We went to Walmart, picked up a couple camouflage jackets and some decoys, and hopped in my boat and headed across the lake. We had no idea what we were doing. I wasn't a very good shot at this point, and I'm sure I didn't hit a thing, but I sure shot at a lot. We had a brilliant time, duck hunting and fishing. Those memories with Mom are some of my favorites growing up. We'd go crappie fishing in the spring and she'd bring a book to read, occasionally asking me how it was going.

"Well, if you don't keep trying, you won't catch anything," she'd say.

She was my biggest cheerleader. I can't imagine a better way to be born into the legacy of the outdoors, learning to fish and hunt.

My mom and dad bought me a trap machine for my birthday one year, the kind you hand-cock and that throws clay targets. We screwed this thing down to our dock on the lake. Mom would pull, and I'd shoot. And that was my introduction to clay shooting. I'm sure we'd get in big trouble for doing that today—check that, we'd be thrown in jail today! But damn, it was cool, shooting over the lake with my mom pulling targets (and probably drinking a gin and tonic).

Living in a small town in rural Michigan, I grew up around guns, and all my classmates had guns. As I mentioned in the prologue, during deer season some of us kept our rifles in our lockers on Fridays. Lots of folks proudly put their NRA sticker on the back of their car. I think they felt connected to a larger, nationwide community, and a lifestyle.

It harkened back to the rugged individualism of our country's pioneers, I guess. The fact that we could hunt and fish, and bring home food for dinner, made us feel self-reliant to some degree. We were very lucky in that sense. And appreciating that kind of freedom is a trait that seems to resonate with the NRA membership then and today.

One of the things I got into as a teenager was skiing—and downhill racing. In the winters, my mom and I would travel all over Michigan, Wisconsin, and Minnesota skiing, going to practice after practice, race after race. Over time I got to be pretty good, and in my junior year of high school I attended Killington Mountain School in Vermont. It was a ski academy, like nearby Burke Mountain Academy that Olympian Mikaela Shiffrin later went to. And I loved it.

As a racer I wanted to be on that edge—crash and burn or join the winner's circle! I had a very up-and-down year on the slopes, but the hard work we put in every day changed my life. My dad would say later it was the best money he ever spent. When you put yourself out there alone on a course, you learn a lot. No one to rely on but yourself. No one to blame but yourself. And in that way, ski racing was the opposite of politics, where you can always find someone else to blame.

My mother had always battled depression, and we were going through a hard time after my junior year away, so I stopped skiing, and didn't go back for my senior year. I felt I had to be home for family. It was probably the hardest period of my life. I was lost without a purpose and worried about my mom.

☆

That summer I got into racing sailboats and made friends with a guy named Billy who traded on the floor of the Chicago Board Options Exchange. One day he took me down to the floor. I'll never forget going down the escalators and how the noise got louder and louder as we drew closer, with bells clanging and everybody yelling. Billy brought me down to the McDonald's and Honeywell pit where he traded for Steve Fossett, the well-known businessman, trader, and adventurer. Billy told me, "Hey, just stand in the back of the pit for a bit." It was electric and I wanted to work there. I was always good at math, and I loved the magic of the trading floor. I thought, *This is what I want to do, hardstop.*

I ended up applying to and getting accepted at Xavier University in Cincinnati for the fall of my freshman year. But by the end of the semester I knew I wanted to move to Chicago and get a job as a clerk on the trading floor. I finished the fall semester, did well, and told my dad I was moving to Chicago. He was really pissed at me, to say the least, but I was determined, and finally my parents accepted my decision. As a friend of theirs said to them, "Look, it's not like he's joining a rock band. He's going to work and going to school at night. What's so bad about that?"

I was off and running. I sort of leaped into adulthood. I worked all day on the floor, and went to Loyola University, and later Northwestern University, at night, studying economics. For me it was great: I got a small paycheck, a small apartment, and some meaning and structure in my life. What more could I ask for?

I thrived on the trading floor. My first job was with Jon Najarian, also known as Dr. J (everyone on the floor had a three-letter badge. His was DRJ. Mine was POW. Or *POW!* according to others). I still see Dr. J all the time on CNBC giving his opinions and thoughts on the markets. He had played football for the Bears back in the day and was a hell of a trader. I had to bug the hell out of him, but he finally gave me a job as a clerk. I was always thankful that he and his brother gave me a shot.

I clerked for a few different firms, and studied markets along the way. My goal was to be a trader when I was twenty-one, the legal age. As a clerk, I'd take my traders' cards and make sure their positions were correct. I became good at this real quick—the importance of getting it right meant real money. Nowadays this job is done by a computer. It was amazing training to be responsible for hundreds of trades a day, and it gave me a front-row seat into how it all worked. I'd study Sheldon Natenberg's book *Option Volatility and Pricing*, the holy grail of option traders, when it was slow, and then I'd grab lunch for the guys and bring it to the floor.

The cadence of the day was typically busy after the open at 7:20 a.m. if we were trading interest rates, or 8:00 a.m. if we were trading other things, and then would settle in by 10:00 a.m. A lot of us would head upstairs until the afternoon trade kicked in. Liar's poker would take over the slow parts of the day. It was basically a game glorified by Michael Lewis's book of the same name. Fold up a dollar bill and play your numbers. Pure poker.

As a clerk working for Dr. J in the Compaq pit (remember Compaq computers?) I shot my mouth off a lot, and one day I made an absurd bet: one game, $1,000, or I shave my head. So here I was, the *entire* trading floor watching me and a guy named Dice. Everyone had thrown their money in the pot, which was now sitting on top of a CQG machine.

And I lost. I was summarily escorted across the street from the Board of Trade to the barber, who shaved my head. Dr. J loved it. We played hard, win or lose. He loved that rap.

Many of the traders I worked for played cards or chess to pass the time while watching the markets to see if they moved. One of them, Greg Baird, was always after me to play him in Acquire, a complicated board game about investing in businesses. He was one of the biggest traders in the Eurodollar pit, second only to Margie Teller, who was all of a hundred pounds soaking wet, but was the baddest trader in the city. Greg was a guy with a giant tolerance for pain who rode his big trades better than nearly anyone in the pit. When everyone else was making pennies on a trade, Greg was taking dollars. I learned a tremendous amount from him. He'd grab me during the down times, and we'd play and play until the markets moved. The games were fiercely competitive, and he would absolutely lay into anyone who made a bad move. Think about that—a competitor who was pissed when *you* made a mistake. He always wanted to play against the best, and it pissed him off when you weren't.

I have ADD, which was a huge plus on the trading floor, because I could absorb a ton of information and make decisions based on it. The busier it was, the better for me. Trading was the great leveler. Only about one of ten guys made it on the floor. As a trader you had to recognize when you were wrong, get out, and move on to the next trade. It also requires a high level of creative thinking, as markets are always changing in response to new realities. It teaches you to be brutally honest with yourself, because if you bullshit yourself, you're dead. If you don't make money you don't get paid. It's capitalism to the *n*th degree.

As time went on, I became bored with studying economics at Northwestern. The truth was, I was living and breathing the market every day on the trading floor. I would listen to some professor teaching us about the theoretical pricing of bonds, and I would be thinking, *A, you're wrong, and B, how is this helping me?* That sounds a little cocky, and I was, but it was also true.

The one thing I did love was game theory. I became friends with one of the professors who taught game theory at the University of Chicago, and we would hang out after work. We'd play chess and talk theory and trading, and I learned more from our conversations than I did from my classes. He appreciated the creativity it took to be a successful trader, as well as the math behind it. Recently I heard Tom Sosnoff, a veteran trader and very successful entrepreneur, say, "I don't know much, but I do know this: Traders may not know much about relationships, or pop culture, but they do know math. Never challenge a trader to a math problem." It became a foundational pillar in my life. You gotta do the math.

So I finally told my parents I was done with school for now. That did not go over well. I had almost enough credits to graduate from Northwestern. But I never looked back. I began trading Eurodollar futures when I turned twenty-one. After working for Greg Baird, I had found someone to stake me, Brad Glass, another trader in the pit. Brad was great. Our deal was simple: He put up the money, I traded, and we split the profits 50/50. He was incredibly nuts and bolts, and passed that on to me. He took advantage of the opportunities that day, made his money, and went home.

I'd trade until 2:30 p.m., go home, take a nap, then park cars for a restaurant in Lincoln Park at night. And the next day, press replay. I remember thinking, *I just want to make enough money so that I can afford Starbucks every day.*

Some trades took place within minutes or less, while other positions I would hold on to for hours or days. I was able to work my way into the pit and really began to learn the nuances. It was one thing to be a clerk, and entirely different to make the calls yourself. I loved the pressure—it was a tough, tough place, with lots of pushing, shoving, and yelling. I realized that if I could survive on the Chicago Mercantile Exchange, where I worked subsequently, I could make it anywhere. It was as cutthroat as it got.

The thing was, you had to be able to do math in your head

quickly, so I taught myself shortcuts. And the more chaotic the market was, the better for me, because somehow I was able to see over the top of it all and make some pretty good decisions. I was good at looking at a screwed-up situation where lots of orders and trades were pouring in and figuring out what was really going on. It's a skill that has served me well in life.

Professionally, my low point as a trader occurred a few years into this when I built a small firm with a couple guys backed by J. P. Oosterbaan, the former college basketball star who won the national championship at Michigan. He and his partner Joel backed our small firm, and we got access to capital and a back office in return.

So I was trading the AT&T and At Home merger and it went completely backwards. And I mean completely. I finally realized how bad my position was and started to unwind my mistake. It took me weeks, and I lost a ton of money, well into seven figures, which was a mortifying amount of money back then. The worst thing was, I kind of messed up the whole group—a few of us had thrown our money in together and I had lost it. I felt really awful and wanted to make it back for J.P., Joel, and my partners.

Incredibly, those guys were great about it. J.P. told me, "Look, go take some time off and get your head straight and we can get it back. Come back when you're ready and not before."

So I did. J.P. realized I screwed up, but it was one out of a hundred positions. There is not a single successful entrepreneur, investor, builder who has not had his or her head on the chopping block at one time or another. It's simply part of the learning curve.

I had gotten married a few years before, and my wife was from Hawaii, so we took off for the islands and I completely checked out. A month or so went by, and when I came back, I made all of the money back and then some over the next few months. It was a great

31

comeback, and I was most happy for my partners, who kept the faith. It's a hard thing to stare into the abyss like that and come back.

But I learned an important lesson—recognize when you've made a mistake and get out. That's very difficult when you're dealing with stock options and you're carrying a large position. It can take time. J.P. had taught me many trading lessons and life lessons that I probably didn't fully realize at the time. Most important: how to deal with people when they make a mistake.

Sure, I screwed up. Badly. He could have fired me. Instead he did the opposite. He offered encouragement, helped me pull myself up by my bootstraps, get back in the pit, and win.

I had been in Chicago roughly ten years when I went back to the Chicago Mercantile Exchange, the world's leading market for derivatives. Basically I was trading short-term interest rate futures for Eurodollars. It was great to be back on that floor. I'd matured and grown as a trader and was able to deal with more complex positions and stomach more risk.

Soon afterward, the exchange announced that they were going to have computerized trading. I told the head of the firm I had joined that we needed to have somebody on a computer upstairs, to trade against what I was going to be doing on the floor. So we talked about different strategies of how to build out this high-frequency trading desk. And we were one of the first to do it. We hired a programmer, and he and I worked together to create what later became the model for the entire firm.

No matter how you cut it, trading is like life. You need to pay your dues. It takes time.

★

And then one day, driving home, after giving it a lot of thought, I felt it was time to move on. I walked away cold turkey.

Part of me felt liberated—I'd been staring at the markets 24/7 for fifteen years. There were times when I second-guessed myself, when I would think I should have stayed. But honestly, it was an intense life that is somewhat myopic in its focus. Most traders just cared about if the markets moved—it didn't matter which way or why. (Ironically, as I write this book in Montana I'm now back to trading the markets again in the middle of the COVID-19 pandemic.)

But I intuitively realized I needed to get out and see more of how the world worked, rather than just trade markets. I also wanted to get serious about pursuing clay shooting, and began to practice four days a week. Mentally, for me it was important to be successful in the sport. I love it to this day. I'm fortunate that it's taken me to tournaments around the world, from Dubai to England to half a dozen European countries and throughout the United States. On any given day I find myself competing with the top amateurs in the world, and even nipping at the heels of the pros at times. One of the unique aspects of shooting is that you compete alongside the best in the world; to put it in golf terms, you get to compete alongside Tiger Woods or Rickie Fowler. I plan to chase around flying targets until I can no longer pick up my shotgun. Nothing beats being tested alongside the best, seeing how you stack up.

And I had decided to make a complete left turn professionally, starting a high-end outdoor clothing company, a kind of Orvis meets Ralph Lauren—authentic, adventure-oriented, really high-quality stuff. Expensive, but cool. And we created a catalog to sell it.

I had met Burt Avedon, who had owned Willis & Geiger Outfitters—he must have been eighty at the time—and Susan Colby, his partner and chief designer. Susan was a powerhouse and an incredibly talented woman who was born in New York and had been at the pinnacle of fashion throughout her career. Willis & Geiger was an expeditionary outfitting company that made safari jackets for Ernest Hemingway back in the day. They made the first flight jacket. They supplied people like Amelia Earhart, Sir Edmund Hillary, and other explorers. The company was bought and sold, most recently to Lands' End, which discontinued the line in 1999.

Anyway, Burt was an elegant, handsome, stylish man straight out of central casting. And he explained the whole business to me. So I decided to go for it. I found some investors, raised a chunk of money, and we launched the catalog. Burt had been very successful with his catalog at Lands' End, so he helped me put it together. I wrote all the copy myself, and I made it incredibly irreverent. And I used myself as one of the models for the clothing we sold (you can ask my investors if this helped or hurt our cause). But somehow, I went from being a trader to writing catalog copy! What was great about the business was that ultimately it was all about math: The cost to acquire customers, their lifetime value and stickiness all played a part in being successful in that business. And that math would hold me in good stead later at the NRA.

I sort of modeled the catalog after J. Peterman, whose catalog became famous in the 1990s as a result of being spoofed on *Seinfeld*, and because a number of celebrities, such as Paul Newman and Clint Eastwood, Tom Hanks and Oprah Winfrey, bought their stuff. This was their description of a flapper dress: *Enter the new woman: rebellious, out there, living life on her own terms... Feels like a whisper in silky crinkly georgette. Which could be the only thing about it that whispers.*

In fact, John Peterman appreciated our catalog enough that he called me one day to compliment me on the copy and layouts.

Anyway, it was a hell of a lot of fun to build something, and we got off to a great start.

And then the 2008 economic meltdown hit, up to that point the biggest economic downturn since the Great Depression. I remember we were right in the middle of raising capital for the company, and all at once the funding stopped as the market imploded. Suddenly I had inventory bills that weren't getting paid. A lot of businesses went under, and like many of them, we found ourselves working with our vendors to reschedule payment terms. It was a very tough time navigating through it, but somehow we kept it alive; I renegotiated this and that to keep it going.

Around this time my second wife and I separated and we finalized our divorce a few years later. Certainly the pressures of keeping the business afloat had taken its toll on us. We had two young daughters, and we both poured ourselves into supporting and raising them. It certainly didn't come without its difficulties.

In the end I had to sell off half of the company to a group of investors, Bruce Willard and some others who had been in the catalog business at L.L.Bean. Bruce and his team had been very successful in building Territory Ahead and Athleta. We were very optimistic about the partnership, and I stayed on for a couple of years, but Bruce and I did not see eye to eye.

So I left in 2011, although J.L. Powell continued on for another eight years, and started another clothing company and built a private equity consulting team focusing on the retail industry. That business got me in front of a number of private equity firms and the opportunity to work on turning around a number of projects for them. A lot in my life was changing. And one of the biggest was that I met my soul mate, partner, and wife, Colleen.

☆

When I first launched the J.L. Powell clothing catalog in 2006, it became very popular and built a cult following, especially within the gun and hunting community. I still hear from folks to this day, and back then it landed me an invitation to the Safari Club in Reno, where I met Tony Makris.

Tony was the president of the Mercury Group, the political subsidiary of the PR firm Ackerman McQueen. And he and I hit it off. We bonded over hunting. He sort of looks like a more mature version of Val Kilmer as Doc Holliday in the movie *Tombstone*—same beard and goatee, same boyish, loving-life kind of face. He was a modern-day Teddy Roosevelt and could tell a story with the best of them.

Tony was basically Wayne LaPierre's right-hand man and closest friend for over two decades. Their relationship went back to the 1980s, when Makris served as a deputy assistant defense secretary under Caspar Weinberger in the Reagan administration, and Wayne was lobbying gun rights on behalf of the NRA on Capitol Hill.

As the head of the Mercury Group, Tony was the guy who brought Charlton Heston into the NRA—they'd met back in the early '80s as part of a coalition against a nuclear-freeze referendum, and stayed in touch ever since. Heston had become a champion of many defense and foreign policy issues and Makris was his main adviser. They talked every day in the '90s, when Heston became an NRA vice president, and later president. Tony was with Moses at the NRA convention in 2000 when he so famously held his rifle above his head and said to the audience, "From my cold dead hands."

Tony told me that before the speech, he had talked to Heston to suggest what he should say to the annual conference crowd, and Heston told him, "I've got this."

Apparently he did. His response to Tony as he walked off the stage, after the crowd erupted in response to what would become one of the most iconic NRA speeches of all time, was, "Well, how was that?" A delivery that only Charlton Heston could pull off.

Walking into Tony's private party at the Safari Club was straight out of a Scorsese film, with all the gun makers from England, professional hunters from Africa, the wealthy who wanted to be just like them. I walked in and there was Tom Selleck talking to Wayne LaPierre. Tony introduced me to everyone. He'd brought me into the gun community sphere and I was very thankful. At some point I struck up a conversation with Wayne, who had been something of a hero of mine—he helped to lobby for and twist politicians' arms to pass most of the gun laws that gun owners today take for granted. And living in a city like Chicago, which at the time had the highest number of murders in the country, I was a huge gun rights advocate.

So Wayne and I hit it off, and talked for some time about previous gun rights battles, and the initiatives to come. He was telling me about a program in Richmond, Virginia, begun in the late 1990s, that was incredibly effective. Project Exile brought down the murder rate by 33 percent the first year it was implemented, and 21 percent the next year. He and I talked ad nauseam about this project, and how we wanted to bring it to Chicago.

At this point, Chicago was a war zone. There were three thousand shootings a year, and over five hundred homicides. We needed real solutions to the gun violence problem, so I was hugely interested in Project Exile.

At the end of our conversation, Wayne gave me his private phone number, so that we could stay in touch, and we did. And of course, Tony and I got together all the time. His longtime award-winning show, *Under Wild Skies*, which he hosted for NBC Sports Network and then later the Outdoor Channel, was his pride and joy, and I got to join him on a few trips. He and I traveled together to Patagonia for a photo shoot for the J.L. Powell catalog—there is a picture of us together smoking cigars and gazing out at the sunset. We spent two weeks there fishing and hunting. The copy I wrote for the catalog, under our picture, was *Bags of Cubans, bottles of Scotch, enough red meat to appease any man, and certainly enough fresh air to make you wonder why you settle for the norm.*

A few years later, Tony called me up and said, "Hey, Wayne LaPierre and I are going to shoot ducks in Kansas—you ought to come." Well, you don't have to ask me twice about duck hunting! Two weeks later I piled the truck full of gear and dogs and met the guys in Kansas. We stayed at a lodge and got up early, at 5:00 a.m., had some coffee, and drove half an hour or so to a flooded timber hole, before making our way to the blind. Wayne and I would talk in the predawn dark about the NRA and what he wanted it to look like. He would tell me about his efforts at the NRA in the '80s and '90s, before it became the powerful lobbying group it was now. And I loved hearing about the history of the place. Sandwiched between Tony and me, who were both competitive shooters, Wayne was in for a challenge. He had gotten a bad rap over the years for not being much of a shot. And of course, we're busting each other's balls over who's shooting well, who's not. It was great fun. But Wayne held his own, and knocked down his birds. I had brought out a young dog named Baron, and despite Tony's badgering he got the job done. The more Makris teased Baron the more my dog would try and make him his pal, as if to say, "Okay, here's another duck, Ace. Can I get some love now?" Later, back in the lodge, Tony, Wayne, and I sat around a massive table and Tony held court, telling one story after another about hunting ducks on the Chesapeake, lions in Africa. Our duck hunting outing had been filmed for Tony's show, and we looked at some of the footage we shot that day, interspersed with a constant banter over who shot better. It became a running joke.

Through Wayne, and especially Tony, I made a lot of connections to people in the NRA world, including Wally McLallen, the guy who put the original deal together to form the Freedom Group, who had been a huge fan of J.L. Powell. In 2012, I started a consulting group, and one of my first clients was the Freedom Group. The company was owned by Cerberus Capital Management, headed by Steve Feinberg. They had bought Remington Arms and renamed it the Freedom Group, and acquired some manufacturers and brands, including Mountain Khakis, Para, and others to add to the Freedom Group umbrella.

They asked me to come in and help think through a rebuild/ rebrand of Remington, and work with the Mountain Khakis team to launch their catalog and build out line extensions within the Freedom Group Portfolio. Remington is a very old, historic company, created in the nineteenth century—it's America's oldest gun manufacturer, and the largest producer of shotguns and rifles—but had suffered a gap in quality over the past decade. The Freedom Group believed they could really rebuild the Remington brand, and bring it back to some of its former glory. Ultimately it was an incredibly difficult task to retool the manufacturing side, reinvent the brand, and achieve the growth that was expected. In May 2018 the company had to file for bankruptcy, burdened with an overleveraged debt structure, and had to be restructured. No CEO could have worked through the amount of debt placed on it, together with other challenges. It was a classic example of private equity attempting to borrow the bank—so that it was overleveraged with debt—and they paid the price.

They were one of our clients in 2012 when Adam Lanza opened fire in Sandy Hook Elementary School, and I got pulled into the maelstrom of Remington's and the NRA's response.

Wayne and I continued to talk, and in 2013 he suggested that, given my background in finance and my interest in gun rights and the Second Amendment, I run for the NRA board. The NRA has a byzantine board structure—there are seventy-six board members, which is almost unheard of. Trying to get the board to agree on anything was like convening the Italian parliament. And as Wayne admitted to me in confidence, they exercised almost no genuine oversight on the NRA executive leadership. Wayne or senior members of the NRA indicated who they wanted nominated to the board when there was an empty seat, and that recommendation went to the ten-member nominating committee, was placed on the ballot, and essentially whoever was on the ballot was voted in. Voting is limited to lifetime members and members in good standing—those who have paid dues for a minimum of five consecutive years.

I joined the NRA board in 2014, when I was appointed to the finance committee, the investment oversight committee, and the shotgun committee (which was not about overseeing shotgun weddings, but maybe it should have been). It wasn't a lot of work. We didn't get paid, although our travel expenses were reimbursed, and only got together three times a year, twice in Washington at the NRA headquarters and once at the annual convention.

I discovered that the finance committee was more of a rubber stamp. We weren't really there to question Wayne's expenditures or Chris Cox's lobbying efforts.

The NRA's board of directors was established half a century ago, which is why there were so many board members. Nobody with half a brain would set up an organization like this today. It had led to the lack of oversight that plagues the organization to this day. That said, the board is made up of an incredibly diverse group of people, but it acts more like Congress than an oversight board.

There are something like fifty different committees that board members sit on. There is an audit committee. There is an urban affairs committee, which actually did have a positive impact, I felt, on the NRA's attitude toward civil rights and inner-city communities, but in light of where the country is today, the NRA spent next to nothing on the effort. Talk is talk. There's a silhouette target committee. There is the aforementioned ten-member nominating committee, a shotgun committee, the Annual Meeting committee, and probably a committee on committees—we had committees for everything. Only one-third of the board is up for reelection in any given year.

While the board members are not paid, a number of them have lucrative contracts with the NRA, which leads to enormous conflicts of interest. The NRA itself, as I would discover, did a horrible job of compliance. The place—and Wayne especially—operated with pure politics as the first consideration in their decision making, which included the quid pro quo way of operating, which led to all the contracts with board members. *If we do this, so-and-so will be happy and they'll vote with us for this or that.*

I'll give you an example: A couple of years later when Oliver North had been dismissed as NRA president, I was listening to Wayne and his aide, Millie Hallow. They were talking about who to put in as vice president to fill the void, as Carolyn Meadows would be sliding up to be president. The guy they were talking about was absolutely wrong for the position. We needed a really steady hand, someone who understood the legal challenges in front of us. But that was the thing. Every decision made at the NRA was a political calculation. Wayne and the leadership were constantly playing the inside game about who to appoint, versus finding who's right for the position. Even Dean Cain, the actor who played Superman in the TV series *Lois & Clark*, was thrown into the turnstile of board members, and Wayne would regularly say to me, "He could run the place someday." I'm thinking, "Uh, okay, why? Because he's kind of famous, or is it the fictional cape thing? Or maybe, just maybe, the board ought to run an actual process to get a qualified CEO?" It was about who liked who, and always stacking the board in Wayne's favor. Many times I found myself thinking the same way, rather than if the person was a good fit for the job. But this time was different. So I stuck my head in and said, "Guys, are you kidding me? What are you talking about? This is the kind of stuff that got us in trouble with the state attorneys general in the first place. Can't we just appoint someone who's good at the job and not make it a contest for homecoming king or queen? How about we put in Charles Cotton? The guy is super bright, runs the audit committee, and knows the playing field regarding all the litigation. Heck, the guy is a lawyer himself."

Cotton had been on the board for a number of years. He was steady, but politically astute. We wouldn't have to worry about him going off the reservation the way North had. Wayne quickly agreed, and he was able to get Cotton to take the position.

Every time I came to Washington for a board meeting I would have a private meeting with Wayne and we would discuss all things NRA, in particular the larger strategic stuff. Where did he see the NRA in the next twenty-five years? How do we get there? For me it was intellectually stimulating. During that time we got close, sharing ideas like moving the organization out of Washington to the Midwest where it would be easier to find people who wanted to work at the association. Nashville and Houston became our top contenders. Wayne wanted to move and personally wanted to get out of the Beltway. He had grown to really despise the place.

My connection with Wayne around this type of thinking ultimately led to a bigger role for me, within the NRA itself.

CHAPTER 2

The Wizard of Oz

In the spring of 2016, I got a call from Wayne LaPierre. I remember
I had just dropped the kids off at school—it was a cold day—and
I was in South Bend, Indiana, driving home on I-80. And out of the
blue he asked me, "Hey, I was wondering if you would be interested
in coming in as my chief of staff here."

Of course I was interested—it was like having Vince Lombardi
say, *Hey, do you want to come help me coach the Packers?* After a lengthy
conversation about his thoughts on what he wanted to accomplish,
I suggested, "Why don't I come to Washington and let's sit down
together and put down on paper what our goals for this would be?"

We spent a number of sessions in a private room above Landini's
in Old Town Alexandria, working on what he wanted to achieve in
a very thoughtful effort to make sure we were on the same page. I
consulted with friends and mentors about taking the position and for
a general reality check. One of them was a very prominent guy who
had shepherded nearly all the secretaries of defense into the Pentagon.

He had strongly recommended that we approach the job in this fashion: "Wayne has to fully buy in to this from day one—if you guys are not aligned every day, you're dead. Simple as that." Prophetic words.

As an NRA board member, prior to working for him, I talked with Wayne all the time about how the NRA needed to be modernized, how it needed to be streamlined and brought into the twenty-first century—how we needed to implement systems and measure our efforts on marketing and membership, measuring ROI (return on investment) and applying basic business practices. Wayne knew the way the NRA spent money was out of control, and the decision making was very political in nature. Whenever short of money, his answer was to pull another rabbit out of a hat by raising more money, which he did for many years until the numbers simply became too large.

Over dinner, Wayne and I talked a lot about what he wanted to do with the association. We agreed that I'd commit to three or four years, tops, and I would move on, and he was more than amenable to that. He had talked about leaving the NRA and I wanted to go out with him, if not before. He knew it was dysfunctional, really on every level. From ILA—the Institute for Legislative Action, the lobbying group that Chris Cox ran—to the public relations–driven Ackerman McQueen, to all the other internal engines, from membership to marketing, no one knew what anyone else was doing; everyone operated in his or her own silo. Every division had its own website and marketing team. There were all these fiefdoms and everyone was constantly fighting over keeping or expanding their control over each other.

For example, "General Operations," which includes the education training department, the competitions division, the Friends of NRA, and other stuff, had a completely separate marketing and PR team from the one that reported to Wayne. We were holding firearms competitions in some of the most arcane shooting sports in the country. These were completely out of date, with negative growth, but they still existed because somebody on the board cared about them, even if only 150 people competed. And God forbid we stopped spending money on a sport that had zero interest and put it into other competitions like trap shooting, which was outpacing every other high school sport in the country.

You simply could not overcome the bureaucracy that had grown up around the NRA. Every decision was based on politics, and small tit-for-tat politics at that. But I wanted to help; this was my chance to do something I believed in. In most ways, Wayne saw the same problems I did—a bloated, outdated association that was run by board politics and acted a lot like Congress, where once a program was in place you couldn't get rid of it.

So I would be the number two guy under Wayne. We had three or four meetings that spring to make sure we were aligned, and I had some real authority. When I brought up personnel, Wayne was a bit evasive. I later discovered he was sort of micromanaging people, while not really managing them at all. He never had big staff meetings, and no one really trusted anyone else. His management style was, as his wife, Susan, would say, "no management style at all." He'd meet with people separately, yes them to death, and then he'd disappear. What he called the "rope-a-dope."

And Wayne, bringing me into his fold, did much the same to me.

★

I flew into Washington one rainy night in June 2016 to begin my career at the National Rifle Association. The NRA headquarters is located at 11250 Waples Mill Road in Fairfax, Virginia, about twenty miles west of Washington. The front of the building is relatively nondescript architecturally, a six-floor modern building with a blue-tinted glass façade with two V-shaped arms reaching out to each side.

While I had been there several times in my capacity as a board member, that first day I felt like a fish out of water. It was the first job I'd had in decades where I would have a boss I reported to. I had been a successful trader on the Chicago Mercantile Exchange for over fifteen years, and had had partners, and had built and sold other businesses, but I put all that aside to work for Wayne.

To enter the building, I needed an electronic key card to get past two security gates; there was a security desk in the middle of the reception area. And to the right, there is a huge, fourteen-foot stuffed polar bear that had been shot a with a pistol by Bob Petersen, the guy who founded *Motor Trend* magazine. Bob had been a huge supporter of the NRA and had donated a ton of money to the organization with the shepherding of Tony Makris. For years, Tony had a dual role as Wayne's consigliere, and someone who arranged high-dollar donations to the NRA.

After clearing the security gates, I made my way to the elevator bank. The senior executive staff of the NRA—the "Royals," as I discovered many of the staff referred to us—were located on the sixth floor. The NRA has about six hundred employees. And honestly, I have no idea what most of them do. I'm positive it could be run with 20 percent of that number. On the other hand, it's an incredibly diverse workforce—we had a lot of women, people of every background, religion, and sexual preference. In spite of having an old white guy reputation, inside the NRA was a lot hipper than you might think. And every one of those folks believed in the NRA's mission.

We didn't have an open floor plan. Instead, we had this bizarre, cavernous labyrinth of offices that allowed for zero facetime. Most of the senior people had large offices, all of which were adorned with some type of bronze statue or art piece. It felt like I'd gone back in time to the 1970s.

What distinguishes the place from most corporations or

nonprofits is a ton of folks there have guns, which they either carry to and from work, or that they keep at their desk. The place is armed to the teeth. People open carry their Glocks around like John Wayne—which is completely legal in Virginia, and some employees made a point about exercising that right.

In other words, folks had their gun displayed on their hip, or in a shoulder holster like Sonny Crockett from *Miami Vice*. To be fair, I occasionally put mine on as well. I kept a 9mm Glock in a safe in my office. It was just part of the NRA culture. And there has never been an incident involving firearms at the "building," as NRA staff members refer to headquarters, other than, ironically, one security guard accidentally discharging his firearm into his thigh at the shooting range.

That said, the joke among the security guards is that God forbid we have an active shooter in the building and everyone starts shooting at each other. It would turn into a standoff scene out of a Coen brothers movie. On the other hand, if you are an active shooter, this is not the building to enter.

Another thing that makes the NRA building unusual is that there is a big shooting range in the basement of one wing of the building, which is open to both staff members and the public. We had two auditoriums, one in the sub-basement and another on the second floor, where we had visitors, and award ceremonies for NRA commendations and plaques and medals at the end of the year, which I discovered were a big deal. Outside citizens like a police officer in a high-profile shooting would be honored at the board meeting. The cop of the year was a major NRA award, and the question was always who was going to introduce it and who was going to win. But there were plenty of awards given throughout the year—it was an inexpensive way to motivate the staff and membership and give everyone a feel-good moment.

The lobbying arm of the association—the Institute for Legislative

Action, or ILA—which was run by Chris Cox, was located on the fifth floor. And the rest of the executive team—Wayne, his executive assistant Millie Hallow, the office of general counsel, and General Operations, including my office—was located on the sixth floor.

Membership and publications—*American Rifleman*—were on the third and fourth floors. And there is an amazing museum open to the public on the first floor in the other wing, filled with firearms and shooting paraphernalia spanning hundreds of years—rifles from the American Revolution, the French and Indian War, the Civil War. They've got a Gatling gun, Annie Oakley's F. Hambrusch shotgun, and the largest collection of Parker side-by-sides in the country. Guns used in Hollywood movies, rifles from World War I, World War II, Korea, Vietnam, Iraq, you name it—it is one of the most highly regarded collections of firearms in the world, a kind of celebration of the allure and craftsmanship of finely made handguns and rifles and their place in American history. And the museum director, Phil Schreier, who runs it is super knowledgeable. He is also the co-host of the NRA's *Gun Gurus* show on YouTube, exploring the stories behind history's most famous firearms. Over the years, when I needed a break, I would call him up at times just to shoot the breeze about the difference between the Remington 3200 and a K80 or the Parker collection.

Phil was a scholar and a heck of a nice guy. Once I called him up needing a serious mental break and said, "Phil, I hear we have a few safes in the place. You got any time for a quick tour?" Of course he did, and so I went down to where Phil opened a giant door and showed me all these Remington prints and war memorabilia, and on and on. I ended up borrowing a very cool Beretta print with multiple engravings of revolvers to decorate my office. But I never fully got moved into my office and I never really felt like it was mine.

The dress code at headquarters veered toward the formal. The directors of the different departments would wear a suit and tie—but most folks there wore suits and ties or jackets and ties. We dressed more casually in the summers, but it felt like I was entering a time warp, where the employees looked like FBI agents from the '70s and '80s. The place had almost a military bearing to it, in a way—everyone who wasn't a director called me "sir." And I would tell them, "Please, just Josh." One of the things I tried to do was to encourage Wayne to get people to let their hair down a little more. We should make the NRA a more fun place to work, I told him. We got the education and training department some cool tactical wear, and they seemed happy about it. It was hard enough to hire smart, talented people, as most people didn't want to be associated with the NRA, much less work there.

As the chief of staff to Wayne, I did wear a suit and tie. But I was a senior executive, and I'm also someone who liked dressing well; to me, it was like putting on armor. It allowed me to fit into any situation, from meeting with lawyers to dealing with banks to sitting down with board members. So I wore nice suits. (That said, I bought them myself, on my own dime.)

That first day of work after my appointment was announced, Wayne wasn't there. So I asked Millie Hallow, Wayne's executive assistant, which office was mine. (Millie's official title in the org chart is Managing Director, Operations Outreach.) Millie was like the office mom—she was about in her late sixties, always calm, and had been with Wayne for almost the entire time he was there. She also served as a liaison between Wayne and the board, and for a time as a liaison between Wayne and Chris, and was a fixture within many conservative political circles. I would call her the board whisperer. Many folks would tell me I couldn't trust Millie, but I did completely. For me she had a good heart, and that was in rare supply around that place. Her currency was information and she always had the latest intel. I'd heard later that Melania Trump had taken a run at getting her to join the First Lady's staff, which is no surprise, knowing Millie's connections in the Beltway.

But Millie had no idea about my being hired, or my position. Wayne hadn't told her—or anyone else—anything. "Let me figure it out," she said.

Usually, when Wayne makes an important decision, he tends to lobby the whole world. For whatever reason, when he hired me, he didn't tell anybody.

Millie soon decided the office next to Wayne's was mine. My office was about ten feet from Wayne's, and when I walked in for the first time it was like I'd opened the door to a time capsule. There were stacks of videotapes, ashtrays—all it was missing was one of the original Commodore 64 computers. The office of Wayne's *former* chief of staff had been archived, stuck in the 1980s, and left untouched ever since. Charming, but in need of an update.

I asked the folks in our office, "Hey, how about we throw everything out, put some new paint up, maybe some new carpet, and start there?" My wife bought me one of those fancy espresso machines that in later years achieved something of its own celebrity as the news outlets trounced us when the free coffee service to the employees was removed. Anyone who knows me knows I pretty much mainline coffee all day long right up to bed.

The response to the office renovation was an overwhelming yes. It was time for some changes.

✯

Later that week, Wayne came into the building and I went into his office to report in. While he had a big bureau desk, he never sat behind it, as I would discover. There was also a big eight-person conference table, and that is where Wayne held court. There were no pictures on the walls or on his desk, even of his wife, Susan, no books or memorabilia, no computer monitor or television. His desk was bare. He did have a big bronze eagle that seemed to regard the room as if it were looking for prey. He had a private bathroom, and behind his office was a smaller room filled with six-foot-high stacks of yellow legal pads. That was how he recorded his notes. He didn't keep a filing drawer or draft memos. He didn't use a computer, let alone text or email. It was a strategy that made things nearly impossible to manage, but the net effect was a limited paper trail. Now, I could text him, but he never replied by text or email. He preferred to talk in person or over the phone. In fact, he was on the phone all day long, one call after another, in almost manic fashion. It was how he kept his ear to the ground on Second Amendment issues. Angus McQueen, the CEO of Ackerman McQueen, would often call several times a day, and Wayne always took his call. Millie handled his daily schedule to some degree.

But don't get me wrong, it wasn't as if he didn't have a system. In one late-night conversation I was talking with Wayne about Bernie Sanders's position on guns back in the 1980s. So he went in the back room, pulled out a notepad from one of the stacks, and emerged a minute later with an ad placed by Bernie's election campaign from 1988.

Incredible. Lesson learned. Wayne was shrewd, he had a system. I would call him chaotically organized. Later, I learned Wayne's garage was also filled with yellow legal pads, and I mean filled.

Wayne never drank or did drugs. His one vice was ice cream. To me, he was this mad scientist kind of character: awkward, shy, introspective, not someone who gravitated toward the limelight. There was a joke around the office that the only way to make eye contact with Wayne was to lie down on the floor while talking to him.[1] But he was also someone who read everything you put in front of him. He would go through every word of a speech or piece of copy, letter, or ad. He was meticulous but also withholding and avoidant of any sort of conflict. And while he was often reticent when among strangers or in an environment that felt unsafe or unfamiliar—he had a finely developed sense of paranoia, undoubtedly a result of the constant stress he felt as the firebrand behind one of nation's most powerful lobbies—on the flip side he could be outgoing and effusive in working the room among people he knew and felt comfortable around.

The real Wayne, of course, wasn't this flame-breathing, terrifying, all-powerful wizard. In fact, he was meek and surprisingly approachable—he would talk to anyone. There was not a dash of snobbery or elitism to him. In fact, I found Wayne evinced more of a "poor me" quality, perhaps after decades of having to play the part of the NRA's hard-fisted gladiator, defending gun rights against an onslaught of antigun zealots. He had devoted his life to the NRA. He had no children, no other hobbies. In many respects he probably felt he was the NRA, and there was a part of him that was a little tired of it.

From our talks together over the years, I learned that Wayne never really had any plans to lead the NRA. He grew up in Roanoke, Virginia—his father was an accountant for GE. He got his undergraduate degree from Siena College in New York, and entered a PhD program at Boston College in political science, only to ditch it to help a Democrat run for the Virginia legislature.

So, funnily enough, Wayne started out as a Democrat. The guy he helped elect was a huge gun rights supporter, which brought Wayne to the NRA in the late 1970s, just about the time the association was shifting from its roots in hunting and gun safety and training to become more of a lobbying and political organization. The association started its political action committee, the Political Victory Fund, in 1976. By the 1980s, the NRA started to use Wayne as a spokesperson in the media on Second Amendment issues, despite the fact that he was quiet and shy in person, more of an absentminded professor than a rabble-rousing firebrand. Radio shows became his testing ground, and Wayne worked hard at developing his oratory skills and media personality over the years. He became executive director in 1991 almost by default. As he said in an interview in the *New York Times Magazine*, "I never set out for any of this to happen."[2]

★

I had met Chris Cox, our chief lobbyist, years earlier, but I wouldn't say I knew him well. He was always skeptical of me, for reasons that became clear pretty soon on my arrival at the building. I had been labeled an Ackerman guy, although I didn't know it at the time. Chris had been at the NRA his entire career, and had been the association's chief lobbyist and principal political strategist for ILA since 2002. In 2016, ILA had seventy-eight staff members and a budget of $30 million.[3] Chris was a smart guy, polished, good-looking, a terrific speaker. But he was very territorial, and was clearly freaked out by my addition to the association. He saw himself as the heir to the throne when Wayne left or retired. Period. Hardstop. That was how everyone saw him.

Wayne had been around so long that there was a constant undercurrent of who's going to succeed him. At this point Wayne was in his mid-sixties. And Chris saw me as a threat to his succession. I had Wayne's ear, most of the division heads reported to him through me, and I became the gatekeeper to his office and schedule. So Chris and I always had a strained relationship, which was never my intention. My hope was that we would be this incredible team together. That's one of my top regrets about my time there. While we didn't agree philosophically or tactically, we both had an unwavering commitment to the mission. Together, we could have really fixed the mess at the NRA and led the place into the future. I think he misunderstood me, and I didn't understand that folks viewed me as an Ackerman plant.

Wayne made it clear to me that ILA was to be treated like a black box. "Don't mess with that. We don't want to upset Chris." ILA was tasked with running all election campaigns, including direct support for candidates, the presidential election, lobbying the House, the Senate, and all state-level lobbying. Chris had his hand in a lot of things. While the institute is just a division of the NRA, it was completely hived off, with its own accounting, which was the epitome of a black box. It was by far the sexiest and most interesting part of the NRA. Chris was a terrific salesman, which went hand in hand with being a lobbyist. Skills that worked well on Capitol Hill and with the board of directors. Managing people was another thing. He came from a well-to-do family in Nashville. But his weakness was that he couldn't stand to have failures on his record. He was a deeply political animal, and his viewpoint was that losing a political fight was a bad thing, whatever the loss. And I found him to be insecure, and as such he didn't generally deal with the congressmen or senators directly.

At the Capitol Grill in Georgetown, Chris was one of the top lobbyists with power, money, and swag. But he didn't run around with celebrities, or the politicians themselves, for the most part. His connections were mostly to their back office—not the people who voted, but the staff who got things done. And his power, and the lobbying power of the NRA, came not from the money we spent, but from the roughly thirty thousand NRA voters in every congressional district. And all the tens of thousands of other gun owners in each district who weren't members but who voted our way on gun issues. The NRA was one of the top three lobbying groups in Washington, behind only big pharma and the chambers of commerce.

Chris pretty much ran his own shop and kept Wayne sidelined. And that's the way Wayne's whole world operated—out of fear. He didn't like to upset people. He hated confrontation. And if you yelled loud enough and carried on enough in front of him, you could usually get a green light on whatever the issue was—approval of an ad, money for whatever. And part of my new job was to make sure that didn't happen anymore.

The guy who became my best friend at the NRA was Andrew Arulanandam. He had worked for the association for a long time, but under Chris. And he pretty much came to despise Chris and the way he operated. Chris would berate people in emails—he seemed to have no filter. When Andrew told Wayne, "I'm going to quit. I'm not working for this guy anymore," Wayne brought him over to our group. Andrew is a PR shop's pro. If you can handle the daily PR grind at the NRA, you can handle anything. It's the ultimate proving ground.

Shortly after I started, Chris blew up at Andrew over something PR-related in a long, intimidating email couched in language that talked down to Andrew and made it clear that Chris thought he was better than him. I was furious, and went in to talk to Wayne. "I'm not going to put up with people bullying other employees. This has got to stop. It's a company-wide problem and I can't in good conscience do nothing. My title is chief of staff, right? If this goes unanswered now it will never stop." So I fired off an email to Chris, saying in essence, "If you have a problem with Andrew, you can address it directly with me from now on. And please do not talk to my employees like this moving forward; if you have an issue please bring it directly to my attention." Chris of course refused to accept blame. He would deflect any blame and put the onus on the other person—they were the ones, in his mind, who had screwed up. And I'm sure he was right much of the time. My point was, however, whether a mistake was made or not, you just can't treat people that way. There has to be a better, more humane, more effective approach. It's just good management.

So Chris was on notice with me, and I was on his radar too. Andrew appreciated what I viewed as simply doing the right thing, and I continued to have his back. And while Chris stopped treating the people directly under me like this, his overall behavior—including going around me and Wayne—didn't improve. He constantly complained about and berated Randy Kozuch, one of the nicest people I've ever met, who did a superb job reaching out to the state governors and the current vice president. But Chris was so insecure, he had to constantly prove he was top dog. He hated the fact that Randy had his own relationships within the White House. Once again I went to Wayne to complain. "This bullying at the NRA has to stop." But Wayne seemed to throw his hands up, "I know, I know," as if saying that was enough. Heck, I wanted him to do something about it. Chris and his chief of staff's behavior toward other employees bothered me deeply.

So began our contest of wills.

★

The NRA is pretty much a nine-to-five culture, although Wayne and I would work late many nights. I'd get into work at 9:00 a.m. and stay until 5:30 or 6:00 p.m., or if Wayne was there late, until the boss left. I'd hold a couple of meetings with staff, which unsettled Wayne, oddly enough, because he rarely called staff meetings. His management style was to let the place run on its own, in a kind of free-for-all approach.

I would check in with Wayne every day at 10:00 a.m., whether he was in the office or not. We'd talk over whatever was going on, and as he said, make sure I didn't "get in front of" him—in other words, to make sure Wayne knew what I was working on. Which was great. I didn't want him to ever be surprised with me. As far as I was concerned, I worked for Wayne, and I strictly honored that chain of command. I was maniacally transparent with him on everything. Wayne knew everyone I was talking to. Why? Because we had plenty of other headaches to worry about, without worrying about each other.

But I wasn't above joking around with Wayne, at the right time. He was particularly interested in reaching out to the membership, because that is where our money, and our clout, came from. I remember walking in late to one meeting, and Wayne and Gurney Sloan, the head of Membership Marketing Partners (MMP), which handled our membership, were standing at Wayne's conference table with a big contact sheet in front of them, showing all the new potential NRA member cards with the logos they were considering. And without even looking, I said, "I don't know, guys. What do you think this time? Flags? Minutemen? Are we going to do eagles?"

And they took me seriously. "I don't know," Wayne said. And I looked at them with a straight face, and they both looked up at me and realized, "Oh, you're just messing with us."

I mean, we're the NRA, like what else were we going to do? What else did we ever do?

At the end of the day, I would head over to a well-known watering hole nearby that was known simply as "the club," where everyone from Paul Manafort to John Boehner to Tom Cole, the congressman from Oklahoma (and a great guy)—the whole conservative gaggle—seemed to go to have a drink or two and unwind. I would see guys from the CIA, some ex–FBI agents, a few Pentagon folks, some former assistant secretaries of defense. The place had a couple of floors, maybe ten thousand square feet, and a walk-in glass humidor, and you could sit and have a drink or order dinner, with your cigar, while catching up with your friends. It was a political junkie's hangout. I never ordered off a menu, and the food was the best in town. I often had meetings there, and I was on my phone constantly working until I left. That was a given with me—my cell phone bill was $500 a month, rolling calls 24/7, following up on work. That was just the nature of the job and I really enjoyed the pace of it.

I tried to keep up my competitive clay shooting as much as I could, but it became harder and harder. Although we had that huge shooting range in the basement of the NRA building, I never seemed to have the time to use it either.

Ultimately, as chief of staff, I gained oversight of pretty much everything over time, except for Chris's shop at the ILA. Almost everything that came to Wayne would come through me. I would talk to the division heads, until I shifted my focus in 2018 to the litigation in New York, working with our outside counsel Bill Brewer, and basically disconnected from all of the operational duties.

Wayne would come in sporadically. Not always on Mondays, never on Fridays. And of course he traveled a lot. I worked out my deal with him before I started, because my kids were back in Michigan. So every other Thursday through Monday I would be back in Michigan with my kids, and on the phone, of course, with Wayne, Ackerman McQueen, or one of our seventy-six board members—a constant barrage of calls that didn't end until I went to bed. But that was fine, it was the job I signed up for, and I knew I was there for a limited time and did not want to look back and regret not trying to do more.

☆

What I quickly learned about the NRA was how bloated it was. Rather than a sleek high-tech lobbying organization, I found it was actually a low-tech, cumbersome bureaucracy. It didn't measure or invest in its marketing to customers or potential customers the way a typical direct marketing company would. It was a very shortsighted, short-term outlook. The problem was the CFOs we had didn't take the time nor have the skills to do that. What was the lifetime value of new customers acquired? How did we manage a budget to build a larger membership base? There was no conversation around ROI when it came to the money we spent. Instead, the thinking was, *Well, if we've got $300 million in revenue, we should have $300 million in expenses.* And there was virtually no oversight. We didn't bid out contracts, so our vendors overcharged the heck out of us, just because they could. We had a call center in Ohio that was getting paid many times the normal rate, in an absurd contract we had with them. It is but one example of the lack of governance and oversight on the part of the finance committee and the board in general. No one at the NRA knew any better. Woody Phillips, our longtime CFO, appeared completely absent.

This "system" evolved in part because the NRA isn't a for-profit institution. The attitude among the senior execs was, *Hey, if we break even, and the cause is just—fighting for Second Amendment rights—we're doing okay.* Leadership's calculus on money was different from the private sector. The entire accounting department were bookkeepers; they did not understand how to actually partner with divisions and provide support to grow and build a business. Just add and subtract. To be fair to them, that sort of approach comes from the top, from the CFO, and that philosophy was simply nonexistent. I'd regularly take calls from membership marketing folks complaining that they had yet to meet with the CFO and explain what they do. Which was to generate over $100 million a year. And yet the folks at the top—Woody, and later Craig Spray—seemed to have no interest in understanding just how that worked, how to support it, and how to grow it.

Wayne had been there thirty-five years, and as I discovered in the first few weeks, he couldn't run an organization on a fiscally sound basis to save his life.

Is he politically smart? One hundred percent.

Did he help to make us what we are? Of course.

Should he be involved? Absolutely.

But he shouldn't be running operations, not even close.

And this is something the NRA's board has known for decades. Wayne was almost tossed out in the late 1990s for fiscal mismanagement. I remember having a conversation with him, telling him we had to measure our return on our membership dollars: If we invest more to acquire more members, what does that look like downstream, twelve, twenty-four, or thirty-six months from now? What's the lifetime value of that member? And how do we prospect for new members much more aggressively, like any other modern direct marketing company? And Wayne's eyes would glaze over—it was like I was from outer space, speaking an alien language.

During the eight years of the Obama administration, we had a ton of membership money and donations coming in. It was driven by the fear factor—our members were afraid that Obama was going to take away their guns, pass a new assault rifle ban again, and expand background checks. After Sandy Hook, gun owners on eBay were auctioning $15 AR-15 magazines for five times that price. It was a crazy time. The membership money and donations were an open spigot at that point. And if we needed more, Wayne would just pour "gasoline on the fire," as he put it.

But that was exactly what had gotten us into the position we were in. We only knew one speed and one direction: Sell the fear. Pour gasoline on the fire. It worked to excite the most extreme faction of our membership—they ate it up.

Case in point: When Wayne said famously at the Sandy Hook press conference, "The only thing that stops a bad guy with a gun is a good guy with a gun," America exploded.

Outside of it simply not being true, it is tone-deaf in terms of talking to upset parents, politicians, educators, and even gun owners. The media went berserk. Even inside the NRA, there was significant division on the press conference, which was panned by the media as tone-deaf and seen as the worst PR move of all time.

But if you measured success by money in the NRA coffers, and ultimately beating back the suggestion of universal background checks, it was a huge success.

It was classic, high-octane "gasoline."

In the long run, however, Wayne became unapologetic and extreme. And he did nothing to broaden the appeal of the NRA with the ninety-five million gun owners who weren't members. Peddling fear on top of fear was damaging our perception with the rest of the public. The NRA gained a million members—and alienated millions more. And the fact is the association could have achieved its goals without turning off the general public. Wayne's speech after Sandy Hook was a watershed moment that put the NRA directly in the crosshairs of the gun control politicians, and it is paying the price now. It will take years and new leadership to fix the damage.

★

The year I walked into the building and my new job, 2016, turned out to be another watershed moment for the NRA politically. It was clear from the onset that Hillary Clinton was going to be the Democratic candidate, even if Bernie Sanders gave her a good scare and made her nomination more contested than anyone expected.

Hillary Clinton hated the NRA. She had promised to fight for more gun control—banning assault rifles, calling for universal background checks. If she were elected president, it would be open season on the NRA and our members.

The NRA party line was Hillary was the Antichrist. We couldn't let her win. On the Republican side, there were seventeen candidates running for president, almost enough to field two baseball teams—including Marco Rubio, Ted Cruz, Jeb Bush, Donald Trump, Carly Fiorina—and every one of them was pro-gun. It was pretty difficult for them to set themselves apart on the issues, and initially the pundits would talk up their most obvious choices. *Jeb Bush is our man! Marco is the conservatives' answer to JFK. Ted Cruz is the legitimate successor to Reagan.* But to no avail. Obviously, we were going throw our entire weight behind whomever the Republican nominee was—but who?

Enter Donald Trump. Typically, we got behind a candidate once it was clear who would win the nomination. But for the first time in NRA history, both Angus McQueen and Wayne (eventually) felt we had to get behind Donald Trump early, before the primaries had completely played out. Trump was way ahead in delegates, had become an unstoppable force disposing of "Lying Ted," "Little Marco," and "No Energy Jeb," and we needed to be behind him.

Not everyone was. Karl Rove's PAC, American Crossroads GPS, which spent over $115 million on Mitt Romney in 2012, refused to back Trump. The "Never Trumpers" were in full revolt at this point. By April, the Republican nomination came down to Trump, Cruz, and Ohio governor John Kasich, as everyone else dropped out.

Wayne and Chris were initially opposed to supporting Trump—we had never backed a candidate so early in an election. When Wayne talked to Angus he was for Trump, with Chris he wasn't, a never-ending flip-flop. Chris was very reticent to back Trump at this point but ultimately he landed on the side of endorsing him. And we wanted to make it clear to Trump that the NRA was his biggest supporter. And that the NRA expected the same in return.

We made the announcement supporting Trump on Thursday morning of the 2016 NRA convention in Louisville, just before the Donald took the stage to a raucous crowd. We had nearly a hundred thousand people there that weekend, and they were fired up. Remington, Magpul, all the big gun manufacturers show up for the NRA Annual Meeting, and this one was packed. Next to the SHOT Show in Vegas, the NRA convention is gun central. The aisles were elbow to elbow with families from the so-called flyover states, some of the most down-to-earth folks in the country. For many this was their once-a-year vacation. It was a social event, a political show, and a religious experience all rolled into one, by far my favorite event of the year, and walking the floor meeting the members was a highlight for me and my wife.

And Trump delivered the goods in his speech: "Crooked Hillary is the most antigun, anti–Second Amendment candidate ever to run for office."

And Wayne doubled down: "If she could, Hillary would ban every gun, destroy every magazine, run our entire national security industry right into the grave, and put gun owners' names on a government registration list."

Chris waltzed into the NRA board finance committee during the Annual Meeting in the spring of 2016, to talk to us about the upcoming presidential election and troll for more money.

"Look," he said, "this is high-stakes poker. If we don't go all in on Trump now, everything we worked for will be wiped away by Hillary Clinton." With his Tennessee Southern drawl, he did an incredible job selling the committee that now was the time, or we'd be answering to the Clintons for the remainder of our lives, the Second Amendment would be burned to the ground, and it would start raining frogs. Picture a dozen or so mostly old guys in a room ready to lose their minds over the prospect of Hillary Clinton winning the election. It was their worst nightmare. At this point Trump was something of a Black Swan to the Republican Party, before he took it over and made it his own. Chris made it clear that Trump was going to be the Republican candidate, and we needed to back him to the hilt.

And that's what we did. By the end of that meeting the attitude among the board members was, *If we have to sell the building to back Trump, that's what we are going to do.* The NRA went all in, and that credit goes to Chris. It was a risky move that really paid off.

Some people were concerned that Trump wasn't really a gun guy. But we were confident he would take a hard line on the Second Amendment and gun rights. Trump's sons Eric and Don Jr. are both NRA members, accomplished hunters and shooters in their own right. They *were* gun guys; Don Jr. would regularly tell the world about getting out of the city every weekend to hunt and shoot—that it really kept him on the straight and narrow. So we were convinced they would help pull their father along. As Trump said in a campaign rally in April, the "eight-year assault on your Second Amendment freedoms has come to a crashing end."

I did raise a red flag, however. As did board member Pete Brownell, who ran a very successful hundred-million-dollar family-owned gun parts business.

"Okay, we can kick in more money, but we'd better have a plan for what happens when we win. When Trump wins, the members will not be pouring money into the NRA. We're going to have 30 percent less revenue coming in." But it fell on deaf ears.

And that's exactly what happened. In 2016, revenues climbed to $365 million, fueled by $31 million in non-dues contributions. In 2017, revenue plummeted.

It was a problem you could see coming from a mile away, for which we did zero planning. With a Republican president, the fear factor went way down, as would the donations. The NRA had been built over the past twenty-five years on fear: "They are coming to take your guns." When that went away, what would happen to member donations? Did our budgets get taken down in light of that? Not one bit.

Officially we reported to the Federal Election Commission that we spent $55 million on the 2016 elections, including $30.1 million on Trump's election campaign—much more than we'd spent in 2008 and 2012, which included funding for forty-five of the most competitive Senate races and 145 House races. Most of the money—$35 million—went through ILA, Chris's lobbying group. ILA, as a 501(c)(4), doesn't have to disclose the donors. Labeled "dark money" by the liberal press, the 2016 donations were as much as we had spent in every previous election going back to 1992, *combined.*

And the actual amount was higher. We typically put our money into TV ads and direct mail. But in 2016, we spent a lot more running the Freedom's Safest Place ads on Fox (that were in theory nonpolitical in nature), internet ads, and grassroots campaigning among our members, all of which doesn't get reported. Our overall spending that year surged by $100 million, a huge new record.[4] Our total expenditures that year ballooned to $419 million. Legislative programs and public affairs accounted for 75 percent of the spending increase. In the two previous presidential election years, we had spent $204 million (in 2008) and $261 million (in 2012). One board member on the finance committee claimed we spent more like $70 million in support of Trump.

And the results speak for themselves. The "deplorables" showed up and whisked Trump into office. We paid for a ton of ads, most showing that Hillary was a threat to everything holy. The message was simple: If she was elected, she would appoint Supreme Court justices who were anti–Second Amendment, and the individual right to bear arms would disappear. In one of the wilder days of the campaign, Donald Trump said, "If she gets to pick her judges, nothing you can do, folks. Although the Second Amendment people—maybe there is, I don't know."[5]

Trump knew what gasoline was, and how to use it to his

advantage. He was the *Exxon Valdez* of such rhetoric. We pushed the fear button pretty hard ourselves in our ads, calling Hillary an "out-of-touch hypocrite. She'd leave you defenseless." We pigeon-holed her as wealthy and elitist.[6] We knew from long experience that fear always worked. According to one research organization, we sponsored one out of every twenty ads in Pennsylvania, one out of every nine ads in North Carolina, and one out of every eight in Ohio, all battleground states. At every corner we made it clear that the election was about being able to protect yourself, and about safeguarding individual freedom. The ads that On Message, the political advertising shop that Chris used, created even won an award for that campaign season. We spent most of our money on Trump, and six competitive Republican Senate races, and we won six of the seven. We spent $6.2 million in North Carolina alone, to back incumbent Richard Burr.[7]

The night Trump was elected, Wayne called me up at 3:00 a.m. to tell me, "I can't believe he pulled this off." Despite our massive support, Clinton was expected by the pundits and polls to run away with it. And instead, Trump won. And NBC proclaimed the NRA had just bought themselves a Supreme Court justice.

★

How did the NRA become such a massive sponsor of one political party? For decades, and as late as the turn of the century, about a third of our lobbying money was given to Democrats.

You read that right.

After all, 41 percent of all gun owners are Democrats.[8] Historically, Republicans had always been more supportive of guns and gun rights, and for multiple reasons, it's now become a one-sided issue. However, that can and should change, although it will take work and compromise from both sides.

In the 1970s, the NRA was transformed from a group focused on gun safety and training, with an emphasis on hunting, to a political lobbying organization pursuing gun rights for Americans everywhere. As Jim Porter, former NRA president from Alabama, said in his speech to the Annual Meeting in 2014, the NRA "had reached a critical crossroads" back in 1977 on whether it should be a sort of "national hunt club," or take a more active political role. (Jim's dad had served as president of the NRA, too—as well as played for Alabama's legendary football coach Bear Bryant—and I sat next to him as a board member. Jim bled the NRA, and I can promise you he is as distraught over the current circumstances of the organization as anyone. A lawyer by trade, he was incredibly knowledgeable about NRA history, and shared much with me regarding the NRA and its machinations.)

So here's a short history of how the NRA got its political game on...

The Gun Control Act, which came in 1968 after the assassinations of Martin Luther King Jr. and Bobby Kennedy, went a long way toward restricting gun rights. It was passed by a bare handful of votes. And people within the NRA felt it passed for only one reason—the NRA "was not in the game" in terms of lobbying Congress. As Jim Porter put it, "There was no Institute for Legislative Action. We didn't even have a registered NRA lobbyist...We weren't even on the playing field."[9]

The NRA got rolled. And that was the inciting political event.

In 1976 the NRA established the Political Victory Fund, and decided to pivot from preserving hunting and access to hunting lands to lobbying and protecting Second Amendment rights. Wayne LaPierre joined the NRA a year later. Its new mission was to advance individual gun owners' constitutional right to keep and bear arms.

In 1980, the NRA backed a presidential candidate for the first time, endorsing Ronald Reagan over Jimmy Carter.

In a move that proved to be very politically savvy, the NRA also started to grade politicians in terms of their support for gun rights, with a grade of "A+" indicating a candidate who has "not only an excellent voting record on all critical NRA issues, but who has also made a vigorous effort to promote and defend the Second Amendment." A candidate at the other end of the scale, with an "F," is considered a "true enemy of gun owners' rights." Now members had a way to message to everyone concerned with gun rights, NRA member or not, what an individual candidate's position was on the issue, whether they were running for a seat in the House, for a seat in the Senate, for governor, or for a seat in the state legislature. We were able to reward candidates who favored gun rights by giving them campaign money, and target those who opposed. Grade them out and hold them accountable. It was a brilliant strategy.

Wayne was elected executive vice president in 1991, and he quickly realized that the way to arouse the base of the NRA membership was make his rhetoric and his positions more extreme, more uncompromising, more fiery and fierce. In a way, he was Trump before Trump. People in the NRA saw Wayne as an essential counterweight to what was happening in Congress, as gun control efforts seemed to capture political currency. In 1993, Democrats controlled both houses of Congress, and President Clinton was able to sign the Brady Bill, mandating background checks, into law, as well as implement a ten-year ban on the sale of assault rifles a year later. That changed the equation, once and for all, and what set off the schism between Democrats and the NRA's political support was the assault weapons ban in 1994, which President Clinton and a Democratic Congress voted into law by a mere two votes in the House.

Gun owners were apoplectic.

Wayne was furious, as was the entire membership.

Hillary's husband had banned the AR-15 and the Clintons would pay.

And while the Democrats and gun control people celebrated, having won the battle, they would ultimately lose the war. Nothing galvanized gun owners like the assault weapons ban. For the first time, the NRA started to target their support for Republicans over Democrats.

In 1994, Wayne teamed up with Republicans in the midterm elections, and helped them take over the House for the first time in almost forty years. The NRA won nineteen of twenty-four priority races that they targeted, leading to a House of Representatives in which the majority of its members were "A" rated on gun rights.

In 1995, Wayne signed off on an NRA mailer referring to ATF—Alcohol, Tobacco, and Firearms—agents as "jackbooted government thugs." Former president George H. W. Bush resigned his NRA membership in disgust, but Wayne got everyone's attention. The language actually came from something Democratic congressman John Dingell said in a 1981 NRA promotional film. Wayne went on *Larry King* to shift the blame and walk it back, but it was too late—the tone and the direction of the NRA was set. The bottom line was that NRA EVP Wayne LaPierre had called a government agency Gestapo-like thugs. While Wayne attempted to shift the blame, it would stick, as it should have. It was a pivotal moment for the NRA, and one that pushed the association further to the extremes.

And the money continued to pour in. Fear, Wayne discovered, sold. And while Dingell was an important supporter of the NRA, increasingly the association moved away from Democrats and aligned itself with the Republican Party.[10]

The NRA also became an increasingly powerful, if strident, voice for Second Amendment laws nationally. The first fruit of that was the passage of the Firearm Owners' Protection Act of 1986, which allowed gun owners to carry their firearms with them across state lines. Most people with guns had one stashed in their house for protection, or in a gun cabinet if they use a rifle for hunting. The laws were a mess. They couldn't carry a gun around with them on the streets for protection. In 1987, only ten states had "right to carry" laws on the books. Twenty-three years later, four-fifths of the states had concealed carry laws.

The NRA really came into its own as a political force as we entered the twenty-first century. First, Wayne helped derail an attempt by the Clinton White House and HUD secretary Andrew Cuomo to forge a comprehensive gun control agreement with the gun industry, in an effort to impose new safety regulations and limits on how guns were sold. Next, Wayne flexed his muscles in blocking a gun show loophole, by tromping the bill in the House after it had passed the Senate by one vote (with Vice President Al Gore casting the deciding vote).

To punish Gore in the 2000 election, the NRA threw its weight behind former Texas governor George W. Bush, and Bush narrowly won the presidency.

That was the year when Charlton Heston issued his bold taunt to fellow NRA members—"from my cold dead hands."

The NRA had become a force to be reckoned with.

As President Clinton would acknowledge, "I believe Al lost Arkansas because of the National Rifle Association, and maybe Missouri, and maybe Tennessee, and maybe New Hampshire. . . . I don't think the NRA got near as much credit as they deserve for Bush's election. They hurt us bad."[11] Gun owners who voted for Bush beat gun owners for Gore by 25 points.[12]

For Wayne, it was payback.

And what did the first pro-gun administration in eight years do for us in return? Bush appointed John Ashcroft, an NRA supporter, as attorney general, and in the summer of 2001, Ashcroft announced the Justice Department's adoption of the view that the Second Amendment gave individuals, not just militias, the right to bear arms. Two years later, in 2003, Todd Tiahrt, a Republican congressman from Iowa, tacked a rider on to an appropriations bill, called the Tiahrt amendment, that forbade the ATF from sharing data it collects on gun crime. In 2004, the association successfully opposed the renewal of the assault rifle sales ban, crushing a compromise bill by a vote of 90 to 8.

As Wayne said in a 2002 speech, "There are no shades of gray. You're either with us or against us."

And in 2005 the NRA supported and helped pass something Wayne had been pushing for years, the Protection of Lawful Commerce in Arms Act, which prevents gun manufacturers and dealers from being sued for the use of the guns they make. It saved the gun industry and was a big deal politically.

Also in 2005, Marion Hammer, the chief lobbyist of the NRA in Florida, helped to pass the first Stand Your Ground law in Florida, making it legal for a person who is attacked or feels his or her life is in danger to protect himself with lethal force, not just in his home but wherever he or she is. Since then, twenty-four other states have passed similar laws.

And finally, there was the *D.C. v. Heller* decision, which constitutionally guaranteed something that we had been successfully advocating in Congress and the executive branch for years: the individual right to keep and bear arms, the cornerstone of the NRA's efforts to advance the Second Amendment.

As Washington became increasingly partisan, the NRA focused

its lobbying even more heavily on Republicans. After the association defeated the renewal of the assault rifle ban, and successfully lobbied Congress to pass the Protection of Lawful Commerce in Arms Act of 2005, Democrats' enthusiasm for gun control was dampened for years. After losing again and again, the Democrats in the 2006 election cycle stopped even proposing gun control measures. Gun control had become a third rail of national politics. The NRA, they decided, was too powerful to buck—even for the newly elected president, Barack Obama.

"His view was that such moves [against the NRA] would be largely symbolic because of the power of the gun lobby to stop them," said Obama political strategist David Axelrod. "In early 2009, after Attorney General Eric Holder casually mentioned that renewing the Assault Weapons Bans was a priority, Rahm Emanuel, then the president's chief of staff, sent a characteristically profane message to Holder on the gun issue: 'Shut the fuck up.'"[13]

Classic Rahm Emanuel, and proof that the NRA had become all-powerful in its perception on the left.

Still, as recently as 2010, the NRA supported 63 Democrats for Congress, out of 435 seats. But those Democrats had high NRA ratings—"A" or better on the issue of guns, and 61 of them were incumbents, with a huge edge in winning reelection. Since then, our funding and our lobbying efforts have skewed even more Republican. The rating a candidate receives is based on his or her voting record, or if he is not currently an elected official, on the results of a questionnaire that the NRA sends out. If the Brady Campaign to Prevent Gun Violence or another gun control group like Everytown for Gun Safety supports a candidate, he or she automatically gets an "F." The grades go out to members during election season and are posted on the NRA website.

For three decades, Wayne had successfully advanced the agenda of the Second Amendment in the NRA by pushing the fear button.

As Wayne said at the 2012 NRA convention in St. Louis, hammering home the fear message, "We live in the most dangerous of times." He warned that terrorists and criminals could "freeze our transportation systems, black out our cities, shut down our distribution of fuel and food," and lead to an "unprecedented breakdown of social order."

We are, he told gun owners, on our own. And the solution? "Anticipating dangerous times and . . . responding in the only sensible, logical way possible"—by being armed.

★

And then came Sandy Hook, and a slew of mass shootings, some at schools, some at churches, nightclubs, and even on the streets of Las Vegas. And the anger, the fear, the frustration at finding a solution to these senseless tragedies has rekindled a debate that receded but never went away.

How do we stop school shootings? What kinds of solutions can we offer?

And what I could see from sitting next to him every day is that this is where Wayne's vitriolic rhetoric came back to hurt the NRA. His sole response to any issue on gun control was: *No. Absolutely not.* The NRA said no to every effort to rein in gun rights, no matter how modest or reasonable. The association blocked any legislation that would infringe on our members' rights, from universal gun checks to any limitation on magazines or on the types of weapons that people were allowed to own or buy.

Now, we might have had good reasons that have a basis in the realities of gun ownership. But the net result was that the NRA became the organization of "No." We didn't offer to become part of the solution. We didn't pose suggestions on how to stop gun violence. We just became known for inciting riots on any effort that would impact the rights of gun owners. And as a result, we were seen as the problem. Even by gun owners.

In a *Washington Post*/ABC News poll in January 2013, only 36 percent of Americans had a favorable opinion of the NRA. And in a poll conducted by the gun control PAC Americans for Responsible Solutions, less than half of gun owners said they believed the NRA represented their interests. Sixty-seven percent said the NRA had been taken over by lobbyists and gun manufacturers and had lost its way.

And that, I knew, was a problem. We were in trouble, I realized, if we weren't seen as part of the solution. After all, we were the most knowledgeable experts in the country on the issue of guns. But Wayne wasn't listening to me. He wasn't interested in fixing any problems— the success and triumph of the previous twenty years had swollen his self-regard. What I realize is hard to fathom is that the NRA didn't think ahead to how to deal with the next shooting; it simply reacted that day to the crisis.

As the ancient Greeks would say: Nemesis follows hubris.

★

In 2013, in the aftermath of the shootings at Sandy Hook, Congress and the president were desperate to take action, to do something, anything, in response to the death of all these young kids. So senators Joe Manchin of West Virginia, a Democrat with an "A" rating by the NRA, and Patrick Toomey of Pennsylvania, a Republican, revived a bipartisan bill that would increase background checks. And it looked for the first time in ten years that there was something Republicans and even the NRA could get behind. Eighty percent of our members supported the bill.

I didn't think the background check bill would have much impact on school shootings or gun violence, honestly, but I thought it was a way to show the world that the NRA could agree and work toward a package of solutions. The parents of the kids who were killed at New-town made a tearful, poignant plea on behalf of the bill.

But in the end, Wayne weighed in against it, saying that it was the first step on a slippery slope to gun registry. Chris Cox and his ILA team pressured Senate Republicans and killed it. And not only that—the NRA ran out a full campaign thrashing Manchin, one of the few remaining Democrats we endorsed. The bill needed to win sixty votes in the Senate to overcome a filibuster, and in the end all but four Republicans voted against it. The NRA had once again flexed its muscles. We had won.

Or had we?

★

One of the things trading taught me is to question your previous moves and the downstream effect: In this case, what were all the limiting factors of a single-minded scorched-earth strategy?

One of the many things I wanted to look into when I started at the NRA was the School Shield program. Wayne had introduced this idea in response to Sandy Hook—he had stood up in front of the entire country to say that the NRA is in business to protect schools. So we put together a blue-ribbon group, chaired by Asa Hutchinson, who is now the governor of Arkansas, to figure out how to define the details of the program and scale the footprint.

Basically, the School Shield group got a number of security specialists together and they came up with the criteria that we should assess with the school to make it safer. There are about four hundred criteria in all. The group had based their work on what the Israelis do to fortify their schools. (And they don't have school shootings in Israel, in spite of the fact that it arguably has more security issues than any country on earth.)

The group talked to school administrators, they talked to local police, they talked to the local FBI. It was thorough and really well done. In the end School Shield would deliver a security assessment to schools free of charge. And then we could make recommendations on what they could do, customized for each individual school and budget. But you needed everyone to make it work—local law enforcement, the principal, all the players.

We had launched the program right after Sandy Hook, and when I came on at the NRA I tried to find out where things stood. I was really excited about the program—it seemed like a genuine part of what we could do to protect our schools and our kids and be part of the solution.

Kyle Weaver, the head of General Operations, was running the program, so about six months after I started, I met with him and asked, "Hey, can you tell me where the School Shield program is at?"

Kyle handed me a nice brochure, and I saw that they had changed the logo to a little schoolhouse. So I asked, "How is the program coming along? This is supposed to be one of our big initiatives." And Kyle said, "You know, it's like a Ferrari in a garage."

I was lost; what did he mean?

He said, "It's ready to roll."

"Good," I said, "But it's been a number of years. How many schools have we assessed?"

Kyle told me, "You know, it's just getting going. It's going to be great."

"Great news, Kyle. When?" And he admitted he didn't know exactly. So I asked him if the guy under him knew. And he said yes, so we went to talk to him. But when I asked this guy where things stood, he trotted out the same nonsense—"It's a Ferrari in a garage."

What the fuck? So I gave it another try. I said, "Okay, guys, I just want to know how many schools we've assessed for the program. It's a number, and it's somewhere between zero and I don't know. Ten thousand? Whatever it is, I'm just curious."

And Kyle finally admitted to me: three. They had assessed three schools. In four years.

I went directly to Wayne's office, in sheer terror. I told him, "Do you know how many schools the School Shield program has assessed?" And of course he had no idea. I told him, "It's not three hundred, it's not three thousand, it's three. The media is going to kill you when you go on TV and some reporter leaks that number out. They will dismember you on live TV. Unless you tell me you don't care."

Wayne was equally appalled, and soon afterward I fired Kyle. I was put in charge of operations.

So now I was chief of staff and head of General Operations, which I did for about two years. It was a move that pissed off some people, like Chris Cox, because according to the bylaws, if something happened to Wayne, the person who ran General Operations took over the NRA.

So while trying to clean things up, I had placed a target on my back.

As for School Shield, I met up with Sheila Brantley, who was one of the more effective, can-do administrators in our organization. And I said, "We need to run this thing like a proper program. You have my full support, and whatever you need, let me know." And she was ecstatic. She could never understand why it was being held back. She took the program from three to three hundred school assessments in less than six months. I was excited, and happy for her and her team. One of the roadblocks Sheila ran into was some pushback because the program was supported by the NRA. People's perception of our extreme stances on guns was holding the program back. So Sheila would work with the attorney general of the state, whether it was Ohio or Oklahoma, and then have the attorney general push it out. And that really jump-started it. It was a great example of government and in this case a nonprofit working together and actually moving the ball.

The School Shield program is telling of the NRA's culture in so many ways. It had gotten caught up in politics and bureaucracy. The managers of it were just wasting time and members' money. And not everyone in the NRA believed in it. Chris didn't seem to believe in it. And I'm sure he was telling Kyle, *Don't do anything with that. Just leave it alone.*

And in the meantime, Wayne was out there selling the program to our members, raising money off it, claiming we were protecting kids' schools. It was another example of the wizard behind the curtain—lots of inflamed rhetoric and fireworks and noise, but very little effective action on countering gun violence, or promoting gun training or safety. And unfortunately, I could see that a lot of the reason for that was Wayne's management style. He didn't delegate, or lead, or hold people accountable, which led to all the political infighting and paranoia. No one was on the same page. Everyone retreated to their silos; everyone was out for themselves. I was there for three and a half years. And yet I sat down with Chris Cox less than half a dozen times. I would tell Wayne, "Let me know when you want me to sit down with you and Chris to talk things through." And Wayne would say, "Yeah, yeah," without meaning it, his eyes on the ground. So while Wayne presented himself as a fierce, forceful leader to the public, it was a part he played, like the Wizard of Oz.

And behind the curtain, Wizard Wayne let the chaos reign, and when we needed him most, he seemed to disappear.

CHAPTER 3

The Puppet Master

What a lot of people don't know is that there was a puppet master behind Wayne LaPierre who dictated and choreographed his every move. He had started working with Wayne and the NRA thirty-five years before, crafting every speech, writing every ad, putting together every commercial, directing every aspect of the NRA's brand and strategy. And his name was Angus McQueen.

The firm he worked for, Ackerman McQueen, was cofounded by his father, Marvin McQueen, as a family-run business out of Oklahoma. First as creative director, and then as CEO, Angus, with a staff that grew into the hundreds, handled the advertising, marketing, PR, branding, messaging, communications, web design, and social media for the NRA. For over three decades, the firm had written Wayne's speeches for CPAC and the annual NRA convention. In addition to Oklahoma City, they had offices in Dallas, where we would meet with them regularly; an office in Alexandria, Virginia, where Tony Makris worked as the head of the subsidiary Mercury Group; and an office in Colorado Springs. While Ackerman McQueen had a number of clients, including Six Flags amusement parks, the Integris health care system of Oklahoma, and the Chickasaw Nation, a large portion of their revenue came from the NRA. In 2017 we paid them $40 million, between Ackerman and NRATV, which they funded, and in 2018 the figure ballooned to $50 million.

Now, Angus wasn't really a gun guy. But he was a hard-core conservative. And a bully. He knew one way. His. Back in the day, he was the advertising director who tried to mainstream the NRA. Before Ackerman McQueen came on board, the NRA was more a hunting and training organization, although it had a small radical fringe of the gun community. It had never had a glossy marketing agency behind it, and it was Angus more than anyone who shaped the perception of the NRA. He shifted the messaging from gun ownership and the Second Amendment to "freedom." It was a brilliant move. Who doesn't believe in freedom? This messaging culminated in what became the Freedom's Safest Place campaign, a phenomenally successful series of ads that ran throughout the 2016 election. Ending that campaign was a strategic failure; folks from both sides of the aisle could relate with many of the ads.

Angus played such a huge role in the NRA, advising Wayne and telling him what to do and say, and the NRA became so famous for Wayne's fireworks and polemics that over time I think Angus came to see himself as the power behind the throne. And in many ways Wayne abdicated decisions to Angus or just gave in and did things the way Angus wanted them done.

Angus wasn't a tall guy—he was probably five foot nine—but he always came across as deeply serious and in charge. With his success "running" the NRA, he spent less time with his other clients, which he left to his son Revan. Angus wore bespoke suits from London, had the finest dress shoes and a predilection for $250 Charvet ties, which he would toss away after wearing once. I don't think I ever saw him without a jacket or tie—he always presented himself in the best possible light, and his clothes were part of that branding, part of his puppet master performance. He was either driven in a black Suburban or drove his Bentley convertible. He lived well and wasn't afraid to show it. When I started coming down to Dallas to see him, he and some of the others from Ackerman would take me out to exquisite dinners, always in private rooms if Wayne was with us, at the best steakhouses in town—Del Frisco's, Morton's, you name it; Angus loved to command the room.

One of the first campaigns that Ackerman McQueen came up with was "I'm the NRA," introducing everyday people who were members: a firefighter, a teacher, a mom. There was a sprinkling of famous people, as well—Tom Clancy, Roy Rogers, Tom Selleck, Karl Malone. The campaign was incredibly successful, showing the world that the NRA was made up of ordinary people—that it wasn't an organization of crazies. Angus helped to turn the annual NRA conventions from a "pipe and drape" show held in county fairgrounds to multiday family outings, with food and exhibitions and "acres of guns and gear" on display, country music acts on a stage, prayer meetings and political speeches focused around freedom and the sanctity of the Second Amendment, all held in huge convention centers around the country. The NRA conventions were transformed into the largest conservative political gatherings in the country, drawing everyone from Ted Cruz and Rand Paul to Donald Trump. The conventions were also used to wine and dine high-dollar donors from the Golden Ring of Freedom— people who had contributed a million dollars or more—with the best in bourbons, cigars, a whole VIP spread. It was a hell of show.

And of course Angus and Tony Makris had brought Charlton Heston to the association, where he served as president for five years.

The election of Heston had rescued Wayne from a board uprising in the late '90s. Even back then board member Neil Know claimed Wayne "did not have the capacity or tools to manage the NRA, and had overseen years of mismanagement, no-bid contracts, and wasting money." In other words, Wayne's inadequacies managing money and people were known twenty years before.

Heston's star power would usher in a new era of mainstreaming the NRA. He was a legendary Hollywood figure who had not only stood up to Joseph McCarthy and his communist witch hunt in the 1950s, but marched side by side with Martin Luther King to the steps of the Lincoln Memorial. Heston believed in liberty, equality—for African Americans and whites, men and women, whatever their skin color or beliefs, to have equal access to education and the tools of success—and the freedom to bear arms. Go down, Moses.

☆

I first met Angus soon after I started in the summer of 2016. I went down with a group of NRA executives including Wayne and Woody Phillips, our CFO. Angus was about seventy at the time. He had been married to his wife, Jody, forever, whom everyone described as an amazing woman. She died in 2013 from the same type of brain tumor my mother did, a glioblastoma. Angus donated funding for a cure to Duke University, one of the leading institutions in brain cancer research. It was something we bonded over; I had enormous empathy for his son Revan, who had been about the same age I was when my mother died. Angus had had three kids, and Revan had become co-CEO of Ackerman McQueen; Angus's plan was to pass the firm on to him eventually.

We always went to see Angus; he never came to Washington. I remember I had booked a room at the Sheraton in Dallas. Tony and

Wayne called me out on my rookie mistake: "We all stay at the Ritz. Move your room."

The Royals—Wayne, Chris, Woody, and later our next CFO Craig Spray, and I—always stayed at the Ritz when visiting Ackerman McQueen in Dallas. I quickly discovered that everything the executives at the NRA did was first-class. And the next thing you know, Tony and I are drinking Pol Roger champagne in the lobby of the Ritz. (Wayne rarely drank much beyond tonic water or Kill Cliff.) There seemed to be a sense of entitlement when it came to travel and hotels; they were "sacrificing" to work for the NRA "and this is how we roll." I felt like Ray Liotta walking into the Copacabana in the movie *Goodfellas*. That is the seduction of living the life, and it's easy to forget the little guy with his $45 membership dues who is paying the bill. When everyone is doing it, it doesn't feel like cheating. And that's how I started to become part of the Establishment—everything I had hated about Washington and politics.

I got the same sense of unrestrained luxury when I entered the Ackerman McQueen building, an incredibly beautiful high-tech office with marble floors and floor-to-ceiling glass windows, looking out over the Dallas skyline. I guess what I wasn't thinking about, right off, was that we paid for all this. We walked into a big conference room with ten-foot-tall TV screens, six across, that was like entering the NASA command center. And then Angus made his entrance, very grand, very formal, in his bespoke wool suit and Charvet tie.

"Nice to meet you, Josh. Congratulations on joining the NRA."

And he led us through a long presentation on the history and relationship between Ackerman McQueen and the NRA, for my benefit as Wayne's new number two. It was a brilliant, glitzy introduction. They had around a hundred people working on the account. Somewhere around 60 percent of their total revenues came from the

NRA. But this was fundamentally an odd relationship. Ackerman was our vendor, but they acted more like partners, with Ackerman being the primary, majority owner. From the get-go, I saw an arrogance about them—that we were expected to do what they said and fall in line.

The meetings were always long, all-day marathons, from 9:00 a.m. until the end of the day. And then we would go out to dinner together. And the sessions were amorphous and unfocused, with no agenda provided—not the way I would run a railroad. The joke was they would bring something up—an ad or a commercial—and Wayne would say, "Yeah, that looks good."

And to Ackerman, that was code for: *Send the NRA an invoice.*

Eventually Angus would "confide" in me: "You know, I'm not close to Wayne like you or Tony, or friends with Wayne."

But that was nonsense. He talked to Wayne every day and sometimes five times a day. And he never held back what he thought, ever. Maybe it was his definition of what a friend was.

With Angus, everything was a constant, near-apocalyptic fight—the messaging and, of course, the politics. He was at war with the world, and constantly imagined black helicopters swooping in from the ATF and the FBI ready to take over his house, his office, the country. In the wake of a school shooting, Angus's immediate reaction and advice was that the NRA say nothing, and then at the right point go on the attack. Like his puppet Wayne, he refused to concede anything, an attitude that has come back to haunt the NRA.

Ackerman had little interest in expanding the NRA's base—in reaching out to the other ninety-five million gun owners who weren't NRA members. In a country with over one hundred million gun owners, the NRA's membership had been stuck at five million for years. But Angus knew it was the existing members who were the most extreme and most vocal and most motivated faction. And that these were the people whom he and Wayne could activate in a time of crisis.

That said, his strategy was effective, and Ackerman McQueen helped the NRA win a lot of fights. In the days after the horrific shootings at Sandy Hook, Angus's response was, *We're not giving a fucking inch. We're gonna have Wayne hold a press conference and say that the only answer to a bad guy with a gun is a good guy with a gun.* That was Angus's fuck-you mentality.

Angus was super territorial. If you didn't agree with him on an ad or a direction or a policy, he had a long history of going to Wayne and telling him point-blank, *You've got to get rid of this guy.* Angus and I met a lot together in my first two years—he intervened in NRA affairs all the time. He was a total tyrant, charming and incredibly intelligent one minute, and a bully determined to get his way the next. He had no problem excoriating Wayne in front of a crowd, or screaming at any of our people, however senior or junior, to get what he wanted. God forbid an invoice hadn't been paid quickly enough—which happened all the time, given all the stuff they were invoicing us for. You didn't want to be on the other end of that call.

☆

That said, Ackerman did come up with some powerful and provocative ad campaigns while I was there. The Freedom's Safest Place campaign, in 2015 and 2016, which ran during the election, was, as I mentioned, a particular success. Each ad told the story of an ordinary citizen, determined to protect him- or herself.

In one, a woman says she can't "afford a nice house in a safe neighborhood," and that gangbangers and drug dealers walk her halls every day. "We called the police...but they can't keep us safe."

She recollects how she walked behind Martin Luther King at Selma. "Now I have my gun. I am the National Rifle Association of America, and I'm freedom's safest place."

You clearly get the sense this woman is under siege. You feel the urgency of her message. Ackerman found all sorts of folks like her, did a ton of spots, and ran these through the NRA and the Trump campaign.

But that wasn't enough. Angus wanted to blow up the world, and any sense of winning over a larger audience through advertising campaigns like Freedom's Safest Place wasn't part of his agenda.

Just after the Parkland school shooting, Angus and the folks at Ackerman worked on a speech for Wayne to give at CPAC, which was a very big forum for the NRA and garnered a lot of attention. Getting these speeches done for Wayne was always a nightmare. They were a circus to produce. Wayne and I would fly down to Dallas to meet with Ackerman a week in advance. And after Parkland, particularly, things were extremely tense. Tony Makris was there for this, along with a whole entourage of Ackerman folks. Usually, Angus would have his team draft the speech in advance, and then come in and put on a big show, subtitled: *This is what you are going to say.*

In this case Angus put together the most extreme far right speech you can imagine, with stuff about fentanyl from China, and drug addicts on the streets, killers coming up from Mexico, the FBI working to take over the government, jackbooted troopers jumping out of helicopters, and so on.

Initially Wayne and I would try to whittle it back to something that sounded somewhat palatable, or plausible—at least to Fox News. Wayne would constantly ask, "Do you think I sound crazy?"

Makris and I would sort of laugh, "Well, I think attacking the FBI could be problematic, but hey, maybe that's just me!" Translation: *Of course you sound crazy!*

Angus and his team would write two major speeches a year for Wayne, the CPAC speech and the Annual Meeting speech. I was the only person from the NRA, outside of Wayne's longtime assistant Millie, who was ever brought inside the inner circle to work on Wayne's addresses. Wayne would go up to a podium at Ackerman to practice, with ten people in the room. And everyone would constantly throw out comments, worried about the time and the pacing. God knows what these rehearsals cost us.

And there were plenty of times when Wayne was uncomfortable with Angus's hard right stance. Some things we just took out later without telling him. And at other times Wayne would get into fierce fights with Angus over the wording—Angus would start screaming at him, as if *he* was the head of the NRA. Angus was always pushing Wayne, and the language was raw—"fuck this" and "fuck that." Angus didn't know how to hold back: "You're a fucking poodle," he would yell in a meeting, pushing Wayne to go on the attack. Angus was someone who just bristled with anger. It was very uncomfortable for me to watch. Why did Wayne put up with this? But Wayne kowtowed, and never fought back. Usually I would remove myself from the whole circus. It was hard to watch Angus berate Wayne in front of everyone. It was so far out of any normal behavior I could imagine.

Angus bowed to no one. And Wayne would turn to Tony and me and ask, "What do you think?"

Wayne was so afraid of coming off as a crazy man, although ironically, that is exactly what he became to the media.

★

During all of this, I had sort of taken over the consigliere role with Wayne that Tony had had before I got there. Which was fine; Tony and I worked closely together. But one of the weird things I discovered was, when Wayne had an issue with me, he would never tell me to my face. Tony would tell me. Wayne, I discovered, would never tell you that he wasn't happy with you; if he wanted to do something different, he'd have someone else talk to you.

I'd always go out of my way to make sure he was happy with whatever I was working on—in fact, I became almost maniacal about it. "You cool with this, Wayne?" And he'd say, "Yeah, yeah, yeah."

But then I'd have to ask myself, *Does that mean yes, or not really or no?* It was crazy. And then later I'd hear from Tony that, no, he didn't like it.

I would scratch my head and mutter some four-letter expletive under my breath.

And Tony would nod, laughing, agreeing with me. "I know, I know, I know. Hey, it wasn't my idea for you to join this insane asylum, Ace. No one asked me."

I would tell Wayne, "Look, I work for you. *Talk to me.* This won't work if you can't be straight with me one hundred percent of the time."

I just wanted to do right by him.

★

Often Angus would tell me, "This is my last year doing this," which I would hear at times from Wayne as well. I'd give them both my "come on, man, Warren Buffett is eighty-five, you are just getting started" speech.

Over time I became close enough to Angus that I'd call him up and talk through a whole host of issues, from policy to board fights, even staffing and personnel. At the time it seemed normal. Angus had been the chief architect of the association's image since before I was born. I think from his perspective, he was constantly concerned about how he was going to keep all of this going. Most of his firm's money came from the NRA, and Wayne was not going to be around forever. What would happen when he left?

Chris Cox, the heir apparent to Wayne, hated Ackerman, and hired his own PR firm to handle publicity and marketing for ILA. Angus and Ackerman were not happy about this in the least. For my part, I appreciated much of the work that Ackerman did, because they really understood the issues. However, working with them was a challenge.

But Angus didn't care about the NRA or its membership. In fact, Ackerman didn't really understand who the members were, what made them tick, let alone the nuts and bolts of our direct response campaigns for new members. Angus would say to me, "I don't know what the fuck those guys do, and I don't really care." Case in point, Ackerman created few, if any, commercials focusing on broadening the base for the NRA.

Angus's focus was on the brand and the image. And billing the place for every dollar he could. He could care less about measuring an ROI. But it's not rocket science—you run a commercial, the phones ring, and people join. The equation is simple: The cost of time on air plus cost of ad equals the cost of acquiring new member.

But that kind of measuring just wasn't Ackerman's style. It didn't serve their purpose. They had too much of a good thing going, and Angus was doing all he could to preserve that.

In one of my first meetings with Gurney Sloan, the CEO of the marketing firm we used for membership drives, he told me, "You have a very big task. You have to get the place to measure what they do, including Ackerman McQueen. They will fight you tooth and nail." Gurney had worked at Ackerman McQueen, and detested Angus.

I think he knew already that I'd fail.

I do think Angus was ready to step away—he talked about it a lot. But he also realized he couldn't—that Wayne's connection was through him, and the two shared a weird parasitism and symbiosis. Wayne didn't think Angus's son Revan was competent enough to trust him going forward. Angus must have been concerned that if he retired, Wayne and the NRA would drop Ackerman. And he was right. Wayne would constantly tell me, "When Angus goes, so goes Ackerman. Revan doesn't have the chops."

The puppet master and puppet did not know how to quit each other.

★

I was down in Dallas quite a bit, especially with the kickoff of NRATV during the 2016 election year. We were also using Ackerman to launch Carry Guard, one of my major projects, as I'll discuss in a moment. And as Wayne's chief of staff—and the executive responsible for nearly all the operations outside of ILA—at some point Angus raised what I guess was an obvious question for him: Did I want to run the NRA someday? I'll tell you, when Angus McQueen talks to you about one day taking over the NRA, it's a pretty seductive conversation. I told him honestly that I was there to work for Wayne, through the period of my contract, and then return to the real world.

Did I think about running the NRA? Sure, I guess so. But right then, I wanted to be exactly where I was—helping Wayne modernize the association.

But honestly, what this conversation with Angus really showed was the dysfunction between Ackerman and the NRA. They worked for us. They're a vendor. And yet they had no problem plotting behind the scenes about who was going to take over for Wayne. They acted like kingmakers, deciding who was going to run the shop. And to

Angus, that was perfectly normal. He really felt he ran the NRA, and he was testing to see if I could be turned into a puppet down the line.

☆

The reason the NRA stayed with Ackerman McQueen so long is that Angus had made Wayne who he was. Were they overpriced? You betcha. But we were paying for a lot of history and trust.

That said, the Ackerman people lived in a total bubble, well dressed, incredibly well paid, working out of beautiful glass offices in downtown Dallas. They lived and breathed their own exhaust all day long. On trips to the Annual Meeting, I didn't see them walking around the floor, and they had no interest in connecting with the NRA members. Sure, they would come to the meetings at the annual convention, but they stayed at the Four Seasons and went to Michelin-starred restaurants. They weren't holding prayer groups or ogling the guns and ammo at the exhibition hall. Like Angus, they really weren't gun guys. (The one exception was Tony Makris, who knew how to use a gun versus looking at pictures of them on a Mac-Book. Born in Alabama, Tony was a shooter, a former cop, and a hunter extraordinaire. He understood the membership and the politics. At times Ackerman listened to Tony, but more often they didn't. Their arrogance was palpable.)

There was no real approval process in working with Ackerman. Wayne verbally approved stuff. And there were many times when we'd get an invoice later and ask Ackerman, *What is that for?* And inevitably their reply was, *Oh, we talked to Wayne.*

In other words, there were no controls over their expenses at all. And if I dared to question some charge, Angus or someone else at Ackerman would just go right over my head. Our CFO, Woody Phillips, was a very nice guy, a kind of grandfatherly figure who had been with the NRA for twenty-five years; some saw him as a complete space cadet as a financial officer, and people took advantage of him. Ackerman, of course, loved him.

For example, there were countless instances of me asking Wayne, "Did you approve this magazine ad?"

He would say, "What are you talking about?"

"Ackerman said you approved it."

And then he would remember. "Yeah, I walked in and somebody waved a magazine in front of me and said, 'Did you see this and do you like it?'"

And Wayne would answer, "Yeah it's great," and that was his approval.

Everything with Ackerman was always last-minute, and always too late to make any changes. But that was the point. They got it done their way. It felt like they were showing their work product to us out of courtesy. It was not a collaboration.

By 2016 we were paying them $25 million a year and they managed all of the marketing, the advertising, and the publicity campaigns. They ran a number of the websites and created content for those websites, and they handled parts of our social media.

In truth it was a complete mess. Very unorganized, with no central management or direction. There were all these different NRA portals for different divisions. Membership, lobbying, everything built separate and redundant. And everyone had their own database—membership, publications, Chris and ILA, the NRA Foundation. And you couldn't access one page from another. Zero coordination, nada. There were multiple stand-alone social media pages. They popped up like weeds. It was insane. There was no cohesive brand or communication because none of those folks worked together.

Prime example of this: I remember a time when Wayne had filmed some video response. And somebody from Ackerman called to say it would be great if we could get this video up on Chris's Facebook page.

"You mean his personal page?" I asked.

The Ackerman person said, "No, no, the NRA-ILA Facebook page."

So this is how I found out that Chris was running his own Facebook page for the NRA-ILA, which it turns out had five million followers. I finally went to Wayne and told him, "This is dumb. We're going to get an NRA Facebook page, because I want to build membership off of it." And Chris wasn't doing that. He viewed it as just a political platform.

So Wayne says, "I'll talk to Chris about it."

And I countered, "No, let me do that." Because I knew now that Wayne doesn't like confrontation.

So I called up Chris to talk about my plan to consolidate our presence on Facebook, and he threw a shit fit, called Wayne to complain about me, and around it went. This was never-ending. It was as if the NRA was made up of two separate wings, and Chris would brook no interference with his wing, ILA. He refused to cede any ground. He would end up staging these long, exhausting filibusters with Wayne, explaining his position, bludgeoning him with words. And Wayne put up with it, rather than just closing down the discussion and issuing an order. They were like a dysfunctional couple. And Wayne would complain to me afterward. And I would implore him to just tell Chris what he wanted him to do. But he wasn't capable of that kind of leadership. At one point, as a joke, Tony Makris and I had business cards made up that said, "What can I say that I haven't said before?"

Ultimately the ILA renamed their Facebook page, and we took control of the NRA page with the folks at MMP, the outside firm we used to do membership and fund-raising, even measuring an ROI with a little tool called Salesforce and, you know, twenty-first-century technology. It was a one of the few initiatives we actually got off the ground in spite of the daily infighting.

I'll never forget what Gurney Sloan, the CEO at MMP, told me about Chris Cox's reaction to launching the page: "I hope you fail."

That was the NRA—everyone undercutting each other, everyone watching out for themselves. It was the result of years of mismanagement by Wayne. If you never hold staff meetings and get folks on the same page, you foment distrust, discord, and so on. That was how he managed. He will deny it, but you won't find a single person at the NRA who, if asked confidentially, would disagree.

The national media thought we were this deep, dark, powerful lobbying machine, high-tech and streamlined, with tentacles everywhere. I had to laugh. It was more like a tuned-out guy sitting in a room full of other tuned-out guys, saying, *I think I'll put this up on Facebook today.* Totally random, with zero coordination, zero analysis, much less a sophisticated tactical approach.

I think the NRA had over twenty social media channels at one point. One day I wrote them all out in front of Wayne on a piece of paper. And I asked him, "Do you know how many Facebook pages Coke has? One. They don't have a separate page for Coke, Diet Coke, Coke Zero. They've got the Coke page, that's it. Do you know how many Facebook pages AT&T has? One."

I said all of this has to be collapsed into cohesive brands, and then we test, measure, and use them as tools to raise membership.

Wayne said, "Yeah, yeah, I agree." But it was hard to get the organization to change.

Angus told me early on, "Josh, the NRA is like a country full of warlords. And now you're one of them. We'll see how you do."

So I turned to him and asked, "Well, we're all on the same team, right?"

He replied, "Fuck that, it's every man for himself." And he started laughing. "The NRA has this been like this forever. Always has been, always will be."

★

That said, I was able to make some progress at fixing our processes. We implemented Salesforce with the membership folks at MMP, and that really started to hum. I told them to just keep testing and learning and when you see the right thing working, scale it up. And they did. They made some great headway in spite of folks rooting against them. There's a reason why Salesforce is worth billions—their software gives you a tool you can use to measure results, as opposed to just throwing ideas up on the wall and writing checks and wasting tens of millions of dollars on marketing. You could now run an automated, measurable process across multiple channels. Simple but brilliant. And not rocket science. This was basic stuff, just blocking and tackling.

At the beginning of each year, Ackerman McQueen would come to us with their budget, giving us a presentation, saying this is what we want to do, pitching all kinds of ads and commercials and other things. And they would have a price tag. But itemizing all of it was impossible to decipher. And they would negotiate exclusively with Wayne and Woody, our CFO, who pretty much said yes to everything.

So I came in and I was in a difficult position—I knew I needed to keep the gears moving, but long-term we had to fix this process. And then a crisis would come up and we would get caught up in it, with no time to spare, and fixing things became impossible. We continually lurched from crisis to crisis.

For example: I hired a senior executive in 2017 out of one of the big tech companies to do high-level analytics and start to measure everything we did. She was going to help connect all of our systems together—where and how the ad spend was working, audience engagement, site content trends, traffic sources, and so on. Basically, modernize the NRA platform. She was very bright, had great credentials, and was very impressive. I brought her down to a meeting in Dallas with Ackerman about two weeks after I hired her. She was working for the NRA's digital director, reviewing the NRA's existing marketing strategy development and service with Ackerman McQueen. Her job was a tall order, to wire all of the NRA, including our relationship with Ackerman, together. In retrospect, it was probably unachievable.

In that meeting and others, she discovered, as her lawyer later put it, that Ackerman was charging exorbitant fees for services that were unnecessary, or not provided at all.

In that first meeting with Ackerman, I had asked her to listen, just soak up information. But she was so taken aback at what the Ackerman people were saying that she texted me her shock and dismay during the meeting. I was sitting a few chairs away from her, and basically she was texting, *This is completely fucked up and the NRA is getting screwed.*

And I nodded at her—*I know, I get it.*

But the point was to ask some questions, for her to learn as much as she could about the relationship. This is a big, complicated behemoth, and it's going to take some time to sort out.

But she didn't do that. She immediately became aggressive.

And Revan, Angus's son, of course was a total prick and basically said fuck off. "What do you know? I don't need to listen to you, you've been here fifteen minutes."

The exchange just escalated right away—it was a nightmare.

I went out to call Angus, who was in Oklahoma City. And he didn't come right out and say he wanted me to fire her, but that is where he got to. And I have to admit I was concerned about whether this was going to work out. I had told her what to do, and she had done the exact opposite—not a great sign. However, her synopsis was dead-on; we just needed to work on the approach part.

So Angus and I called up Wayne to talk about whether or not we should fire her. "You know, you hire all these new people, and they waltz in and don't know shit, and start questioning us on how we do our jobs. Everybody wants to be in charge of the messaging. We've been doing this for the NRA for thirty-five years..."

This perfectly illustrates the dysfunction—Wayne and I were willing to have a conversation like that with our vendor. Moreover, we were inviting the fox to guard the henhouse—we were allowing Angus to weigh in on whether or not to keep the very person we hired to do a deep dive into the money that we were spending with Ackerman. That was how entangled the relationship had become.

Later, I told her I get it. Let's go have a drink tomorrow and talk about it in a more relaxed setting. I told her I thought she had come on too aggressively. Revan's reaction was predictable. She didn't seem to get that this was a relationship that had been in place for over thirty years, and it would take more guile to fix it. In the end, we let her go.

Another reason I mention this is that there was an article published in the *New Yorker* in 2019 about the NRA, accusing me, unfairly, of two sexual harassment claims. And this was one of them.

I think she worked for us for about six months. And she asserted a claim against the NRA. And one example she cited was that, on her second day of work, at a meeting, she asked a question and I dismissed her, saying, "You sound exactly like my wife."

The irony is that I was complimenting her: My wife, Colleen, is a brilliant consultant with a thirty-year background from IBM and Ernst & Young, and one of the most astute people I know. What I was trying to say was, "I totally agree with what you're saying. That's exactly why I hired you."

But she took it as a criticism and misogynistic. Well, that was not what I intended, and for that I apologize. She also said she was promised a title that she never got, and that my suggestion that we meet after work in a bar the next day to talk more casually about what had happened at the Ackerman McQueen meeting was inappropriate.

At heart, her accusations were part of a claim to get the NRA to pay her a bigger severance package. And it worked. We settled, to make it all go away.

In truth, she was let go because no one at the NRA wanted the sort of measurement we were looking to implement. For me, personally, it was a failure on a couple of levels. We didn't achieve our goal of implementing system-wide controls and measurements. And I came away with the hard realization that the kind of reform I had wanted was not likely to happen. How could I bring in folks with experience and know-how when Wayne, Angus, the NRA, and Ackerman didn't want to change?

★

Where things really started going off the rails between Angus and me was over NRATV.

NRATV was Angus's brainchild. The NRA had had a cable show

for some time, airing recorded segments about people using their guns to protect themselves. But Angus advocated for a live-streaming channel, and bringing on board a ton of media talent to broadcast live content and opinions 24/7. And ultimately he convinced Wayne that this was the mechanism to reach younger viewers.

NRATV live launched in 2016. It didn't require a subscription, but it was enormously expensive. Ackerman hired Dana Loesch from TheBlaze—she had previously been an editor and reporter at Breitbart—offering her a seven-figure salary. She was super controversial, very much in your face. And there was division on the board about hiring her—half of the board hated her, and half of the board felt she had just the right amount of moxie and sexiness in the vein of Fox News.

In addition, Oliver North was hired away from Fox for over $2 million a year. Those headliners came with a whole pool of on-air talent and production people who were getting paid a lot of money. And part of Angus's thinking was that with Wayne doing less and less in the media, we needed more bench strength to do messaging for the NRA. These would be our spokespeople, our NRA surrogates.

The second problem with NRATV was that nobody watched it. So we were spending all this money, ultimately $25 million a year by 2018, and for what?

When I asked Ackerman for the number of unique viewers, they couldn't give us that. That's as basic a metric as you can get.

Then a third set of problems began when NRATV quickly morphed into this far right, extremist rant about immigration, about how Hillary Clinton was going to march into your house and take your AR-15, about burning down the *New York Times*, and so on. We had abandoned our focus on the Second Amendment and basically became an outlet for far right cant.

Sure, Wayne came out and said that the one thing that stops a bad guy with a gun is a good guy with a gun (even if it is not the only way to stop a bad guy). But having Dana Loesch propagate this dystopian fever dream on a daily basis, coupled with conspiracy theories of socialists taking over the country and gangsters entering from Mexico, was taking the toxicity to a whole other extreme. NRATV made us look racist, and there was a racist, xenophobic element to it. (And one thing Wayne is not is racist.)

Dana Loesch's show, *Relentless*, in particular, turned up the flame in terms of the craziness, with her extreme viewpoints and the sheer fury with which she delivered them. Controversial before, she went full bomb thrower. That had always been her schtick, but now she was calling the mainstream media "the rat bastards of the earth.... I'm happy to see them curb stomped."

One particularly incendiary Dana video that Ackerman produced, and that Wayne signed off on, was "The Violence of Lies." It went viral, and made us look like jackbooted stompers ourselves.

"They use their media to assassinate real news. They use their schools to teach children that their president is another Hitler.... The only way we stop this, the only way we save our country and our freedom is to fight this violence of lies with a clenched fist of truth."[1]

Good Lord.

Always ready to go exothermic, Dana tended to see the world through a lens of violence and fear. And NRATV became her bully pulpit for this. In 2012, in one of her previous stints as a spokesperson for CNN, she said on her radio show that she didn't have a problem with Marines who urinated on dead Taliban soldiers. "I'd drop down and do it too. That's me, though. I want a million cool points for these guys," she said, according to the *Huffington Post*. "C'mon people, this is a war. Do I have a problem with that as a citizen of the

United States? No, I don't." Why we would be surprised by her rhetoric was beyond me.

And then she really crossed the line. What really turned into a media firestorm was a segment in which she portrayed Thomas the Tank Engine, the kids' cartoon character, in a white hood, mimicking the Ku Klux Klan, to criticize the show's effort to add diversity to its cast.

Personally, I was appalled. The outrage was universal. And she was officially the chief spokesperson for the NRA, and special assistant to the executive vice president for public communication to Wayne himself!

We were catching flak that we did not want or need. Wayne was furious when he talked with Angus. But ultimately nothing happened. No statement, no firing, no punishment for putting a Grand Wizard KKK hood on a children's cartoon character! Wayne rarely held anyone accountable.

Things boiled over for me when she posted a tweet in 2017: "Spent my weekend preparing to move due to repeated threats from gun control advocates." The security team called me up and said hey, what's the deal, is Dana moving? Because she just posted this tweet telling people she's moving because of threats to her safety. Sighing, I replied, Go ask her husband and get back to me. Dana's husband, Chris, handled her security. Well, they checked with Dana's husband and they were not moving anytime soon. They talked about it, yes, but they weren't moving. So I called Angus and said, "Look, we can't have her out there just making stuff up." And his response floored me. "Well, if the members respond positively, that's a good thing and maybe you can raise money off it." I didn't need to hear any more. I followed up with Wayne. In truth, Wayne didn't want to deal with it, but I told him, "Look, I do not want any part of raising money off of Dana making shit up. I can't believe it."

The next day I was on a plane to Dallas to try to sort this out, which was an incredible waste of time. Dana could not understand why I was upset. She had zero remorse.

Eventually when the pressure from the media and the board became too great, Wayne started pushing back on the cost and the content of NRATV, and asked me to dig into it. And Angus went ballistic.

I was just asking basic questions that anyone who is paying $50 million for a TV channel would ask. Wayne and I flew to Dallas to push back on spending. I remember we were sitting in the Ackerman Death Star, and Angus just blew up at Wayne and me, screaming profanities and claiming we didn't know what we were talking about.

"Wayne, I will cut your fucking tongue out if you do anything to NRATV!"

I thought, *Okay, that's a new one. Cut your fucking tongue out?* Angus refused to budge an inch. I got up and started walking out. And he yelled, "Where are you going?!"

I said, "I got it."

He said, "What do you mean, 'I got it'?"

"Angus, you are crystal clear—I've got the point and I'm good." I was not about to be talked to that way. I wasn't going to be their puppet. And I walked out. I wanted nothing to do with their dysfunctional circus.

After that, Angus wanted to get rid of me. I don't think I talked to Angus again after that. And several months later, they found a way to push me aside.

CHAPTER 4

The Hammer

I was at "the club" having dinner one night in early 2017, when someone came up to me and said that Steve Bannon, the chief strategist of the Trump administration, wanted to meet me at the White House as soon as possible. He passed me his direct number and I called him. Steve answered and quickly asked, "Hey, can you come over to meet me tomorrow at the White House?"

I replied, "Absolutely," but checked in with Wayne to get clearance.

Wayne said, "Of course, yes, take the meeting, but don't tell anyone else."

The last thing Wayne wanted to deal with was Chris Cox finding out that I was at the White House, stepping on his turf. Classic Wayne. Never tell anyone anything and let's keep everyone in the dark and at each other's throats.

The next day I was off to the White House. Once I was through security, the guard instructed me to go up to the building. To my surprise, I was walking by myself for a hundred yards on the White House grounds. Once inside, I entered a beehive of activity. A woman behind a very nondescript desk addressed me straight away: "Josh, right? You're here to see Steve?"

I nodded yes.

"Take a seat and I'll let him know you're here."

The vice president walked by as I was waiting to see Steve. I guess Steve had told him I was coming in that morning. And he graciously thanked me (I know . . . weird?) for coming to see them.

"We love the NRA," he said, which really meant he loved Randy Kozuch, the NRA's lobbyist to all the conservative governors and attorneys general, who knew the vice president very well.

I was shown in to Steve's office. Steve famously had his whiteboards listing numerous strategies, tactics, plans, and positions up on the wall: Move the embassy to Jerusalem—check; Build the Wall—check; Taxes—check. He pulled his chair straight up to mine. "I've heard a lot about you."

He couldn't have been more gracious as he took out some index cards for notes and said point-blank, "What do I need to do for you guys?"

Remember, the NRA had been one of President Trump's biggest, most vocal, and most generous supporters.

"Number one, we need money." We truly did bet the bank on the election. "We're broke—we spent every dime on the election supporting the president.

"Number two, we need national reciprocity. Honestly, that's our legislative priority."

And Steve asked, what is that?

I told him, "The number one thing all of our members want— they want to be able to carry their guns from state to state without having to worry about getting a basketful of licenses, dealing with the patchwork of state laws, hoping they didn't break laws while driving across the country. Ideally it would work like a driver's license. If you have a concealed permit in Ohio, that permit would be honored in every other state of the union. Our members do not want to be pulled over because they live in Ohio and New Jersey doesn't recognize their Ohio permit."

"Is there a bill on it?" Steve asked.

"Yes, it's in the House now."

His response was, "Well, nobody here knows about it."

So I'm thinking, *You've got to be kidding.* Clearly Chris Cox, our chief lobbyist, was not creating enough noise. Yet inside the NRA he was claiming, "I've got this covered." Well, he didn't.

Jared Kushner stuck his head into Steve's office, and Steve introduced me. He told Jared, "We've got to do this reciprocity thing. Look, all the guys driving a truck across the country need this. It's *the* thing the NRA is fighting for."

And Jared's reaction was similarly clueless. "What is that?"

So I discovered this huge disconnect between the Trump administration's support and what we wanted to do. The fault for that didn't lie with the administration, but we needed to be on the same sheet of music.

And Steve said, "I get it, I've got it"—and we met for forty-five more minutes and talked about Chicago, the application of federal gun laws, a range of things. He and I hit it off quick. He had no idea what was on the NRA's Christmas list. As he admitted, he was not a gun guy and didn't fully grasp the issues. But he fully appreciated the part that the NRA and the Second Amendment played in the election and the connection between our membership and his "deplorables." Bannon was and is the spiritual leader of the populist movement that he and Andrew Breitbart launched. He respected the fact that this was *the* issue our folks voted on, and the importance it played in American life. He immediately metabolized the gun politics of Chicago and what could be done to stop the violence and bring law and order, with over three thousand shootings a year there. We nicknamed the initiative Project Gotham (I'm not sure who is the Dark Knight in this scenario . . .).

Going forward, Steve became a great friend and adviser to me. He's one of the few I've found who can be counted on where loyalty matters. We were both now Washington warriors in the business of fighting for the little guy, trying to advance our agendas, and we became kindred spirits in a way I never would have expected.

The NRA's ties to the White House were reaffirmed that spring when President Trump became the first sitting president in history to address the NRA at the 2017 annual convention. "The eight-year assault on your Second Amendment freedoms has come to a crashing end," Trump told our members. Gun owners now "have a true friend and champion in the White House. I will never, ever infringe on the right of the people to keep and bear arms. Never ever."[1]

The members ate it up. Why wouldn't they?

And the president didn't just talk the talk, he walked the walk. In February, he quietly signed an executive order that rolled back a regulation imposed by President Obama that made it harder for those receiving Social Security checks for mental illness and people deemed unfit to handle their own financial affairs to purchase a gun.[2] As Chris Cox said, this "marks a new era for law-abiding gun owners, as we now have a president who respects and supports our arms."[3]

That said, we would find the president at times to be an uneven, unreliable ally. I would never say that we had buyer's remorse, but without question he could take us to DEFCON 2 in a heartbeat. But to his credit, he was pushing on the issues we felt were important. As Chris would say, the president had a very freewheeling approach to these issues. At a televised meeting a year later where he convened a bipartisan group of legislators including Dianne Feinstein, Pat Toomey, and Marco Rubio to talk about gun control bills, he told lawmakers he wanted to produce "one terrific bill" on guns that expanded background checks. He even invited Senator Feinstein to throw out her proposed ban on assault rifles and add it to the final bill. Feinstein "almost levitated." Our own reaction was one of shock in Wayne's office as we watched it play out on national TV. Wayne's reaction was, "Oh my God, this is a disaster. What is he doing?"

"It has to be very, very strong on background checks," Trump told the lawmakers. "We want to pass something great. I want a strong counterpunch."

Was this the same guy who promised to back the NRA as a friend and champion? Not only that, but he called out the lawmakers for being afraid of the NRA. It resulted in this exchange with Toomey:

TRUMP: I'm just curious as to what you did in your [2013] bill.
TOOMEY: We didn't address it, Mr. President.
TRUMP: Do you know why? You're afraid of the NRA.

Ultimately, the NRA came out on top, Trump's waffling was quickly corrected, and he parroted the NRA company line within days and remained a consistent defender of the Second Amendment. But that was our guy. You never knew what was going to come out of his mouth.

One weekend Wayne and Chris were having lunch with the president at the White House. After the meeting Wayne called me. I asked, "How did it go?"

Wayne laughed, and said, "Well, I don't know. I'm not sure he heard us. I'm really not. He kept telling us what an amazing menu it was, and asked his staff for a Sharpie so that he could sign it for me. It was all he could talk about."

Later, Trump seemed to be waffling on red flag laws, which we opposed, because they could potentially take away an individual's right to bear arms without due process. These laws are far from being one-size-fits-all. But when the president brought it up, Wayne of course replied, "Well, it truly depends on making sure in every one of these cases there was proper due process. We can't have a situation where people's guns are being taken without the right process."

The president replied, "Come on, nobody gives a shit about due process."[4]

★

One of the big initiatives I wanted to start up when I joined the NRA was the Carry Guard insurance program, with the idea that the NRA would become a leader in the conceal carry space. It would include a training component focused solely on the self-protection space and a liability insurance program that would cover you in the event you had to use your gun to protect yourself or your family. In today's world, if you end up having to use your firearm there is a very good chance you'll end up with significant legal costs. There is a company in Wisconsin called the United States Concealed Carry Association that was making $70 million a year and performing identical services.

It was obvious to me that the NRA was missing this opportunity to grow and support membership. Virtually no one within the association had even heard of USCCA.

When President Obama came into office, there were about four million concealed carry holders in the country. Four million

Americans had a permit to carry a concealed firearm with them wherever they went. In most states, you go through a day or two of training to get a concealed weapon permit. In Washington, D.C., it's a three-day process of training to obtain a permit. For the most part, what you have to go through is pretty rigorous. On the other hand, there are some states, like Vermont, that give gun owners a concealed weapon permit without requiring any training or a special application. New Hampshire and Missouri do not require a permit at all.

I have a permit-to-carry card, and many states provide reciprocity. So if I'm in Michigan, and I carry my firearm in Florida, my permit will work there.

By the time Obama left office, there were fourteen million concealed weapons permits in the United States. The numbers exploded simply because gun owners thought the president was going to take away their guns, although Obama and Congress never actually tried to do that. There is no doubt that that is what drove so many people to buy more guns, and to obtain concealed weapons permits. They're buying them basically for self-protection.

In terms of reciprocity, it depends on the state—there are a patchwork of laws across the country. The National Reciprocity Law that was introduced in Congress would solve this problem and allow a person with a concealed carry permit to travel from state to state with their firearm, and know they are not running afoul of any laws. But it has been stuck in Congress for a number of years, well shy of the votes needed to pass it in the Senate.

In my conversations with Wayne and others within the NRA, I was told, "Right now we are an afterthought. We're not even on the radar in terms of concealed carry." As of 2019, the number of concealed carry weapons permit holders had reached nearly nineteen million, and only a fraction of them are currently NRA members. It's the beating heart of the market. Nine out of ten guns sold in the country are sold for self-protection. Hunting and sport shooting is minuscule in the scheme of overall sales.

In conversations with Wayne I told him that "this is one of the reasons you brought me in, to come up with new programs and grow the membership." All of which he agreed with; he wanted to fast-track the entire program.

So I set up a meeting with USCCA. They had built this $70 million company, and what were they selling? They were selling a magazine focused around personal protection, carrying a concealed weapon, and all that implies, and the equivalent of a personal liability insurance policy in the event you use your firearm for self-protection. They had built an incredible business, admittedly with help from the NRA.

And I really wanted the NRA to get into that business. Because if you are a gun owner and you use your gun in self-defense, most of the time you're going to end up in some sort of legal situation— maybe not litigation, but there will no doubt be lawyers involved. It can get really costly very quickly, even if you use your gun in your own defense. If a criminal breaks into your house and you shoot him in self-defense, you will most likely end up in a legal fracas.

So this insurance is no different than any other kind of insurance. In fact, if you have a liability clause in your homeowner's insurance, you're probably covered for this eventuality. Carry Guard was the same concept. You're covered in such a case. Just like a homeowner is with his or her insurance.

It made a lot of sense on all sorts of levels. From a business standpoint it looked lucrative for the NRA. And more important, this could be the kind of grassroots initiative that would bring new people into the membership rolls. Think of a woman carrying a gun for protection in inner-city Chicago; how is it, I argued, that she's not an NRA member? Today, there are eighteen million concealed weapons holders in the United States—the numbers have gone up. Which is three and a half times bigger than the current membership of the NRA.

Tim Schmidt, the president and founder of USCCA, was laser-focused on customer service and had built an amazing apparatus. I was exploring what relationship if any we could forge with them. After meeting with Tim and USCCA, I was very interested in how we could form a joint venture with them. Angus quickly beat back any notion of that and Wayne followed suit. USCCA had an incredible team that looked like a modern NRA. They were entrepreneurial, had an incredibly motivated staff, and had already done much of the heavy lifting. It was about as sound a fit as you could think of, but that's not how things operated at the NRA. (The irony is that today USCCA is positioned to fill the void the NRA ultimately left behind. Tim has poked his head out a few times doing national publicity, including a piece on *60 Minutes*, and he did a darn good job. As it turns out, the market is his for the taking.)

So I was committed to building this into a great program for the NRA. We brought in Lockton Affinity, the world's largest privately held insurance brokerage, as our partner. The program was underwritten by Chubb, the insurance giant. And Angus McQueen was hugely excited about it and viewed it as an obvious path to go down. We worked on it for most of 2016 and early 2017. We launched it at the 2017 NRA annual convention, in a big way. And we had a spectacular kickoff.

We had a great insurance product that we were selling, and created a training program to go along with it—which struggled to come to fruition. The training program was built around a simple premise: that people want to feel confident walking around with a gun in their bag and know how to handle it. They have developed the skills to use their firearm in a life-and-death situation, and have had training to understand how that unfolds in real time—and the consequences of such an action.

But how do they get trained to do that? A lot of the training out there is really disconnected from everyday experience. It's not set up for this. It's all over the map in terms of what it offers a gun owner. I wanted something that was easy and accessible, so that gun owners, especially women, felt comfortable coming in and getting trained in this fashion, to become proficient in how to use their gun. It's one thing to own a gun and it's another to really know how to use it.

Like anything else, you have to practice, right? It is the Law of 10,000 that Malcolm Gladwell writes about—the 10,000 hours of focused practice to master a skill or subject. Otherwise, you're not going to be great at resorting to your training, or relying on it in a situation that will require split-second decision making under an incredible amount of pressure. So we built this training program with the idea that it would evolve and adapt over time. And it would be female-friendly. And we launched this in record time. There was a lot of demand for it. The issue was, it took a lot of time to develop the trainers to the level we wanted, and would be a slow rollout to scale it to size.

Carry Guard was everywhere at the 2017 Annual Meeting. It was my baby, and, good or bad, it would be on me. The project was nothing more than another way for the NRA to connect with the people who have guns but were not members already. According to the numbers I was seeing, the fastest-indexing person to purchase a firearm for protection to get a concealed carry permit is an African American woman in an urban area. And so there was always this constant question at the NRA: How do we connect with women in urban areas? And I felt Carry Guard was our pathway to reach them.

And honestly, that is the future of an association for gun owners in America, whether it's the NRA or another organization that takes its place. That is the membership to chase. If you decide that you're going to walk out of your house with a firearm every day for protection, you're pretty serious about it. Those people care about their right of protection.

It was also high ground for the NRA to stand on. It's a human right to be able to protect yourself. And if you look at the statistics of the eighteen million who have concealed weapons permits, only 0.8 percent have committed any serious crimes (while 8.6 percent of the U.S. adult population has a felony conviction, or about one in twelve).[5] They are law-abiding, which makes sense if you think about it: They've gone through the trouble of getting a permit card so they can carry. They bought the gun legally. By definition, they are following the rules.

These people are the future of the gun rights movement, and they vote. That was why I felt the Carry Guard program was so important. It went over like gangbusters among the members at the Annual Meeting, exceeding all of our expectations.

And I couldn't believe the amount of shit I took for backing the program.

I guess all of this falls under the rule of no good deed goes unpunished.

Chris Cox at ILA was going nuts over it, pointing out every photograph that had a problem, or this or that. You can't imagine the amount of time we spent going over a photograph where a guy had his finger resting on the trigger as he is moving between shots. You'd have thought we were trying to replace a heat shield tile of the Space Shuttle while in orbit. He hated it for God knows why. Probably because it wasn't his idea. Without question he was worried about the threat to his position as heir apparent. Now my success with Carry Guard out of the gate was a threat to him. Also, Chris was someone who always wanted to be in the know, so the fact that I had created this whole program without his knowledge made him crazy. He was like a little kid stamping his feet and holding his breath. Wayne suggested, "Why don't we take Chris down to Ackerman and show him the whole program." But Chris wanted nothing to do with it.

The other problem with Carry Guard was how I got it done. Wayne and I chose to create Carry Guard mostly outside the NRA, with Ackerman McQueen. I knew if I did it internally, it would never get done. Remember: The NRA is enormously bureaucratic, and folks there just didn't have had the tenacity or the vision to create Carry Guard from scratch. It was not in their DNA. Many corporations set up skunk works projects to launch an innovation, and that's in effect what we did.

For the training part of it, I ended up hiring four guys—an ex–Navy SEAL police trainer, a retired law enforcement officer with decades of training experience, another firearms trainer, and a Green Beret guy who had his own training shop and had carried concealed for the duration of his deployment. These guys were all former military and law enforcement professionals. They trained people for a living, were incredibly disciplined, and focused on safety first and foremost. And we came up with a really interesting program.

But I created this whole thing outside of the NRA structure. And people within the NRA started to get wind of it. I had no idea, in retrospect, what the blowback would be on me. And I completely underestimated the sheer hate within the association toward Ackerman. The buzz around the office was, ironically, *Josh is an Ackerman guy.* Everyone was seen that way, everyone got a label: *You're a Chris guy, you're a Wayne guy, you're an Ackerman guy.* (Wayne too was seen as an Ackerman guy.)

And so I got a lot of blowback for Carry Guard inside the building. Nonetheless, we got off to a great start. The demand for the insurance product far exceeded our modeling.

The training was going slower, however. It was something that we wanted to get right. The biggest issue was developing the trainers up to the level we all had hoped for. It just took some time building that pipeline. One of the things that slowed us down was that we had to find gun ranges where people could move around, to simulate real-life conditions. In most ranges, there are blinders, and you stand and shoot in place. So you learn how to shoot being really still, but that's far from realistic in a real-life situation, in your home or out on the streets. We wanted owners to feel comfortable in all sorts of conditions, from low light to pouring rain.

Ultimately that dramatically narrowed down the number of ranges we could use. We put together a three-day program. People would come in to train, and we would give them different tests, to grade them on time and accuracy. And eventually the program really started to get going, until it was killed by the bureaucrats at the NRA, led by Joe Debergalis, the head of General Operations. Joe seemed to spend more time concerned with where to put his bronze statue of Charlton Heston, rather than focusing how to grow the place. He was someone we hired who Wayne and I went back and forth on, for these very reasons—he wasn't as innovative as I felt we needed. I could imagine him dreaming of himself as the next Wayne LaPierre, smoking cigars in a big leather chair, while having his ankle biters do his bidding, and repeating his schtick to the board that he's trying to do more with less.

★

My hope now is that someone will think through what we were trying to achieve and pull it off themselves. We need more available training in real-world situations than is readily available. The folks at Thunder Ranch, Gunsite, the ICE Training guys, along with USCCA are doing great things in the training world, but there needs to be a larger effort to scale that level of sophisticated training. Unfortunately the NRA is nowhere near where it should be in this space. They lag far behind the aforementioned groups, which is tragic considering the yearly budget of the NRA and low single-digit spend on safety and training. It's due to nothing more than a lack of leadership and a bureaucracy that has calcified into a do-nothing apparatus.

Along with training, we did a marketing push where people would give us their email and we would send them a guide for free. The most popular one was the aftermath guide: What happens if you use your gun in defense, after the fact? We were getting thousands of emails asking for the guides, and we would then turn around and market back to them. This is not some cutting-edge tactic but rather modern e-commerce marketing. It was a very engaged audience.

By the end of December, we had twenty-five thousand customers. They bought policies that gave them $150,000 in criminal defense reimbursement, and $1 million in civil liability protection. And they were paying $400 a year, driving $8 million in revenue. All the customers were acquired in the first six months of the program. The program was on a solid trajectory, well above our initial projections.

Lockton and Chubb were ecstatic as we surpassed their own internal modeling, which laid out a multiple-year downstream revenue stream of all the customers. Folks don't just cancel their insurance policies. It's a sticky business; there is a reason why Manhattan is filled with skyscrapers adorned with AIG and the like. We were just getting it going and our project showed signs of growing into something of real value. And we were pulling in new members too. Little did I know what lay ahead.

★

For the past ten years the NRA at the federal level has run into a brick wall in terms of advancing gun rights. But at the state level it has continued to be extraordinarily effective. And no one epitomizes the political power of the NRA at the state level better than Marion Hammer.

I could make the argument that Marion has had a bigger influence on gun lobbying than Wayne LaPierre. She is nothing short of a legend, tough as nails, and an unwavering gun rights advocate. She is eighty years old, diminutive in stature, with the heart of a lion. Millie Hallow, Wayne's longtime assistant, described her as the firebrand of the NRA board, a moniker she wore with pride.

Marion, as you may surmise, is not always loved by everyone. I'm quite sure that's just how she wants it. If you cross her, she will not forget it, as she let me know early on in our relationship. She's also a gun-packing mother and grandmother—she keeps a Smith & Wesson .38 Special in her purse. She once told the *Orlando Sentinel*, "If you came at me, and I felt that my life was in danger or that I was going to be injured, I wouldn't hesitate to shoot you."[6]

Having spent a good deal of time with Marion, I can assure you that is a fact. She has been such an effective lobbyist that the Sunshine State is referred to as "the Gunshine State."

Once a competitive target shooter, she described her first experience shooting a .22 as a five-year-old. "I remember seeing a great big red tomato right on the front of that can," she recalled on CNN in 1995 as she rose to the presidency of the National Rifle Association. "And on my first shot, I drilled the tomato dead center."

Marion was the architect of the Stand Your Ground laws. In an impassioned speech before the Florida state legislature, she proclaimed, "You can't expect a victim to wait before taking action to protect herself, and say: 'Excuse me, Mr. Criminal, did you drag me into this alley to rape and kill me or do you just want to beat me up and steal my purse?'"

That's classic Marion.

Once I had settled in as Wayne's chief of staff, she and I used to talk every other week, depending on what was going on. And during contentious times, every day, including Sundays. She was a huge supporter of Wayne and would do anything to help him. She thought of him as one of her own. If we needed board votes on something for Wayne, she was our go-to person. She was also the person I went to when I had a problem with the board—she would know what to do or how to deal with it. She was super effective, feisty, opinionated. She and I had served on the NRA board together, but I really got to know her working with Wayne.

She served as the first woman NRA president, from 1995 to 1998, and has been the NRA lobbyist in Florida since the fall of Rome. She in effect ran the NRA in Florida all by herself.

And she was always at loggerheads with Chris Cox. Chris wanted to control her—as he wanted to control all of the state lobbyists. And in fairness, that was part of his job. But Marion wasn't having any of it. Chris was constantly trying to look over her shoulder, and she would just not put up with that. She was too powerful politically and always got the job done. And Florida was one of the biggest states in terms of NRA membership and concealed carry membership in the country. She was always lobbying Wayne and me to get rid of Chris. In conversations, she would express her frustration or exasperation with Wayne over his reluctance to fire Chris. I told her, "Welcome to my world." Chris was deeply suspicious of people who were really effective at their job. She ran Florida, and Chris was always getting in her way. "Asshole," she would say of him in one exchange after another. With the email blasts she sent out, NRA headquarters and her boss, Chris, had to approve the language, and he was constantly changing the wording and taking forever to get back to her. When he finally was let go Marion hooted and howled, and that's how it goes in the NRA's version of *Game of Thrones*.

For decades, Florida has been the laboratory for new gun rights legislation, and that's all due to Marion, lobbying in a state that has a Republican legislature and a Republican governor. "There is no more tenacious presence in Tallahassee than Marion Hammer," said Sally Bradshaw, who was Jeb Bush's chief of staff. "A lot of lobbyists come and go, but Marion is part of a cause, and that means she has real credibility and a stick-with-it-ness that few can match," Bradshaw added. "You want her on your side in a fight."

As Richard Feldman, a former organizer for the NRA, said of Marion, "There is no single individual responsible for enacting more pro-gun legislation in the states than Marion Hammer."[7]

Marion is the ultimate example of the conscious effort on the part of the NRA to focus its lobbying efforts on individual states. Gun control groups tended to pursue national agendas—they didn't have resources to fight state by state. As a result, the NRA's strategy to fight for gun rights at the state level usually went unopposed. David Keene, a former NRA president said, "90 percent of the laws that the NRA has contended with over the course of the last few decades have not been federal laws, but have been state and local restrictions."[8]

One of the first battles the NRA lobby fought at the state level in the '80s and '90s was for what we call "preemption laws." These mandated that the laws at the local or county level could never be stricter in terms of gun regulation than the laws at the state level. Why? It was easier to fight for gun rights at the state level.

Think about that for a moment. The NRA got in front of the local jurisdictions in an effort to make gun rights equal across each state. It was a brilliant tactical move that was little followed by the press or the antigun crowd. Arguably it was one of the NRA's biggest victories.

In 1979, only two states had full preemption laws, and a handful more had partial laws. Marion helped to pass preemption early on in Florida, paving the way for a broader state-by-state push.

By 2005, forty-five states had full or partial preemption laws. Randy Kozuch, the head of NRA's state and local operations at the time, then shepherded preemption across the finish line in many other states in the country. His soft-spoken drawl and low-key approach with the governors and statehouse leaderships smoothed any resistance. His approach was to educate and teach folks and coax them into a yes, not just beat them over the head. Like Marion, he was one of the most effective lobbyists the association has ever had.

Marion also pioneered and passed the nation's first concealed carry laws. Because of her, gun owners can carry a concealed gun in public, and we now have concealed carry weapons laws in almost every state.

You cross Marion, as Florida legislators learned, at your peril. She and I would regularly have heated discussions, but no matter how mad I would get I always ended with "I love you" and always got back an "I love you too." That's how much she meant to me, politics or not.

There were a number of occasions when she'd warn me to be careful of this or that, and she was always right. She was a political operator's operator. She was also one of the few people who could give

Wayne a piece of her mind. Wayne would call me, usually about a Chris Cox issue, to tell me, "Man, did I get it from Marion today. She just won't let up. I told her I'll deal with Chris."

Her office, a few blocks from the state capitol in Tallahassee, is relatively nondescript—it has no leather-covered chairs or fancy waiting room; instead it is full of flyers being sent out, campaign mailers. It looks like something out of *The War Room*. She has a trove of letters displayed from everyone who matters in politics in the state of Florida, and photos from her many victories, including former governor Jeb Bush, who wrote a glowing thank-you to her.

With Marion, you are either on her side 100 percent of the time or you are on her shit list, whatever your transgression, and let me tell you, that is not a list you want yourself on.

As one Republican Florida legislator said, "If you're with Marion ninety-five per cent of the time, you're a damn traitor."[9]

The NRA has three hundred thousand members in Florida, and Marion stays in touch with them regularly by email, sending "alerts" and letting those who follow her know who has been loyal to the cause and who has, in her words, betrayed her and our Second Amendment rights.

It was a never-ending battle to get Chris's approval for these emails, all part of the games and bureaucracy that plague the NRA. One former state Republican senator who worked with Hammer estimated that her emails reach "two or three million" people.[10] With almost two million permits, Florida today has by far the most concealed weapons permits in the country. With 4.6 million Republican voters in the state, one strategist says, "The number of fanatical supporters who will take her word for anything and can be deployed almost at will is unique." With the upcoming election and importance of the I-4 corridor these may be prophetic words. And that is the power of the NRA. It has nothing to do with contributions or money and everything to do with a very large block of committed people who come out to vote on a single issue. It is in fact the definition of democracy. Others might not like it, but the pro-gun voter is very effective in that regard.

Politically, winning and keeping Marion's favor is gold. When Rick Scott was running for a second term as governor against former governor Charlie Crist, Hammer helped steer $2 million and her two million voters to Scott. And not surprisingly, Scott won, by a single percentage point. As Republican state senator Matt Gaetz, a rising star in Trump world, said in an interview, "If you are the governor, and you've won by a handful of votes, and you've got great political ambitions, you're going to take Marion's call in the middle of the night. And, if she needs anything, you do it, and if you don't think you can do it, you try anyway."

The Stand Your Ground legislation was introduced by Republican lawmakers in 2004, but it was all choreographed by Marion. As the Florida state minority leader acknowledged, Marion was "the ringmaster," telling lawmakers what to do.[11] Stand Your Ground justified the use of lethal force—of using a weapon—anytime a gun owner believes he or she is under threat of harm. Critics claimed there wasn't a single instance in which a Florida citizen had been wrongfully charged. But legislators for whom the bill was a bridge too far, or who initially opposed it, decided the law wouldn't have much impact, so why not appease Marion? In the end, only twenty legislators voted against it—all Democrats—and Jeb Bush signed it into law, calling the bill "common sense." It only became controversial after George Zimmerman in 2012 shot an unarmed seventeen-year-old black man, Trayvon Martin. Since then, Marion's Stand Your Ground law has been adopted in twenty-seven states.

To me, it was an example of the foresight and relentlessness of Hammer's approach. Whether or not you agree with the laws, you simply cannot dismiss her success in a world where political victories and real legislation passed is something of a miracle. In 2014, she pushed for a bill to allow people without permits to carry concealed guns during a mandatory evacuation, like a hurricane. An expert witness from the Florida Department of Military Affairs, Captain Terrence Gorman, a highly decorated combat veteran, was asked to testify regarding the legislation at a Senate committee hearing. His testimony did not go Marion's way, saying that the bill conflicted with existing law. Many in the committee felt he did a good job. Marion, however, was furious. "You're on my shit list," she told the expert witness's supervisor.[12] She contacted Governor Scott's general counsel, saying the witness was "'clearly there to kill' the legislation, and demanded to know what was 'being done to undo the harm he has caused with his actions.'" And she came down on the expert witness like a ton of bricks. There was a lot of back-and-forth, but as a Scott staffer admitted, "It was one-sided. It was Marion saying, 'Here's what I want you to do to fix this problem. You're going to do this, and this, and if you don't do any of these things it's going to be an issue.'"[13]

Six months later, Governor Scott signed Marion's bill into law. It was a vivid example of Marion playing hardball to lobby for what she felt gun owners needed.

She never gave up. It was something I admired in her. I learned a lot from her. After Trump won the 2016 election, our members wanted to cash in their chips. As I told Steve Bannon in the White House, the number one priority for the membership was passing national reciprocity—if you had a concealed weapon permit from one state, say Missouri, it would be honored in every other state. This law would in effect federalize concealed carry permits and allow you to cross state lines freely with your gun. The NRA had made a big deal about it in the run-up to the 2016 election. At the 2017 NRA Annual Meeting, an older member came up to me at one of the auctions. "I guess you're one of the important guys, huh?" He poked me with his cane. "So tell me, when are we going to get national reciprocity?"

The NRA had gotten a bill through the House in 2016, but Chris refused to push it to the floor of the Senate, supposedly "because he was told by Mitch McConnell we didn't have the votes."

That's the difference. The Hammer approach would have been, "Mitch, we just spent $30 million to get Trump elected. I want a goddamned vote every month! Make them say no and I'll raise hell and let their constituents know as much! Bring the damn vote to the floor."

Chris's philosophy was he couldn't possibly bring a measure to the Senate floor, for if it were to fail, that would be bad politically for him and the NRA.

At the time it was a fiercely discussed debate on strategy. I was firmly in the "let's charge this hill" camp. And it's hard to argue now, considering we are in year four of the Trump administration and any discussion of the law has evaporated and not a single vote ever happened in the Senate. That said, I have no doubt Trump would be happy to Sharpie that into law in the Oval Office.

The Hammer approach was in fact how Wayne had passed the Firearm Owners' Protection Act, which completely rolled back the laws that were put in place in the 1968 Gun Control Act. He made Congress vote over and over, win or lose. Ultimately it succeeded, and to this day was the last piece of legislation passed with a discharge petition. People bowed to the massive pressure they were getting during elections from the NRA for not cooperating.

Tony Makris would constantly rant that the members wanted a vote on national reciprocity up or down, good or bad. His point was valid: What good is a lobbying association if you don't show that you're out there fighting for the rights of your members? Winning or losing a given battle isn't always the be-all or end-all—that's why they are called battles and not wars. Getting in the damn fight is key, so that you can ultimately carry the day. And making senators vote, even if they vote no, was not a bad thing.

When Chris took over ILA, Wayne let him pretty much run it his way, which was not how Wayne had approached political fights in his heyday. The battles were no doubt different substantively, but philosophically, we chose never to bring forth a piece of legislation that wasn't guaranteed to pass. If we didn't have all the votes, it wasn't going to be voted on.

For me, this fear of failure was missing the larger point. I tried to persuade Wayne of it, but Chris would respond in some overly nuanced way that might not have made much sense, but was a tactic he used regularly on Wayne to great effect. Filibustering, as Wayne put it.

In spite of the media's obsession and the association's supposed clout, the NRA has failed for years to pass any new pro-gun legislation at the national level, nor has it brought any new legislation to the floor. In recent years the NRA's national lobbying efforts have been all defensive.

My instinct was to "use the Hammer" method—make them vote on it. Make it part of each senator's voting record. Use that in the next election to get behind someone who would support your cause. Tell every gun owner in America on the record what you believe in.

And that's the way Marion saw it, too. We were completely simpatico on this topic. One of the things she fought for in Florida was an open carry law—to let gun owners carry weapons openly in public, as well as require state universities and colleges to allow guns on campus. With all odds against her, she pushed forward; to her, a defeat in the legislature was a temporary hindrance.

"Eventually, everything passes. That's why, when folks keep asking, 'What if these bills don't pass?' Well, they'll be back. If we file a bill, it will be back and back and back until it passes."

Marion helped to construct an enhanced Stand Your Ground law, putting the burden of proof in a shooting on the prosecutor, rather than the shooter; it was controversial, as critics claimed it forced prosecutors to "prove a case twice." On the other hand, it would render a defense based on Stand Your Ground "nearly impregnable."[14] Democrats in the house criminal justice subcommittee tied the law up with amendments that would neuter the bill. When the committee voted on the amendments, two Republicans were missing. One was Ray Pilon, a Hammer favorite with an "A+" rating, who was obliged to attend a different committee meeting for a bill he was sponsoring. As he said, "Marion crucified me" for missing the vote. He told her he would have voted against the amendments, but he had no choice but to be present to discuss his own bill. "She didn't believe me. She called me a liar."[15]

That winter, Marion revived the legislation, where it passed the state senate and went to the house judiciary committee. The chair, retiring Republican Charles McBurney, in the end had problems with it and couldn't support it. And the bill went down to defeat again.

A few months after he effectively killed Hammer's bill, McBurney hoped to get an appointment as a circuit judge in Jacksonville. In the spring of 2016, a nominating committee put him on a list of six finalists, which then went to Governor Scott.

For Marion, it was payback time. She emailed her followers that McBurney "had proved himself to be summarily unfit to serve on the bench of any Court anywhere.... E-mail Governor Rick Scott RIGHT AWAY. Tell him PLEASE DO NOT APPOINT Charles McBurney to a judgeship." Thousands did so, and Scott chose one of the other candidates. McBurney wrote an op-ed on Jacksonville .com, complaining that the message to legislators and elected officials is, "If you cross me once, even if the issue doesn't involve the Second Amendment, I will take you out."

And Ray Pilon, who missed that crucial committee meeting vote? His NRA rating was dropped to "C," and Hammer supported one of his House colleagues over him in the primary for an open seat in the state senate. "She sent out thousands of cards telling people to vote for him," Pilon said. "She did for him what she once did for me." Not surprisingly, Pilon lost.

And the enhanced Stand Your Ground bill? Hammer refiled it in 2017, and got forty-five House Republicans to cosponsor it. It passed the legislature, despite vehement protests from prosecutors across Florida, and was signed into law by Governor Scott. That is an example of the power of even a single determined individual taking action and framing the debate. A textbook example of how to play hardball politics. It is *not* for the faint of heart. And it all stemmed from the fact that Marion believed in the cause.

In June 2016, in the wake of the horrific Pulse nightclub shooting in Orlando, where forty-nine people were killed and even more wounded, Democrats tried to convene a special session of the Florida legislature to deal with gun violence, and later introduced a bill to ban assault rifles. Marion called the efforts a publicity stunt, and Republicans beat it back. The assault weapons ban didn't even get a hearing. Most recently, Hammer torpedoed an assault weapons ban before it even hit the floor—the measure failed to get enough signatures to be put on the 2020 ballot for Florida. (That said, ballot initiatives have become a favorite tactic among gun control advocates in many states and will no doubt be a future battleground for years to come. And an opportunity for voters to weigh in directly on their rights in their own states.)

The NRA flexes its muscles successfully in other states, as well. Representative Debra Maggart, a member of the Tennessee legislature, had an "A+" rating. As she said to the *Washington Post*, "You can't get more pro Second Amendment than me."

But in 2012 she tabled an NRA-backed bill that would permit gun owners to keep their guns locked in their cars. Three months later, billboards appeared in her district, picturing Maggart alongside President Obama, with the caption, "Representative Debra Maggart says she supports your gun rights. Of course, he says the same thing. Defend Freedom, defeat Maggart."

She lost in the Republican primary by 16 points.[16] As Chuck Cunningham, the former NRA state and local affairs director, said, "We'll spend the kitchen sink against those who turn on us."[17]

I know what gun control people reading about Marion must think: *This is who we must stop!* But folks, I hate to break it to you. What Marion is doing may be playing hardball, no question, but it is part of the messy process that is called democracy. What people fail to recognize is that the NRA is not successful because it spends a ton of money. It's much more basic than that—it's about the *voters*. When told to vote in a given election, folks who are committed to gun rights turn out and vote. That's the NRA's power; the money is largely insignificant.

Sure, you need to turn the voters out, but when Marion or the

NRA tells Florida gun owners to vote, they do it. Simple as that—and a far cry from the sinister Washington games that I saw play out between Wayne and Chris that did little to benefit the members of the association.

And following Marion's lead, the NRA has done the same in Michigan, Ohio, Nebraska, and many other states. In the grand scheme of things, the NRA spends pennies in elections. Generally if there is an issue around guns, NRA members turn out. Chris once said, "We have a track record of being focused, whether you call it myopic or laser-like. We've been called dogged. I'll accept that. We've been called unforgiving at times. I'll accept that. We are going to do everything in our power to protect this right for our members."[18] Well, that was Chris at his most idealistic in terms of defending gun rights. Unfortunately, his actions didn't always match his words, and he was just as laser-focused on internal politics and turf.

★

The NRA lost $55 million in 2017. As I had feared, revenues plummeted from $367 million in the 2016 election year to $312 million as donations dried up under the pro-gun President Trump.[19] That was a huge problem for us. Cutting costs at the NRA was very difficult.

The NRA at heart was a grassroots organization, and over half our revenue came from the $45 annual fees of the roughly five million members.

The rest of the money came from donations and other income streams. Roughly $10 million comes from our affinity programs with Hertz, Wells Fargo, firearms insurance programs, and so on. The thirty-five hundred Friends of NRA local events, run by volunteers across the country, where folks pay their twenty bucks to have dinner, maybe enter a raffle—those bring in about $75 million a year, half of which goes to the national organization, the other half to the state-run NRA chapters for gun safety and gun ranges.

There is roughly $5 million in contributions from gun manufacturers (more in an election year), and probably another $5 to $10 million from them in advertising in *American Rifleman*.

There is an assumption on the part of the media and the public that gun manufacturers dominated NRA funding. That we were in bed together. It was a silly construct, but the press loved the sound of it. That in essence the NRA was bought off by the Remingtons and Rugers of the world. We did get as much as $15 million a year between donations and ads in the magazine—which is real revenue but it's also paid ad space, not a blank check—but it makes up only 5 percent of the NRA's funding. In my time there, of the seventy-six board members, only two or three owned or ran gun companies. The NRA wasn't run by or bought off by the gun companies. That sounds good in the pages of the *Washington Post*, but it simply wasn't true.

Sure, the gun manufacturers came to the annual conventions and staked their flag there—the convention was the second biggest gun event in the country. It was a great venue to advertise their wares. But that had nothing to do with gun manufacturers providing the majority of revenue to the NRA. In a conversation with Wayne, I had told him, "We ought to consider putting every dollar donated from gun manufacturers straight into the School Shield program, which would serve two purposes, one, to show we were serious about protecting schools, and two, to make it clear the idea that the NRA was bought and paid for by gun companies is simply false."

Without question, the NRA helped to pass the Protection of Lawful Commerce in Arms Act in 2005, which protected gun manufacturers from lawsuits. But that is just because those rights are congruent with Second Amendment rights. In 2016, there was only one gun manufacturer that gave the NRA a lot of money, Ruger, all of which was spent on the election.

A good friend of mine who was the CEO of Remington tried twice to get elected to the NRA board. The membership refused to vote for him because they viewed him as a hedge fund guy from New York.

There are no big junkets, payoffs, or bribes from Big Gun that I'm aware of. Sure, the concealed carry law was good for Glock, and I'm not saying that the NRA hasn't laid the groundwork for manufacturers to prosper. But it's not like their views dominate the NRA's decision making, let alone drive the association's revenues.

The NRA is also well behind on its pension fund payments and has been for years. And in one of the craziest bits of corporate malpractice, the NRA had given employees both a pension and a 401(k) with a 5 percent match. Not everyone who has the 401(k) gets the pension, but everyone who gets the pension also gets the 401(k). So two retirement programs when we couldn't afford one. Okay . . . You simply cannot make this up. I haven't done the math but you can imagine how many millions of dollars yearly of member dues are going to pay for someone's pension *and* 401(k). And that is the overwhelming point—that the association over the decades has lost touch with operating as not-for-profit and became a vehicle that filled many employees' pockets, from the top to the bottom.

In 2018 we finally stopped incurring new pension obligations, and during the pandemic the NRA temporarily stopped any match of 401(k) funds.

In terms of fund-raising the NRA's charter is a membership organization focused on Second Amendment rights and education and training.

The night Trump won in 2016 was followed in my mind by the

stark reality that revenues plunged in 2017 and we needed to retool in a number of places. And Wayne, the board, none of the folks on the sixth floor had a plan for this. Unfortunately, much of it was now laid on me.

Wayne and Woody Phillips, our CFO, and I worked through the entire budget from top to bottom and made substantial cuts, but still weren't close. The place was bloated to the extreme, especially in General Operations. After much discussion, that was when Wayne and I decided to let Kyle Weaver, the head of General Operations, go.

Or so I thought.

The night before we announced the move, Wayne called me up at 2:00 a.m. in a full panic, claiming that I was forcing him into something.

"You made me do this! I always thought [Kyle] might run the place!"

I was stunned. *You're leader of the National Rifle Association and you are blaming me?* I thought.

And I also realized at that moment, *Wow, this guy won't take responsibility for anything. He wants to blame me if it doesn't work out.*

"Slow down, Wayne. If you don't want to do this, fine. No big deal, we can just walk it back."

The next morning, I had our outside counsel, Steve Hart, in my office, and we were looking at each other wondering if this was going to happen. And I couldn't get an answer out of Wayne, who was MIA, on whether to go ahead with the firing or not. He wouldn't call me back.

Then he called Steve's cell.

"So, Steve, what do you think?"

It was absolute silliness. And we were both in my office taking these calls, realizing just how screwed up the place was. Finally,

Wayne reluctantly decided to go ahead, but the decision was up in the air until the last minute. It was a microcosm of thirty-five years of decision making under Wayne—he was unable to let anyone go, he hated confrontation, and he was scared to death of catching heat from the board for making tough decisions.

Once that saga was over, Wayne had asked me to look at the PR department Kyle had built within the General Operations division, which included over a dozen people and outside vendors. The NRA had Ackerman McQueen doing PR work for us, Chris had his own PR department, and Kyle, as head of General Operations, had a third PR arm. In other words, we had three departments all hiring different outside PR firms and staffing up internally to work with those firms; outside of being incredibly redundant, no one communicated with one another.

I had been named the interim director of General Operations after Kyle left, as well as chief of staff, and those people were now directly under me. Ultimately, I removed the entire group in 2017, all great and talented people, but just redundant. And we didn't skip a beat.

This became known as "the Purge," as I later learned.

☆

In the fall of 2017, Governor Andrew Cuomo came out against Carry Guard, calling it "murder insurance." As if the people we were insuring were murderers, and we were paying their legal fees. We didn't insure criminals or illegal gun use. It was ridiculous. But clearly he felt this was good politics.

At around this time, in October, Wayne called me in. Our general counsel, John Frazer, was already in his office, and they showed me a letter from the New York State Department of Financial

Services (DFS). This agency was threatening to open up an investigation into the Carry Guard program, as well as potentially other NRA insurance-related programs that, they claimed, might not be following New York state insurance law, specifically as it relates to marketing versus solicitation of new customers, a nuance that to this day is not clear to me.

Wayne had a kind of Cheshire cat grin on his face as I sat across from him at the conference table reading the letter. He said, "Well, at least Chris will be happy." Translation: Chris finally had something he could blame me for.

All insurance is regulated at the state level. And New York is the toughest state in the union when it comes to such things. Unfortunately, its regulation is highly politicized in nature. It was no secret that Governor Cuomo hated the NRA. At one point he said publicly, "If I could have put the NRA out of business, I would have done so 20 years ago," referring to his time as the secretary of HUD under President Clinton.[20] Everytown for Gun Safety, the anti–gun rights group founded by Michael Bloomberg in 2014, put together a white paper that basically roadmapped this plan for Cuomo to go after the NRA. All of which is fine unless you happen to be an elected official using government resources to damage a political foe that you simply don't like. To me, it lies somewhere between discrimination and tyranny.

The New York State Department of Financial Services began a large-scale investigation into our insurance practices, which ranged from Carry Guard to every other insurance product. New York state insurance law is arcane, but in essence, they were making the case that as a nonprofit, the NRA can't market insurance directly. We could talk about it and direct people to websites and insurance companies, but we couldn't actually sell insurance in New York—that was their claim.

On the other hand, there were plenty of other nonprofits doing what we were doing, utilizing their brand to sell insurance, including AARP, which affiliates with a car insurance company, or a health care company like United Healthcare, or a life insurance company like Travelers.

In similar fashion, the NRA was leveraging its brand. Furthermore, the association had offered insurance related to gun range owners, firearms insurance, and a host of others that supported gun owners' ability to exercise their Second Amendment rights. Without liability insurance, shooting ranges couldn't exist, and the NRA filled that void for many ranges. And now all that was thrown into question. Were we out of compliance with New York state laws? Yes, we were, and Lockton as our provider of record was responsible for the mistake and worked with the NRA team to get into compliance. The solution, though, killed Carry Guard for good, and cost members and the NRA tens of millions in revenue and the ability to provide a much-needed insurance policy to its members. While I had another option on the table that could have guaranteed the NRA insurance programs to members for decades to come, I was overruled by Wayne, as he felt it would be too difficult to get board approval. Ironically, we didn't ask for board approval very often. Outside of being a revenue generator, Carry Guard could have been plowed back into education and training, as I'd originally envisioned. The programs were just not about making money.

★

Perhaps the biggest myth that has emerged from the tragic, recurring nature of mass shootings and school shootings is that the single biggest culprit is the AR-15, what most of us refer to today as the "assault rifle."

Granted, the AR-15 looks scary. Most people think it is a military weapon. Although it does have its origins in the military, the same is true for many guns used by civilians today: Glock, Sig Sauer, Beretta, and more all have pistols and rifles that are carried by law enforcement and military worldwide. The media refers to the AR-15 as this deadly, high-testosterone killing machine, able to fire dozens of bullets in a concentrated barrage. But the exact same thing could be said about 75 percent of the firearms sold in the United States. You can fire sixteen rounds out of a Glock 19, and a round from a 9mm is empirically every bit as deadly as a round from an AR-15. Sales of the AR-15 were banned for ten years, giving it a kind of illicit mystique. The reality, however, is far less sinister. Many people use AR-15s today for competitive sports shooting. And while it has a high-capacity magazine, the same can be said of a large majority of guns sold today, including handguns. Yes, with a caliber of .223, it's immensely more powerful than a pistol. However, compared to other rifle calibers, the AR-15 is anemic.

The AR-15 is certainly as deadly as any gun can be, put to the wrong purpose. But next to virtually every other rifle caliber—.30-06, .270, or .308, all of which are very popular—it's less potent. Typically, the larger the caliber, the wider the internal diameter of the gun barrel, the bigger the bullet, the greater the power of the weapon. And all of these calibers and many more can be found in semiautomatic versions the same as a garden-variety AR-15.

The fact is that assault rifles are used in 1 percent of the gun-related deaths in this country. (Remember that 60 percent of the forty thousand gun deaths in the United States are self-inflicted—they are suicides.) So when we talk about solving gun violence, we are talking about solving sixteen thousand deaths in the country on a yearly basis, of which about four hundred involve an assault rifle.

Over the past twenty years, assault rifles have been involved in 25 to 30 percent of mass shootings. Since 2012, an AR-15 has been used in several widely covered mass shootings in the United States. An AR-15, or a modified version of one, was used to commit the attacks in Aurora, Colorado (June 2012); Sandy Hook Elementary School in Newtown, Connecticut (December 2012); San Bernardino, California (December 2015); First Baptist Church in Sutherland Springs, Texas (November 2017); Las Vegas (October 2017); and Parkland, Florida (February 2018).

So the AR-15 got a sinister reputation as the "preferred" gun for mass shooting. Partially deserved, perhaps, but the highly charged and politicized nature of the assault rifle masks the underlying argument: There are plenty of more powerful guns out there and the damage caused by an AR-15 is not unique to its make and model. Any misuse of firearms, solo or in combination, can lead to tragic circumstances.

I'm not trying to correct the AR-15's bad rap, but to point out the real issue here. And for that, a little history is required...

What is commonly known today as an assault rifle in the United States was created by Eugene Stoner in 1955, who completed the initial design work on what he originally called the ArmaLite AR-10, the precursor to the AR-15. The AR designation stood for ArmaLite; it was the politicians and the media that later came up with the more violent moniker "assault rifle."

The cousin to the AR-15, the AR-10, still exists, by the way. The AR-10 was submitted for rifle evaluation trials to the U.S. Army's Aberdeen Proving Ground in late 1956. And it was adopted by the Army as their basic utility rifle, the M16. The M16 was the infantry rifle used in Vietnam, although the military version was fully automatic and used a larger-caliber bullet. The difference between an automatic (an M16) and a semiautomatic (the AR-15) is that when you squeeze the trigger on an automatic, it fires one bullet after another without stopping. With the AR-15, you have to pull the trigger each time to make it fire. A Glock is a semiautomatic, as is any revolver, as is my shotgun I go duck hunting with. One squeeze, one bullet.

Essentially, automatic weapons like an M16 are illegal for use by civilians—you need a special license to be able to obtain an automatic weapon in the United States, and the permit is both difficult to get and expensive. One of the provisions of the Firearm Owners' Protection Act of 1986 made machine guns Class III weapons, which are not available to the general public. (As you can imagine, there is still a fringe faction of NRA members who are not happy with that.) In addition, a Class III weapon is very expensive, while the assault rifle or the semiautomatic version can cost as little as $750 (although you can also pay $15,000 if you're flush with cash).

Before long, American troops poured into South Vietnam armed with three hundred thousand brand-new M16s. The gun wasn't without its problems, though. Even today, the AR-15 is infamous for not being able to withstand the same rugged conditions as its Russian counterpart, the AK-47, can.

Colt, which purchased the designs of the original AR-10, had erroneously claimed the rifle to be self-cleaning. As a result, it wasn't kept clean by soldiers and kept jamming. But the most common problem was a "failure to extract"—that is, the cartridge would get stuck in the chamber after firing, and a soldier would have to remove the jammed cartridge by hand. Not great for combat.

Reports came in about soldiers who had been killed, their rifles in pieces in front of them, as they desperately tried to put them back together in time to defend themselves. In the words of one Marine, "We left with 72 men in our platoon and came back with 19. Believe it or not, you know what killed most of us? Our own rifle. Practically every one of our dead was found with his [M16] torn down next to him where he had been trying to fix it."

When the patent on the AR-10 expired in 1977, other manufacturers were able to use the basic design to create rifles for the public. And that is what gunmakers did—they took the M16, removed the automatic firing feature to comply with U.S. gun laws, and created the AR-15. It wasn't until 1989 that these rifles began being sold.

The AR-15-style rifle was available to the public for almost twenty years before one was used in a mass killing, in 2007 in Wisconsin.

The gun community decided they needed to come up with a new name for the category, other than "assault rifle," so they called it a "modern sporting rifle," or MSR. Today there are an estimated four hundred million guns in the United States, and about fifteen million assault rifles in circulation, based on manufacturing data, according to Jen Baker, who was the NRA's public affairs director.

It took a while for the AR-15 to become popular. And with the 1994 ban on assault rifle sales, there was no real market until the ban was allowed to expire in 2004. After that, sales and demand started to take off.

In 2007, AR-15s accounted for 14 percent of the rifles manufactured, but they soon became a kind of Lego kit for grown-ups. Gun owners can customize their MSRs by changing out flash hiders, changing handles, and virtually every piece on the gun. That is one of the reasons for its popularity—the AR-15 gave the hobbyist a platform to do all sorts of tinkering, and one of the reasons the rifle looks, to gun owners, cool, modern, and intimidating.

The AR-15 dominates the video game market, in such popular games as *Call of Duty*, *Fortnite*, and *Modern Warfare*. Most folks think they are scary-looking, which adds to the aura of intimidation (and the allure). Even my wife, Colleen, feels that way. I could have my shotgun sitting out in the kitchen and she could care less. But if she sees my AR-15 out, she'll look at me and say, "Seriously? Are you trying to freak our friends out? We've got people coming over!"

The AR-15 platform is still being used by the military in the infantry today—it is now called the M4 in the fully automatic version, and M4A1 in a semiautomatic, three-round-burst variant. But the concept of a gas-powered return is the same. When you fire the AR-15, what happens is the bullet spins as it goes through the chamber, because of the grooves in the barrel. There's a hole about halfway down the barrel where the gas from the explosion in the chamber flows as the bullet passes through. That gas goes up through a little tube and back into the gun, adding to the momentum of the bolt carrier group moving backward, which ejects the cartridge and goes straight back to push the next the bullet forward.

The sequence is as follows: When the trigger is pulled, the firing pin hits the primer, igniting the powder; the cartridge explodes, sending the 65-grain bullet down the barrel, twisting once every seven inches; the gas from the explosion is expelled through the gas tube back into the gun, where it helps to push the bolt carrier group backward, and as it goes back, the shell casing flies out; the bolt carrier group picks up another shell, and the gun is ready to be fired again.

All of this happens about as fast as you can pull the trigger. There's a large spring that pushes against the bolt carrier group and absorbs a lot of the recoil. So instead of it having a hard recoil, the motion is absorbed. You still get a little kick, but not much, making the AR-15 a very easy gun to shoot. Probably its biggest plus is you don't have to be a great shooter to use it. It's forgiving in terms of recoil, and it doesn't require a lot of training or marksmanship. I could get anyone shooting better, at a quicker pace, more accurately, with an AR-15. When Colleen is shooting a rifle, I'll have her shoot an AR because it's so easy that it's like shooting a BB gun.

Another major reason the assault rifle became so popular is because the ammunition is very inexpensive. And that's a plus for guys who want to go out and plink—you know, shoot cans in the woods, that kind of thing.

It's also incredibly ergonomic and, again, easily customized. I've spent many nights changing out the barrel guard, or putting in a new adjustable gas block. There's a giant swath of rifles that fall into this category of a modern sporting rifle. But to put it in perspective, nine out of ten guns that are sold in the United States are for "personal protection," and the majority are pistols, such as a Glock 19. I don't know exactly how many Glocks are sold a year, but it's a high number. Assault rifles make up a much smaller subset of sales. The FBI reported in 2017 that of the 10,982 gun murders in the United States, 4 percent involved an "assault weapon"—less than 450 shooters.

One of the fastest-growing shooting sports in the country has evolved around the AR-15. It's called "3-Gun," where you are running along, shooting at targets with a pistol, an AR-15, and a shotgun. Everybody's dressed up like they're competing in a bike race or 10K run, with Spandex shirts adorned with sponsor logos, baseball caps, and thousand-dollar glasses. The actual targeting and shooting lasts only a minute or so, but people seem to love it.

That said, there is no question the AR-15 has become demonized in popular lore. Why do we need assault rifles? people ask.

My response generally is to flip the question. What would banning assault rifles actually accomplish?

Would it bring down the number of mass shootings, when they are only used about a quarter of the time? Would banning AR-15s really affect gun violence?

I'm all about stopping these mass shootings, but what impact would banning the MSRs actually have?

From a caliber standpoint, there are a hundred different calibers that are much deadlier than an AR-15. A .223-caliber assault rifle next to a .30-06 ("30 ought six" in gun vernacular) or a .30-30 used to hunt deer is a joke. It's like comparing a fork to a hammer or a cannon. And then there is a .300 Win Mag, which is twice as big. Or the .300 Blackout, which is what a lot of the special ops guys use now, because it's got so much stopping power. And the idea that the AR-15 is a high-speed round, well, sure, it is a high-speed round, but less so than most of the rounds out there. And certainly not nearly as deadly as many other guns if you are a madman trying to kill people.

The notion that an AR-15 is a "killing machine" is silly. Of course it is. So is a revolver. So is any gun. And handguns are the most common weapon used in mass shootings, regardless of whether shooters struck schools, businesses, or churches. In the 2009 Fort Hood shooting, the gunman was armed with an FN Five-seven pistol equipped with laser sights.

The perpetrator of one of the deadliest mass shootings in history, the 2007 Virginia Tech massacre, was equipped with two pistols, a Glock 9mm, and a .22-caliber. In the aftermath of the Virginia Tech shootings, *Slate* magazine wrote an article entitled "Thirty-Two Victims, Two Guns?" Its subtitle asked, "How did Cho Seung-Hui kill so many people with such small weapons?" The article went on to state that neither of the guns was particularly dangerous.[21]

Excuse me? A 9mm and .22 are not dangerous? They are *guns*; he killed thirty-two people with them.

My point is that it simply does not matter what kind of weapon you wield if you are determined to kill people, whether it is an AR-15 or a .22 pistol. And any shooter of any handgun or rifle can carry extra magazines and simply reload to shoot more people. That's exactly what happened. As we know all too well, these shootings don't happen spontaneously—they are mapped out in advance. That is what we are up against.[22]

Again, of all the murders that take place in the country, only 1 percent involve a rifle.

So why is the AR-15 so demonized? Again, I get that they're scary-looking. They've become the bogeyman of guns, the one model that is easy to target, if you'll pardon the pun.

And yes, the AR-15 gives you the ability to change magazines quickly. With my shotgun I can shoot twice, then I've got to open it up and pull out the shells and reload. It's very limited in terms of capacity.

People ask, why do you need a thirty-round magazine—the standard magazine size for an AR-15? Well, I would argue, in all these mass shootings, these insane people have multiple magazines on them, and it takes like two seconds longer to run thirty rounds through three ten-round magazines than a single thirty-round magazine. In other words, a smaller magazine capacity is not going to make an appreciable difference.

So what are we really solving by banning high-capacity magazines? Are we hoping that they get through their first two magazines and maybe the gun jams? That's not a solution—that's a prayer.

A recent study by Johns Hopkins Bloomberg School of Public Health found that there was no evidence of assault rifle bans leading to lower "incidence of mass shootings."[23] For a country with only eight million citizens, Switzerland has over two million guns, including plenty of ARs—they have a history of an armed citizenry—and there hasn't been a mass shooting there since 2001.[24]

It's not about the gun, it's about the culture.

Why isn't anyone asking the simple question: What has changed that these guys have decided their life is so awful that they are going to shoot up their classmates? No one shot up classrooms twenty-five years ago, and we had plenty of 9mm pistols and hunting rifles to go around. I honestly don't know why these young men see no other choice but to pick up a gun and kill their fellow workers or classmates. It's a haunting situation for all Americans when we live in a country where the frequency of mass shootings is higher than anywhere else in the world.

And whenever we have a mass shooting in the United States, Senator Dianne Feinstein from California rolls out her whiteboards covered in pictures of assault weapons. It's gotten to be knee-jerk and rote in response. That said, I appreciate her passion. She's been through trial by fire—she was the president of the board of supervisors who identified the bodies of San Francisco mayor George Moscone and supervisor Harvey Milk, who were assassinated at City Hall in 1978.

But again, what exactly are we trying to solve?

Let's start with the data, and change the discussion to finding solutions. I'm happy to have the debate. I think we should. I just want to be sure what we are trying to accomplish as we talk about banning specific guns. Is it to ban something that non–gun owners don't like, or are afraid of, or is it to genuinely solve the problem of gun violence and mass murder? I'm all in favor of doing things that will actually solve the problem, and I have some ideas about that and some steps we can take (see chapter 10).

☆

All that said, the AR-15 played a major role on the night of October 1, 2017, when a retired auditor and real estate businessman and serious gambler named Stephen Paddock opened fire from his suite on the thirty-second floor of the Mandalay Bay hotel in Las Vegas at a crowd of concertgoers below. Over the course of ten minutes he fired over a thousand rounds indiscriminately into the crowd, killing 58 people and wounding another 413.

It was a bloodbath, pure and simple. Several hundred others were injured in the panic that followed. It was the deadliest shooting in U.S. history, eclipsing the Pulse nightclub shooting in Florida eight months before.

Paddock had exhibited none of the usual warning signs of someone who was about to go off the rails. To this day, we don't fully understand why he went berserk. His killing spree had been meticulously planned over weeks; he'd been scouting out the hotel and sight lines, and had brought up an arsenal of weapons over a period of days; he had apparently considered other sites earlier, as well.

One of the reasons Paddock was able to fire off so many rounds so quickly is that among the weapons he had were fourteen AR-15s equipped with bump stocks, which essentially allowed him to fire in rapid succession, similar to a machine gun, rather than having to pull the trigger with each shot. The tragedy led to a political outcry from both houses of Congress, from President Trump, and from the media, on the need to ban bump stocks.

I didn't even know exactly what a bump stock was at the time. But I quickly learned and thought there was just no defensible reason for them to be legal.

Wayne, Chris, and Angus ran around and around in circles for three days about the statement we were going to put out about bump stocks. We couldn't defend them—for all practical purposes they turned an AR into a machine gun, and machine guns are illegal without a Class III license.

But we were terrified of looking like we were backing down on the issue of gun rights to our members, even if the "right" was not something we supported. Chris in particular was very concerned about how this was going to be perceived by the membership. And in some regards, he was much more aware of what the potential backlash would be than Wayne was. But working out what to say was like having fifty-two cooks in the kitchen. In the end, the NRA decided to state that bump stocks should have been regulated by the ATF previously. We didn't suggest they should be banned, or that we needed new regulations against them. We punted that responsibility to the ATF to handle the issue.

The statement that Wayne and Chris put out said, "The NRA believes that devices designed to allow semiautomatic rifles to function as fully automatic rifles should be subject to regulation."[25]

It was a not-so-clever dodge. But the NRA couldn't be seen supporting legislation that would ban bump stocks.

Once we had decided on our course of action, Wayne asked me, "What do you think?"

I told him honestly, "The membership will go absolutely batshit."

"What do you mean?"

"Look, Wayne, you've been telling people for thirty years that the ATF are the bad guys, jackbooted thugs, and now you are going to throw this back on the ATF? Do you honestly think the membership is going to forget what you've said about them in the past? The hardcore guys, the guys on the far right, are gonna think you sold out.

"Now, I'm not saying we shouldn't do it. Or that I think you're wrong. I think we should do it. There is no reason for bump stocks to be available to the general public. But just be aware," I cautioned him, "you are going to get a lot of blowback."

In the end, they put out their statement. And a day later, Wayne came back and told me, "We're getting great responses."

It was delusional—and a classic case of us being in a bubble and not able to measure responses or grasp reality.

I printed out hundreds of Facebook comments and highlighted them. I went back to Wayne and said, "You're getting destroyed. That's the bottom line. The point is, they're conditioned. We've been telling them for decades that the government is going to take their guns. So any attempt to rein in their rights is seen exactly the way we've been telling them to see it, as the first step on a slippery slope."

Las Vegas revealed how flawed our thinking was. If any response had to pass muster with the most extreme elements of the membership, the NRA would never be able to be part of the solution. There was no room for compromise, let alone debate. And in fact, the very word "compromise" is reviled by the membership. We were the organization of "No."

The folks on the extreme right, the bump stock crazies, think, *Well, it's my constitutional right to have bump stocks.* And of course, that's not realistic. We live in a society regulated by laws. So these guys are literally pressuring the association not to concede on anything. These are the same people who are still pissed off that the NRA compromised on the Hughes amendment to the Firearm Owners' Protection Act of 1986, making machine guns a Class III weapon. That is the level of fervor from a very vocal minority of the membership.

Our mistake, I was convinced of over time, was that we paid too much attention to the fringe, and not enough to the tens of millions of gun owners who didn't feel that way. It was a repeat for me of the Kyle Weaver situation with Wayne—he couldn't face the tough call and didn't want to be called chicken, or, worse, that he "wasn't a good leader," or outflanked by extremists on the board. I'm sorry, but it's called leadership; you can't make everyone happy, especially on tough issues.

Ultimately, under intense political pressure, President Trump ordered a review of existing regulations, and in December 2018 he announced a federal ban on bump stocks. Gun owners were required to destroy them or turn them in.

But it was the only time I can think of where the NRA "supported" restricting something gun-related, even when it seemed like a no-brainer. And even then, we didn't really come out and just say what should be done.

Wayne and Chris and Angus had become "Hollow Men" representing nothing but political cant and their own self-interest. It was Washington at its worst—and it was wearing me down. The NRA in many regards had become divorced from effective advocacy, or rather, it had lost focus on advocacy every day and devolved into a never-ending quest for personal power and turf building that had nothing to do with the Second Amendment. The infighting was far worse than anyone knew. It was the result of an institution that was leaderless.

Me at age six, fishing.

With Wayne LaPierre at the conference table in his office, poring over the budget, with a statue of an eagle behind us.

NRA ILA chief lobbyist Chris Cox. *(Credit: Alex Wong via Getty Images)*

With NRA board members Lance Olson and Bart Skelton, outside of Wayne LaPierre's office at NRA headquarters.

After a great duck hunt with Tony Makris. Those are my dogs, Baron and Jade.

President Donald Trump speaking at the NRA annual convention. *(Credit: Scott Olson via Getty Images)*

Bill Brewer, the NRA's outside attorney in charge of litigation, in his New York City office.

The Hammer— Marion Hammer, the NRA's chief lobbyist in Florida, target shooting, circa 1995.

Red Sparrow—Russian spy
Maria Butina. *(Credit: Sergei
Savostyanov via Getty Images)*

With former NRA
president Pete Brownell.

My wife Colleen going through the paces of Carry Guard instruction.

I'm working out the kinks of the Carry Guard program, shooting an H&K VP9 pistol.

Wayne LaPierre at the White House meeting with President Trump. *(Credit: Getty Images)*

Bill Brewer (standing) with Wayne in a private meeting room at the Ritz Carlton in Reston, Virginia, discussing strategy.

Jay Prince, the NRA board member who shouted "We're shutting this down" at the membership meeting at the 2019 annual convention, with Wayne's executive assistant, Millie Hallow.

NRA president Ollie North speaking at CPAC, the huge annual Conservative Political Action Conference. *(Credit: Alex Wong via Getty Images)*

Another thing I love. Shooting at the World Championships in England.

Steve Bannon coaching me during media training. Bannon felt the NRA needed to get me out in the media to present our case, and Wayne bought into it. Steve pushed me as far as I could be pushed, to see how I could handle the pressure. Then Bill Brewer shut the whole initiative down—I assumed because it wasn't his idea.

A funny but spot-on depiction of the state of the NRA under Wayne. *(Credit: Dave Granlund)*

Bill Brewer, with Wayne LaPierre, in a private room of a restaurant, discussing the endless litigation we were involved in.

Doing what I love most—hunting ducks.

CHAPTER 5

From Russia with Love

After the election in 2016, media around the world found itself caught up in the spellbinding connection between an attractive twenty-seven-year-old Russian agent, Maria Butina, and her ties to the NRA. Tall, slim, seductive, Butina had grown up around guns, learning to hunt in southern Siberia with her father. Starting in 2013, she had become an advocate of liberalizing Russia's gun laws, which strictly restricted handguns; she had made a splash in the Russian media three years before when she became the founder of a Russian gun rights group, Right to Bear Arms. It would gain her immediate notoriety. But then she brought her act to America, ingratiating herself with prominent conservatives and a coterie of NRA executives and board members, on whom she made an equally memorable impression.

And after the U.S. presidential election, she was accused of being a Russian agent, working to infiltrate and influence America's political elections.

Crazy, right?

Suddenly we're cozying up to the very people we'd fought the Cold War against? A gun rights activist from Mother Russia? Does a dictator like Putin really want to arm his citizens? I don't need to take a poll of NRA members to know what they think of the Russians...

Honest to God, you cannot make this up.

The question on everyone's mind: Was there a dark money connection between Russian-backed gun groups and the NRA, funneling money from Moscow to support Donald Trump's election? It was an explosive narrative—guns, sex, espionage, and politics—that could have been dreamed up by a Hollywood screenwriter. And the media world ran with it.

And seriously, how could you blame them? This woman ran one of the oldest ops in the KGB playbook, *Red Sparrow* tactics that should have been obvious to all of us. But Butina worked her magic on a number of NRA board members, presidents, and others. She was incredibly appealing and coquettish and knew how to make these guys feel important.

☆

The initial ties between the NRA and the gun lobby in Russia began years earlier. David Keene, the president of the NRA from 2011 to 2013, was a former adviser to Republican presidential candidates Ronald Reagan and Mitt Romney, and a career lobbyist. In addition, Keene was the longtime chair of the American Conservative Union, which organizes the annual CPAC, or Conservative Political Action Convention, in February. Keene had also taken over the job of NRA spokesman after the Sandy Hook shooting, when Wayne, after his Sandy Hook speech, went MIA for months. (Afraid for his life and the political blowback he suffered for the speech, he didn't have the heart to step into the ring. He went low-profile for almost a year.)

Alexander Torshin, one of Putin's supporters and for a decade a Russian senator, with deep ties to the FSB—the principal security agency of Russia, successor to the KGB—had joined the NRA in 2010. Torshin was not a good guy. He had connections to the high-profile Spetsnaz forces, most notably the Night Wolves biker gang, the quasi-military guys who rode into Crimea in the middle of the night with ski masks to take over the peninsula. They reported directly to Putin.[1] And there were reports that Torshin was involved in money laundering with Alexander Romanov, the head of the Russian Tambov Gang, in Spain.[2]

Fifty-seven at the time, and short—five and a half feet—with a barrel chest and a bull-like neck, Torshin, according to the CIA, saw the advantages of establishing a relationship with one of the strongest political lobbies in America, and potentially exploiting it to his advantage. A lifelong gun lover, Torshin was introduced to Keene through G. Kline Preston IV, a Tennessee lawyer, as the man working to change gun laws in Russia.[3] Torshin first met Keene at the NRA annual convention in Pittsburgh in 2011, where Torshin claimed that he wanted to organize their own NRA in Russia. This friendship, like most of these things involving the Russians, didn't evolve by accident.

The two hit it off, and Torshin methodically cultivated his ties with the NRA. At the 2013 NRA convention, he was presented with a rifle as a gift, and attended a ceremony for the Golden Ring of Freedom—a special designation for people who had donated a million dollars or more to the NRA. (At the dinner, you receive a golden dinner jacket with an NRA crest.)

Maria Butina first worked with Torshin as an unpaid intern. By 2013, she had become, through Right to Bear Arms, the face of gun rights in Russia. Torshin supported Butina's rise in Russian gun rights circles, fêting her and toasting her political acumen and beauty. And in late 2013, she and Torshin hosted an NRA delegation that included David Keene, along with other gun activists, to the Right to Bear Arms convention in Moscow. She and Torshin catered elaborate meals, and the vodka flowed freely. Professional models wore revealing shorts, showing off garter belts that also served as concealed carry gun holsters.

As Keene said at the meeting, "I've hosted your senator Alexander Torshin at the National Rifle Association's annual meetings" for the last three years.[4] He went on to tell the audience, "We need to work together."

John Bolton, later Donald Trump's national security adviser, addressed the audience, and Keene posed for a picture with Butina, who was grinning like a gun moll. The function crawled with Russian politicians, and clearly the event had Putin's blessing. (Torshin was a close ally of Putin's.)

A year later, in 2014, Butina appeared in a profile in *GQ Russia* wearing stilettos and lingerie and carrying a pair of pistols. It was softcore gun porn aimed at making her a magnet for the media—and American gun rights luminaries.

But 2014 was not a good year for Russian-American relations. Russia invaded and took over Crimea from Ukraine, and President Obama imposed sanctions on Putin's government. Even here, Torshin left his fingerprints—it was he who helped "steer the legislation that officially annexed the territory."[5] He would appear with Putin at a Kremlin signing ceremony.

Regardless, Torshin's pursuit of NRA luminaries and board members continued, as investigators would later discover from his nearly 150,000 tweets, in Russian, sent since his account was created in 2011.[6]

Maria Butina, in turn, was invited by David Keene to the 2014 NRA annual convention in Indianapolis, where she met with Wayne, presented a Right to Bear Arms plaque and membership to then

NRA president Jim Porter, who succeeded David Keene, and took selfies with Republican presidential candidates Louisiana governor Bobby Jindal and Rick Santorum.

She tweeted at Torshin, "Mission accomplished."

It was Butina's first trip to America, and she made the most of it, including a stop at the NRA headquarters, where she posed for a picture with Keene.

She returned again the next year, where she continued to make inroads with NRA board members, at the 2015 convention in Nashville. Donald Trump spoke, although he had not yet declared his intention to run for president. Torshin would later claim to have met Trump there, although the Trump administration denies it. Butina met several other prominent conservatives outside of the NRA as well, including Republican Wisconsin governor Scott Walker. Two months later she traveled to Wisconsin to attend Walker's official announcement that he was running for president.[7] She wrote an op-ed for *The National Interest*, a foreign policy magazine founded by Irving Kristol, urging closer connections between Russia and the United States. Her cell phone case had a picture of a shirtless Putin riding a horse. Behind the scenes, however, at least one reporter, Tim Dickinson in *Rolling Stone*, claimed she was being paid by the Russian government as a special assistant to Torshin, who had been appointed deputy governor of the Russian central bank.[8]

Butina became particularly close to political operative Paul Erickson, who helped to run a number of failed GOP presidential campaigns—he was national political director for Pat Buchanan's 1992 campaign. He had first met Maria at the Right to Bear Arms convention in Moscow in 2013, and the two were seen together countless times in 2015–16—at a camp for young Republicans, appearing on a podcast together, at the graveside of F. Scott

Fitzgerald, with Butina in a flapper's outfit and Erickson carrying a bottle of rum and one of Fitzgerald's books—and had developed a romantic relationship.[9]

At the end of 2015, Butina and Torshin invited some NRA members to a second Right to Bear Arms convention in Moscow: about half a dozen NRA members and some others, including Pete Brownell; Joe Gregory, chair of the Golden Ring of Freedom; Arnold Goldschlager, a doctor from California who helped to raise big donations for the NRA; Milwaukee sheriff David Clarke; and Paul Erickson.

★

When I heard about the trip, I was shocked, and so was Wayne. I personally witnessed Wayne's opposition to this trip. As he was quoted in a *New York Times Magazine* article, "My attitude was, stay away from her. . . . I saw this itinerary . . . it's got all of these meetings with . . . oligarch so-and-so, and deputy so-and-so. And I'm like: 'You guys are all nuts. Are you crazy?'"

Now, should he have been more vocal about this bullshit, and really put his foot down? Should he have taken a stronger stance? Well, in retrospect, yes, he should have; that's hard to dispute. Wayne objected to the trip, but in the end failed to kill it.

But later, this whole issue of who "authorized the trip" became a major bone of contention. Angus McQueen coined the phrase "it was an unauthorized trip," which Wayne fell back on sometimes.

Tony Makris and I made a stink about this trip from the outset. We both saw that it had the potential to explode in the NRA's face— and in particular Wayne's. But everyone else told us it was "no big deal." Makris in particular (remember, he worked for Caspar Weinberger and had grown up in the Cold War) had the idea ingrained in his brain that the Russians were the bad guys. The politics of just how the Republicans became the appeasers to the Russians and the Democrats became the more hard-nosed party by 2016 is hard to fathom. Distrusting and fighting the Russians was part of what the Republican Party stood for—this just illustrates how much Trump has turned the world and mainstream media upside down.

Anyhow, the NRA guys who were invited had no idea what they were getting into, I thought. I never met Butina face-to-face. The first time I saw her was at the NRA-ILA Auction, a major NRA fundraiser. I remember Susan LaPierre pulling me aside and asking, "Hey, do you think that woman is a Russian agent?"

I told her, "One hundred percent. She's probably with the FSB."

It was clear to a lot of us who she was. I mean, Putin has no interest in liberalizing gun rights—he hates the idea of private citizens having handguns. They don't have a Second Amendment in Russia—it's a communist regime. The whole setup and premise here is ridiculous. As Steven Hall, who served as chief of Russian operations for the CIA until 2015, said, "The idea of private gun ownership is anathema to Putin. So then the question is, 'Why?'"

The answer according to Hall was that Putin was "baiting a trap."[10] These oligarchs and FSB operatives—they were not the kind of people you wanted to hang out with.

I told Pete Brownell, who was an NRA board member at the time, and who was elected president in May 2017, not to go. But Pete and the others appeared smitten with Maria Butina, and I guess enamored of the idea of opening up Russia to gun rights. And I think for Pete it was an adventure—Pete and I were good friends and talked a lot at the time.

I remember him telling me: "I'm going over to Russia. It's going to be great."

I told him, "Nothing good is going to come of this. Come on, man."

He laughed and said, "Aw, it'll just be a bunch of glad-handing."

Neither Wayne, nor Angus, nor anyone else paid enough attention to this until it all came back on the NRA. Wayne had told them to dump the trip, but they were determined. He made it clear the NRA was not paying for it, or so he thought. Those going had to pay for it themselves.

As it turned out, the NRA did end up picking up part of the tab in a scheme of back-and-forth invoicing from some of the various people who went. As the *New York Times* reported, the trip became the subject of scrutiny in several investigations into the NRA's ties to Russia, including Robert Mueller's investigation.[11]

Anyway, off they went. A bunch of old white guys under the spell of a young, sexy female Russian operative, although we didn't know that for sure at the time. Later, she was convicted of being a foreign agent, and Putin made her out to be a national hero.

As Pete told me afterward, in Moscow the NRA guys "kept crossing paths with top Putin cabinet officials" like Dmitry Rogozin, the deputy prime minister of Russia in charge of the defense industry, and Sergey Lavrov, the Russian foreign minister. In a public filing, David Clarke estimated that the Russians spent $6,000 on him alone for hotel rooms, meals, and so on.[12]

For Pete and the others, it was a pure junket, what one reporter later called "fun and guns." Clarke tweeted an admiring photo, saying, "I test fired one of their sniper rifles."[13] One member of the delegation, Arnold Goldschlager, said they visited a Russian gun company, met with a senior Kremlin official and several wealthy Russians. "They were killing us with vodka and the best Russian food. The trip exceeded my expectations by logarithmic levels."[14]

⭐

What was anyone thinking? The Russians have always been trying to manipulate our politics. They've always messed around with our elections and public figures. And Butina was clearly putting on this whole charade. The Russians are constantly looking for an edge to cause disruption and destabilize our democracy. They look for ways to leverage a relationship, to get something on you that they can use later to blackmail you, or make themselves indispensable to you. It's classic KGB strategy.

In that regard, the trip and Butina's operation was an overwhelming success. It begat a media storm, resulted in two congressional investigations, raised questions about the validity of the presidential election—was there Russian dark money behind Trump's election?—and ended up costing us a ton of money in legal bills. And I believe that this was exactly their aim from the outset—to sow discord. It's as simple as that. They play the long game.

Two months later, back in the United States, Butina and Erickson became partners in a corporation called Bridges, established, according to Erickson, "in case Butina needed any monetary assistance for her graduate studies." And sure enough, months later she enrolled in a master's program at American University.[15]

Was it all part of an elaborate cover? She also hung out with Republican presidential candidates, spent Thanksgiving of 2016 at a congressman's country house, took a Trump campaign aide to see the rock group Styx, and "helped a Rockefeller heir organize 'friendship dinners' with influential Washingtonians."[16] After the November 2016 election, she wrote to Torshin on Twitter at three in the morning, "I'm ready for further orders."[17]

Erickson tried to set up a meeting between Trump and Torshin, via email, as Congress discovered and shared with the *New York Times*. Erickson claimed that "happenstance" and his NRA connections enabled him to "slowly begin cultivating a back-channel to President Putin's Kremlin." As the *Times* reported, Erickson suggested a meeting between Trump and Torshin in Louisville, Kentucky, at the 2016 NRA convention, to establish "first contact." The meeting never took place, although Torshin did meet Donald Trump Jr., a longtime NRA member, at a dinner at the convention.

★

All of this blew up in 2017. The media was all over it, and Congress called for an investigation by the House Oversight Committee, and Ron Wyden and the Senate Finance Committee also wanted to look into it. The media ran with the story—NRA infiltrated by Putin's Moscow—and Rachel Maddow jumped on this, investigating and speculating about the possibility of Russian dark money being funneled through the NRA to support Trump in the election.

Wayne called me in to talk about the Russia trip, and he said, "Well, thank God we didn't pay for any of this."

So I called Andrew Arulanandam, our head of PR, just to make sure none of the bills went through the NRA, and I discovered we did pay for part of it.

I put the paper trail together, and it became this whole sordid tale, where we paid for some things but got reimbursed.

At first, Pete's lawyer took a hard line on the trip, claiming that Wayne had approved it, when he had not. This got leaked into the press, in a story in *The Daily Beast*, claiming Wayne had approved all of this, everything. That hyperbole went on for a month, and we were pushing back, making it clear that the trip was never sanctioned by the NRA as an organization.

It was a mess and we looked compromised—just like the Russians had hoped.

It was no secret that Putin supported Donald Trump over Hillary Clinton in the 2016 election. It's been widely reported since that Russian hackers had spent millions on Facebook on fake ads and disinformation to try to tilt social media to Trump, targeting key battleground states and counties. And of course, the NRA had gone all in on Trump as early as May 2016, and ultimately contributed $30 million in federally recorded funds directly to Trump's campaign, probably another $20 million to the Republican Party, and was one of his strongest, most vocal supporters.

So it's not surprising that the NRA/Russian connection got a lot of press.

We conducted our own internal investigation, and Congress investigated the claims, but there was no evidence found of any money being funneled into the election through the NRA.

Of course the conspiracy theory in the media was that the NRA had been treated as a kind of money launderer. As a nonprofit, we are allowed to accept foreign cash. We just can't spend it on American political campaigns. That is illegal.

But as several reporters pointed out, money is fungible, and can be moved around and used to free up other, unrestricted funds that do go to elections. And that was the fear. That said, neither Wayne nor I, nor Bill Brewer nor the audit committee found any evidence of that. Nor did Congress.

Butina herself said her support for gun rights was just that, and not "evidence of the long arm of the Kremlin."

"Sometimes," she wrote in a nod to Freud, "a cigar is just a cigar."[18]

Pete Brownell resigned as president of the NRA, and Maria was arrested, and later prosecuted. Wayne was on his way to the White House Christmas party in 2018, and suddenly I looked up at the TV screen in my office and there was Vladimir Putin on CNN, talking about Maria Butina, claiming she was set up by the National Rifle Association.

It was complete propaganda, but it was on the news everywhere. And I realized Wayne knew nothing about this, and he was about to be blindsided. So I called him up and told him, "You may be walking into a mess. I'm looking at Vladimir Putin talking about Maria Butina, saying she was duped by the NRA."

He couldn't believe it. "You're kidding me?"

I said, "I kid you not. There are pictures of you on TV. The Russians, Pete, everything."

Wayne was pissed. I told him I just wanted him to know before he got ambushed at the party.

Fortunately, he didn't. But he called up afterward to rant about Maria, Putin, and the rest. I couldn't blame him. He had opposed the trip, and had tried to dissuade Pete and the others from going. But they were determined. Yet it all fell back into his lap. I guess that is the downside of being the CEO and the public face of the NRA. When the shit hits the fan, he's the one who feels the breeze. The gun control lobby—especially Michael Bloomberg's organization Everytown—and the media had a field day with that. They kept flashing pictures of Wayne, Rick Santorum, and Maria, and Putin, and Butina posing with Jim Porter, the NRA president from 2013 through 2015. There she was with my buddy Pete Brownell, there she was with Donald Trump Jr.

All of it unbelievably stupid.

Ultimately Butina entered a plea deal with federal prosecutors in 2019, admitting that she was a Russian agent—that she "agreed and conspired" to infiltrate the Republican Party and the NRA to "promote Russia-friendly policies on behalf of the Kremlin."[19] And that her work was directed by Alexander Torshin, in what she called her "Diplomacy Project."

So there you have it. No dark money for rigging the election, just a bunch of old guys who got duped by the looks and charm of an FSB agent and allowed our country to fall prey to these spies, gangsters, and con artists. I cringe when I think of the all damage the Russian election interference has caused our country—the divisiveness, the investigations, the vitriolic rhetoric and no-holds-barred politics. In that regard, the Russians and Putin won a massive victory. They had compromised our integrity. And I'll bet they had no idea just how successful their half-baked operation to sow discord in the U.S. election in 2016 would be.

Creating the illusion that they had infiltrated the NRA was just one tactic in a war against our institutions and ultimately pitting us against each other. And their attempts at *kompromat* also shone a light on the fact that we didn't have our financial house in order. Far from it.

In that sense, they won.

CHAPTER 6

Under Attack

On the afternoon of February 14, 2018, the NRA's world was upended. On that day, Nikolas Cruz, a nineteen-year-old mentally disturbed former student, entered Marjory Stoneman Douglas High School in Parkland, Florida, with an AR-15 and several magazines, activated a fire alarm, and began firing indiscriminately into the crowd of confused students trying to exit the building. Before he was done, Cruz had killed seventeen people, and injured another seventeen. It was one of the worst school shootings in American history. The reaction across the country was a mixture of agony and rage. And a lot of that rage was pointed at the NRA.

In the past—since Sandy Hook at least—school shootings hadn't put the association under financial pressure. In fact, they were a grim opportunity, and Wayne had boosted membership and donations in those periods of crisis.

Parkland was different. I cannot overstate the level of public anger and rage after Parkland. And the Parkland kids—the survivors of Parkland—were just beginning to do national media, and David Hogg took the spotlight. They wanted to create a movement, and they were understandably angry and wanted action. Who wouldn't be after what they had witnessed?

★

Just before the shooting at Parkland, I'd been working on getting a new banking partner for the NRA. The NRA had been with Wells Fargo forever, and it had been decades since the agreement was put to bid. Part of the new process I was trying to implement to make the NRA resemble a modern organization was to bid out certain services and to make sure we were getting the best available costs and terms.

In one day, the entire landscape changed.

The list of banks we wanted to work with and who wanted to work with us was down to about five, including SunTrust, Wells Fargo, and BB&T. And then Parkland happened. Within days, all the banks pulled out, and Wells let us know that it had no interest in changing their pricing. I was really worried about Wells Fargo closing down our credit card processing. That would have essentially shut the organization down, as members used their cards to charge their membership fees and make donations. Customers who applied for an NRA card through Wells Fargo would get points and a lower interest rate. And in return we would get money back from Wells Fargo as part of their affinity partnerships. The affinity partnerships with different companies brought in a fair amount of money, about $10–$13 million a year.

The whiteboard in my office had a daily list of threats and problems. The list was growing. And soon it was overwhelming.

Within ten days of the shooting, we lost nearly all of our affinity partners—United Airlines, Avid, MetLife, to name a few major ones.

First National Bank of Omaha put out a statement that customer feedback had prompted a review of its relationship with the NRA, and as a result, First National would not renew its contract with the association. Rachel Maddow ran a segment as only she can on the fallout, including a screen filled with logos of all the corporate partners bailing on the NRA.

And then, on February 22, in the middle of the investigation by the New York State Department of Financial Services, Chubb, which had underwritten the Carry Guard insurance program, announced that they would no longer partner with the NRA. Chubb had given us notice three months earlier, but they used the opportunity to make some political hay by going public with their decision, declaring, "We're no longer working with you."

Well, no kidding, I thought, *you told us that three months ago.* But this was about public relations for them, no more, no less. But I could feel the ground moving beneath my feet, and everyone was looking to distance themselves from the association. The tragedy of yet another horrific school shooting had a cascading effect that no one internally was considering. Outside of myself and Wayne, it was business as usual, even while the walls started to collapse.

And as we were dealing with those crises, we were hit with a major series of cyberattacks that shut down the association's servers again and again. We had a top cyber team from LookingGlass, which specialized in cybersecurity, that had worked at the highest levels of government and for corporations like Goldman Sachs, working on it. In a presentation to Wayne and me, they told us they hadn't seen this level of sophistication in a cyberattack since the Chinese attacked the Pentagon. It was technically a DDOS—denial of service—attack, but of massive scale.

And speaking of cyber, we found out that some of the online

campaign against us was being driven by a really smart kid who had won a Peter Thiel Fellowship. (I'm not kidding…)

Somebody emailed me anonymously to say, "Robert Legate is your problem. Check it out."

So LookingGlass and I looked into it. Legate had engineered a sort of bot that he sent out to tens of thousands of people, encouraging them to reach out to our partners directly by email. He made it very easy for them to communicate with the companies who worked with us, and to express their opinions (that is, blast with form-letter email complaints about the NRA).

Technically it's not against the law—these were real people sending emails. But he automated the process and facilitated the exchange. So this one kid created all of this, and we could look at his Twitter feed and see him going down the list of NRA sponsors—United, Hertz, and so on—targeting each. He probably got the list of our affinity partners from our website. Pretty simple stuff.

And if you're United and you are getting a hundred thousand emails opposing your relationship to the NRA, and your PR people are screaming bloody murder, what are you going to do? So they severed their relationship with us.

This kid gave all these people a way to express their anger. He's a great example of how the aftermath of Parkland created a new scale of backlash against the NRA. People were fed up.

The attacks on the NRA were fast and furious and we were simply not prepared for this on multiple levels. In addition, our security team was alerting us about a constant stream of threats over social media. So now we were worried about Wayne's security. Wayne hired a full-time security guard to stay at his house. Chris had a full security detail as well, although he wasn't as well known and didn't really need it.

Wayne's safety became an all-consuming issue for him. In the face of a mass shooting, he would inevitably think, *How is this going to affect me?* or *Here we go again, it's never-ending.* He would receive death threats on social media. After a major shooting like Parkland, he would have two security guards stay with him at the house. He refused to have a driver—he loved to drive himself—but he would park at the back of the NRA lot and have a security guard escort him into the building. That said, the threats were real—people would accost and attack him in public. And Parkland took that threat to a new level. I wouldn't be surprised if he suffered from PTSD. Andrew Arulanandam and I would dread having to call him up to tell him there'd been another shooting or threat against him. It required him to deal with the media—and reality—which he loathed. He would often disappear, to God knows where, for a few days, or a week or two at a time, checking in but not divulging where he was. There was never a week that went by when Wayne didn't talk about leaving or quitting.

Wayne was driving around in a Suburban with two armed security ex–Navy SEALs, and they were pretty amped up. You'd flip on a TV and see all this hatred being expressed against the NRA, and then suddenly all of our banks and corporate sponsors have bailed, and it felt like we were under siege. That we were at war.

This was nuts. I was trying to keep my head as everyone around me lost theirs. Little did we know it was the beginning of a movement that would begin tearing the place down from the outside in and the inside out. The infighting would soon begin in earnest.

⭐

Within hours of the Parkland shooting there were protestors around the NRA building, and in Florida. The Bloomberg Everytown group was ready for this. They'd clearly had a plan in place for the next school shooting, and now they were activating it. They intended to use the furor and pain and public empathy in the immediate aftermath to build a movement.

And it worked. Within hours of the shooting, Chris Murphy, the Democratic senator from Connecticut, said, "This has got to stop, the NRA can't keep killing our children."

The gun control folks had decided they were going to use the anger and emotion of the moment to take us on. And that set the stage for the rise of the Parkland kids. David Hogg, one of the survivors, quickly became an activist for gun control, giving speeches and organizing events, marches, and boycotts.

He was very compelling. And it gave those kids an outlet. It was hard to watch them in so much pain. My children were teenagers, and they felt the same anger, pain, and helplessness—every kid across the country felt it, one way or another. I remember sitting in my office late in the night watching the media, which seemed to spend every minute after Parkland devoted to the shooting, questioning, "Where do we go from here?" I had the same questions. Where is this going to go, and how will it end? As a country, we certainly can't go on watching thirty kids gunned down in our schools every couple of months.

President Trump and the First Lady, Melania, flew down to Florida to visit surviving victims in the hospital. Several days later, under extreme pressure from parents and politicians to do something, Trump brought over forty teachers and students and community leaders, including a dozen from Parkland, to the White House to air their concerns and share their grief. He really seemed to want to take action in some form, and some of the ideas he entertained crossed all sorts of political lines. It truly appeared as though he might go where no president had gone before in the gun control fight.

"It's not going to be talk like it has been in the past. It's been going on too long, too many instances. And we're going to get it done."[1]

★

We at the NRA had to figure this out: How do we respond to Parkland? It was a national tragedy, and Wayne had to weigh in.

There was a kind of checklist we'd run through whenever there was a mass shooting. How bad is it? How many people were killed? What do we know about the shooter? Where did he come from, and what was his mental state? Obviously, if kids are killed, the political blowback would be intensified by tenfold. What kind of gun was used? Was it an AR-15?—which was bad politically—or if it's a pistol, then the shooting graded lower on the gun control threat scale. Did the shooter get the weapon legally, with a background check? All of this went into evaluating just how large the political fight would be, as callous as that sounds. That is how we viewed and gamed things out.

But there was no war room. It was always an ad hoc effort, never organized or run the way it should have been. We always had lots of data points from these mass shootings, but there was no real attempt to aggregate or study it. It drove me crazy. At one point I hired arguably the finest retired FBI agent available to organize the incident data and orchestrate a response, but it never went anywhere, stonewalled by NRA bureaucracy and intransigence.

Parkland happened just before Wayne and I were scheduled to fly to Dallas to work with Angus and Tony and the folks at Ackerman on Wayne's CPAC speech, which was little more than a week away. Ultimately, we decided that Wayne's CPAC speech would be the NRA's response. We basically lived in Dallas for the week, crafting the speech, including Wayne's response to Parkland. We would work at the Ackerman offices throughout the day, in their Death Star control room, watching cable news and the aftermath response to Parkland roll in.

Ed, an Ackerman assistant in another room, controlled the TV screens. Angus would yell, "Ed, pull up CNN on three!" And magically we'd be looking at Jake Tapper on a ninety-six-inch screen.

One of my jokes was if we cut Ackerman's budget, poor Ed would have to go, and then how would we change the channel? (Sorry, folks, I had to laugh sometimes in order not to cry.)

At the end of the day we'd head back to the hotel, with security, and go to dinner with Tony. Wayne would walk around with sunglasses and a hat pulled over his head, and he was staying at the hotel under an alias. There was a surreal quality to it all. He even went so far as to buy a bulletproof vest. In restaurants, we always sat in the corner, our backs to the wall, and never missed checking out the next person walking into the room.

While we were down in Dallas, Jake Tapper called Andrew. They were planning a town hall event in Tallahassee—did we want to participate? Wayne was focused on the speech—he wasn't interested in doing it. It wasn't a big enough event. Bringing in Wayne to do a national media event was like rolling Moses down from the mountain. It had to be worth it.

I could have done it, but Chris would have freaked out if I started going on TV, because now I would be encroaching on his world.

There was a real push within Ackerman to build up Dana Loesch as Wayne's official spokesperson. So Dana agreed to do it.

We flew back to Washington the night before CPAC, to stay at a hotel with better security—Wayne couldn't go home; his address was doxed on the internet and it wasn't safe.

Wayne, Tony, and I flew out of Dallas on a private jet the night before his speech. Flying with Wayne always seemed to be a time when we could speak freely, and where I saw the most authentic version of Wayne. As we got settled, I asked him what he thought of the speech.

"I'm happy with it now. I wish Angus wasn't such a pain in the ass on this. But it's good. I'm good with it."

And then we would talk a bit about everyday life, about my kids, and my wife, Colleen, and Wayne's wife, Susan. He always asked about my kids, and he'd send them ice cream at Christmas from his favorite place, Graeter's. That was his thing. One time my one daughter was going through a hard period at school, so we pulled her out for a time, and I brought her into work every day for a month or so. She'd hang out and help Wayne and me, and he was great with her. It really meant a lot to her and to me. He could not have been more supportive of me or my family during that time. It mattered and made a difference.

Millie, Wayne's assistant, would tease me that I was a little in awe of him. No question, part of my attraction to Wayne was that I was working side by side with someone who had changed history.

There truly is an endearing quality to Wayne that unfortunately few see. But he's a complicated guy. He would feel very pained over people leaving him—I think he would feel a little betrayed. It's a shame that the association became so tainted by extremism, and Wayne was perceived as a tyrant and caricature of himself. If he had handled things differently, he might have gone down as the guy who saved the Second Amendment. Instead, I knew, he was seen as a villain by much of America, appealing to the most extreme fringes of the NRA, always pouring gas on the fire.

And as I would soon discover, he had no qualms over betraying those closest to him. That was the hardest thing I had to come to terms with. And I never saw it coming.

★

It was dark and gloomy and rainy when we landed in D.C. We hopped in a black Suburban, accompanied by our ex–Navy SEAL security guy, and were off to the Ritz…

That night Dana Loesch went on the CNN town hall. Dana was working for NRATV exclusively at that point. And she was a firebrand. That was part of her identity. It was a high-pressure event, and it took an incredible amount of courage for her to do it.

Student survivors from Parkland and their parents were there, as well as some of the parents of the kids who had been killed, who spoke out against gun violence. And the sheriff of Broward County was there as well. To say the least, this was not a friendly crowd for the NRA. The kids had just seen seventeen classmates and teachers shot down a week before. They were literally in mourning. And they were angry—they wanted something done so that this never happened again. Several in the audience were calling the NRA murderers.

Dana called me from the green room. "This is crazy. People are screaming and yelling at me, 'You fucking bitch.'"

It sounded awful. I was concerned about her safety. Tony and I were sitting in his hotel room wondering how Dana was going to handle this. It was an angry, emotional crowd, and Dana was not known for her empathy. How would she come off?

Dana held her own. She was sophisticated, sympathetic, and fact-oriented. She always knew her facts cold. We didn't agree on everything, but she did all of her own research—she was not somebody who was fed talking points. She pulled off a great performance and showed a level of empathy and sophistication I'd not seen out of her.

The crowd was hostile to the point of violence. As soon as it was over, CNN anchor Jake Tapper turned to Dana and said, "You've got to get out of here." Security whisked her out while people were screaming at her and throwing things.

But Dana is tough. After the town hall, Wayne called us up, and I told him, "Dana's doing great, knocking it out of the park."

The next morning Tony and I and security met downstairs in the back alley of the Ritz, drinking coffee by the car. When Wayne and Susan came down, they got in the back of the Suburban with Tony.

For some reason the driver didn't show up, and the security guy turned to me to say, "Hey, great news, you're driving!" Although CPAC was friendly territory, it felt like we were headed into a war zone.

Our security guy was sitting in the passenger seat next to me. I noticed he was, of course, carrying. So I asked him, "Hey, man, do you have a gun permit for Maryland?"

"Don't ask technical questions," he replied, which got us all laughing and broke the tension.

And so I drove on. And we got Wayne to CPAC.

★

As we were crafting Wayne's speech in Dallas, I argued that this was an opportunity to acknowledge the depth of this problem in America, and ask the simple question, "Why is this happening that these troubled people, as a last resort, decide to shoot up a classroom, or inflict their rage on their fellow citizens?"

But Angus, as usual, wanted to go on the attack. I'm sure he called me a poodle or a lapdog at the time. No chance of that. We had to go full throttle. He embraced conspiracy theory, nativism, that the FBI was rotten to the core, that black helicopters were about to descend on every major city in the country with orders to take our guns, and everything else you can think of. While Angus and Wayne were going at it, I removed myself from the room to work on other things. When I came back, Wayne was standing at a lectern, and Angus was unloading on him. And I asked, "How's it going?" And Angus replied, "It's just a family argument."

"Okay, you guys, have at it."

We were able to tone the speech down to a certain degree, but in the end, Wayne blamed everyone else for Parkland, from the media to the failure of leadership at the FBI to the "European-style socialists" who had taken over the Democratic Party. The "breathless national media eager to smear the NRA," he claimed, "hate the NRA; they hate the Second Amendment; they hate individual freedom.... Their goal is to eliminate the Second Amendment, and our firearm freedom, so that they can eradicate *individual* freedom."

It was over the top, and meant to be. Moreover, he ended his speech by reiterating what he said after Sandy Hook—that the only thing that stops a bad guy with a gun is a good guy with a gun.

At CPAC, Wayne was preaching to the choir—the NRA had been a major sponsor for years. But to the rest of the world, it came across all too predictably. The Parkland parents and kids were justifiably furious.

We all met afterward at a restaurant, and everybody felt Wayne had done well, a little fooled by the friendly confines of CPAC. And there was a brief moment where we thought, *Okay, we got through this*, and let out a sigh of relief.

But in the political world and in the media, the pressure was only mounting. Even the Republicans in Florida wanted to raise the age you could buy a rifle. And Governor Scott said he'd sign it.

The times they were a-changin'. I could feel it.

In retrospect, I think Wayne's speech was a huge lost opportunity to counter the perception of the NRA. We could have defended

Second Amendment rights while opening a dialogue. We can and should protect gun rights—*and* lead with real solutions. But Angus McQueen was never in that business. He convinced Wayne to sing the same old song.

On Sunday, several days after Trump's meeting with the survivors of Parkland, the president invited Wayne and Chris Cox to the White House to talk about gun control legislation. The president prided himself on being the most pro-NRA, pro-gun president in history. As a candidate, he told the NRA membership, "I will never let you down."

But he seemed to be at odds with us this time. At a bipartisan meeting with legislators the following day, he seemed to support imposing some of the toughest new restrictions on guns in decades, from raising the age you could buy an assault rifle, to discouraging reciprocity on concealed weapons, to implementing a universal background check.

"Some of you people," he told legislators, "are petrified of the NRA. You shouldn't be petrified."

He went on, "Don't worry about the NRA, they're on our side. And you know what, if they're not with you, we have to fight them every once in a while, that's okay. Sometimes we're going to have to be very tough and we're going to have to fight them."

Well, that was Trump on a Monday. But then on Thursday night, he met secretly for a second time with Chris and Wayne. And he was reminded who had helped elect him.

After the meeting, the president did a one-eighty, completely changing his tune. He tweeted, "Good (Great) meeting in the Oval Office with the NRA." The word on the street was that the president thought Wayne was weak. But he represented five million committed voters, and Trump never lost sight of that.

And after the meeting, the president no longer wanted gun control. As Chris tweeted, "POTUS and VPOTUS support Second Amendment, support due process and don't want gun control."

While the immediate threat of political action by Trump and Congress abated, the outrage and attacks on the NRA had not. Parkland had changed the game, and suddenly state governments, and Democrats, felt unleashed.

From that day forward it was open season on the NRA.

★

After Parkland, and with the heat turned up on the association, I got a Saturday night phone call from Dave Lockton, who administered all of the NRA's insurance. He told me that they needed to drop us as partner and that Lloyds was yanking all of our insurance. Lockton is the world's largest privately held insurance brokerage. Dave had been with the NRA for decades and helped build a great program, but at the time the blowback from other clients was just too much.

Ultimately neither Lockton nor Lloyds did abandon us, although, as I mentioned earlier, Chubb, the insurance giant that underwrote the Carry Guard program, did. They informed us they would not be underwriting any new policies.

It was a pretty serious blow. The issue wasn't with the product, it was the investigation out of New York. In the months after the investigations began, the Department of Financial Services fined Lockton, they fined Lloyds, and they fined Chubb, to the tune of, I believe, $15 million. Our backers really didn't have much recourse other than to drop Carry Guard. They couldn't afford to lose their licenses in New York—it would take down their whole insurance business.

Subsequently we discovered that Maria Vullo, the head of DFS, met with Lloyds and told them that if they didn't stop doing business with the NRA, she was going to yank all their licenses in the state of New York.

The DFS came after me, too, for a deposition.

Were you in charge of marketing for Carry Guard? they asked. Did you approve all the messaging?

I *was* in charge of the program; but ultimately all of our marketing decisions were approved by Lockton.

DFS's claim was basically that Wayne and I sat in a room and came up with the Carry Guard "scheme" as a deliberate way to circumvent New York's soliciting laws.

That just didn't make sense. Why would we do that? How would the NRA benefit from an illegal insurance program? This was political and it brought out the worst functions of government oversight. But we complied and cleaned up all the marketing to adhere to New York's arcane laws, and that should have been the end of it.

But this wasn't about compliance. This was all about getting the big bad NRA.

That said, Chubb made a lot of money on Carry Guard—millions—because there were no claims. Which ironically was something of a problem. If you're charging for insurance, you want to prove it's a legitimate product. I knew the claims would be low—the people most likely to buy the insurance were law-abiding. But none of us thought the claims would be zero. And from what I understand, to date, it still is.

But Governor Cuomo had characterized it as murder insurance and that we were backstopping murderers. Anything associated with the NRA was politically radioactive and we were close to a meltdown.

Was I blamed within the NRA for the legal battles that arose because of Carry Guard? Certainly by some, but most understood why it was needed and supported the program. As did Ackerman McQueen, until it became an issue—and then, of course, it was my fault.

Our board obviously felt the efforts of the DFS in New York to close us down were purely political in nature. Multiple other providers existed in this space, including Lockton Affinity, our insurance administrator, and we didn't solicit anything without their express approval. (I can guarantee you that Lockton was unhappy with all this, and the feeling was mutual.)

No one sat in a dark room and said, "Okay, guys, here's a great idea, let's figure out a way to circumvent the solicitation rules in New York State!" It's a ridiculous premise. It was a frustrating end to a program I had created, and that was on its way to being a game changer for the association. But as I would soon discover, Carry Guard was only the first battle in a much larger war with the powers that be in the Empire State.

★

A month or two prior—early 2018—there had been some rumblings that the New York attorney general would open up an inquiry into the NRA. The NRA is domiciled in New York, where it was started. The association never moved it, and as a result its charter was tied like an umbilical cord to New York.

Eric Schneiderman, the New York attorney general at the time, told Tom King, an NRA board member from New York, "You guys have got to get your act together, because I'm being pressured by Cuomo to open up an investigation into you."

So as shockingly divulgent as that news was, we knew that an investigation was coming from the AG, on top of the Department of Financial Services proceedings.

On a Saturday in February 2018, I was on a call with our legal team, and I realized they were way out of their league, missed the bigger picture, and we were in trouble. I asked Steve Hart, our outside counsel, to have our lawyers simply assess our risk. It became apparent they couldn't do it. They simply didn't understand what was coming and how the game against us would be played. All they seemed to offer was theoretical legal speak. This was not a class at Harvard law school. We were not prepared.

They didn't understand that Cuomo was going to use every single political tool in his toolkit against us. He wanted to bring the place down. The governor is a brawler, this was going to be a bloody street fight, and we had to lawyer up, literally.

I called Steve afterward and said, "We're in deep shit. We've got to get somebody else in here. We need a killer."

He totally agreed. "I've got to call [Bill] Brewer and see if I can get him to help us. He can deal with this."

William Brewer III hailed from Texas, but he specialized in New York State law, where he had an office. As a Democrat, he had ties to Hillary Clinton and, later, Beto O'Rourke. And in a bit of "it's a small world," Bill's wife was Angus McQueen's daughter.

Bill was smart as a whip, ambitious, and known for playing hardball. As he told *Texas Lawyer* early in his career in an article criticizing his "scorched-earth" litigation, "We don't believe we should earn our living from being nice to other lawyers."[2]

On the other hand, clients loved his approach. Howard Meyers, whom I'd met, and was the founder of a manufacturing company in Brooklyn, said, "I've worked with Bill for decades....He delivers time and time again."[3]

So Steve and I talked to Bill. And he was impressive—from the moment he walked in the room, he was in command. He convinced me that he knew what to do and could solve our problems. And he had this larger-than-life presence. Later Wayne and I met with him and Travis Carter, his PR guy, in Wayne's office. Bill laid out a very disturbing case about how the NRA had a much bigger problem than an insurance issue.

"These guys are coming for you." Bill went on to lay out how Bloomberg, the New York State Department of Financial Services, and the New York attorney general were on the warpath to take down the NRA. Our fears were being realized, and much of what Bill said that day would be proven true.

Bill was also a phenomenal salesman, brilliant, oozing self-confidence...almost bordering on arrogance. Privately he said to me, "I'll do this, but you gotta get Wayne to let us get into all the issues at the NRA."

In essence, he asked me how bad things were.

And I admitted, "It's pretty bad," and tried to assure him that Wayne would give us full rein to do what we needed to do.

So Bill and I started to poke around to see where we were vulnerable as a nonprofit, in terms of our procedures and compliance.

From that day forward, we were joined at the hip. Every day starting in February 2018, we were on the phone together daily or in meetings. I would take Bill's call over any other call. It was a 24/7 commitment and I'd regularly talk with Bill at 1:00 a.m. and then 7:00 a.m. the next (same) morning. That's how hard we ran. Wayne nicknamed us the Vampires.

☆

After we hired Bill Brewer, I was traveling to New York to meet with Bill over the New York State lawsuits and other litigation and ongoing investigations five days a week. The investigations made Wayne crazy. He loved to say, "New York laws are so complex that no one's in compliance."

But that wasn't true and I would reply, "Well, Wayne, it's pretty basic, right? You've got to bid contracts out. Not just do a deal based on 'I know a guy' relationships. So don't say the New York law is too complex, because that's not true. It's not."

Wayne would claim, "We're being targeted because we're the NRA."

And to a large extent, he was right. But that was the consequence of our extremism, and the flip side of the NRA being targeted by the state of New York was that the NRA was totally fucked up. We desperately needed more oversight, more process, and more compliance.

Now, would the New York AG be looking into us if we weren't the NRA? No. And in the legal world, you can't do that.

Bill suggested that we sue Governor Cuomo and Maria Vullo, the woman who was running DFS at the time, for just that—viewpoint discrimination—for treating us differently because we were the NRA, and because we were a lobbying group whose views differed from theirs.

We got Anthony Romero from the ACLU to sign on to this (of all things). That was a major coup, and Bill sold it hard. Romero realized that this could happen to any organization, and he was right: What if you're Planned Parenthood in North Dakota and some conservative governor does the exact same thing? What if North Dakota tries to take away your banking apparatus or your insurance apparatus? Or use their regulatory powers to squash Planned Parenthood? You can't do that.

In the spring of 2018, Bill was pushing hard to get this lawsuit out. I couldn't get a hold of Wayne that day because he was traveling.

So I told him, file it. I'd deal with Wayne, and I'd take the heat. We needed to go.

And for the short term, it worked! We got a tremendous PR lift as a result of the lawsuit, and the mood music, as Bill would call it, was great. Everyone felt we were on the right track. News of the lawsuit was everywhere, with the media reporting Cuomo was running a blacklist campaign. Brewer claimed in conversations that Bloomberg and the folks at Everytown for Gun Safety were pissed at Cuomo and felt he overplayed his hand. So the governor was getting it from both sides.

☆

So we filed for viewpoint discrimination with the idea that the lawsuit gave Bill, Wayne, and me the leverage and time to fix things within the association, and prepare for the pending investigation.

To my surprise, I heard that Judge Thomas McAvoy, of the Northern District of New York, came into court and said, "Before we get started, I just want everybody to know that I have a Sig pistol. If that's problem for anybody in the room, I can recuse myself."

So there's the great constitutional question, right up front—*Hey, I'm allowed to keep and bear arms, according to the Second Amendment of the Constitution.* The DFS lawyers did not ask McAvoy to recuse himself. And the judge allowed the case to move forward. In other words, he felt there was enough merit in our legal position to proceed with a trial.

To my surprise, I received a welcome vote of confidence from the cops in the courtroom. While I was going through security to get into the courtroom—there was heavy-duty security up in Albany— the security guy asked me, "Are you with the NRA?"

I said yeah. And he whispered to me, sotto voce, "Go get 'em."

Later, when we would get out of court at the end of the day, almost every cop and security guard in the building came up to us and said thank you. I think that they felt they were treated like second-class citizens a lot of the time, and that we were trying to help them.

In the meantime, Bill Brewer and I were attempting to clean up the NRA's business practices. We were fighting the good fight, and I was spending the bulk of my time on the New York legal issues, coordinating the litigation with Bill. I was pleased that Wayne had the confidence in me to drive all of the litigation.

The potential investigation by the New York attorney general was derailed when Schneiderman was accused of abusing several girlfriends, and resigned in May 2018. New York appointed an interim AG, Barbara Underwood. On that front, we had been given a reprieve, but New York City public advocate Letitia James, who had called the NRA a "criminal organization," was running for attorney general, and she was backed by Andrew Cuomo. James won the election in the fall of 2018, setting us ultimately on a collision course.

★

That May, Woody Phillips, our longtime CFO, announced that he was retiring after more than a quarter century on the job. Angus McQueen, in a panic, told him, "You can't do that! You're not leaving!"

Honest to God, the folks at Ackerman tried to convince him to stay on. They loved working with Woody—he was their meal ticket.

I was charged with bringing in a new CFO. I retained Korn Ferry to search for the right candidates, and we ended up hiring Craig Spray, and ultimately he was approved by the board.

Unfortunately, Craig had a really brusque bedside manner, and to my chagrin, appeared to have a Napoleon complex. He loved to run around the sixth floor and proclaim, "Hey, I didn't make this mess, I don't even need this job."

Just the attitude you want from your new CFO while you're headed into a battle.

Within the first month, Craig Spray and Woody went to Dallas to meet with Ackerman McQueen to go over the budget, in a kind of passing of the baton. I was worried that this was going to be a mess—and it was a complete disaster. Craig was supposed to ask pertinent questions and cut the budget. But Ackerman hadn't had that kind of oversight before. When Craig asked for adjusted invoices so that there was more clarity and transparency in terms of what the NRA was paying for, Angus completely lost his shit.

When Craig came back I asked him, "Well, how did it go?"

He was in shock. "I've never in my life ever experienced something so unprofessional and so crazy."

He was taken aback at the defensive anger and hatred he encountered at Ackerman. He looked like he got hit by a bus. Wayne laughed it off.

Ackerman McQueen went completely, pardon the pun, ballistic.

Granted, Craig did not have the best bedside manner. On the one hand, the NRA needed a CFO who would implement much stronger controls. And Craig had the skills to do that. The problem was that he didn't have a marketing background, didn't understand the lifetime value of our members, or the way that membership really worked. I suspected I'd made a big mistake.

Shortly afterward, Angus called Wayne, screaming at him to fire Craig. And Angus was serious enough that Wayne and I actually considered it. We were on the fence. And at some point Craig figured out he didn't actually work for Wayne. According to some revision of the bylaws back in 1994, he was elected by the board. Wayne, as EVP, certainly had some level of control over him. But Wayne didn't exercise that control. He remained hands-off, saying that Craig reported to the board. And Craig didn't want to work with anybody.

And I thought, *You must be kidding. Now I've got another person to worry about.* He approached Wayne about getting me fired so that he could take my job as well, and become Wayne's unofficial COO. Wayne told me all of that, in great detail, about how Craig wanted me out and was mortified by the whole thing. He even pulled Brewer in on the details of the conversation.

And this is the guy I had handpicked for the job. Not my best hire—check that, my worst. I should've asked for a refund from Korn Ferry.

★

In the summer of 2018, there were fireworks from a different front. Andrew Arulanandam, our PR guy, called me.

"This is not good."

"What's not good?" I asked.

"There's something that came out of the audit committee about you."

My mind was racing. *What could it be?*

I was informed there were a number of whistleblowers from our internal accounting team, six of them, and they had the audit files and records for the last few years. They had all worked at the NRA forever. And they had all signed off on all these reports over the years, but now there were irregularities they were suddenly bringing to light.

The NRA accountants had written up a list of complaints in a page-and-a-half memo called "List of Top Concerns for the Audit Committee." In the memo, they enumerated a number of business transactions involving NRA vendors and executives, starting with the invoices from Ackerman McQueen.

The audit members claimed they were forced to sign the audit reports. But they were raising a red flag now, and as such, declared themselves officially as whistleblowers. The list spelled out specifics behind an earlier handwritten memo from a week before, dated July 12, that had been written by Emily Cummins, the NRA's managing director of tax and risk management. The whistleblowers claimed that the NRA lost millions of dollars to Ackerman. *(So that part was true.)*

Emily went into a meeting with Bill Brewer and told him, "I'm a whistleblower." And whipped out the policy for him to read. Meaning she fell under whistleblower protections. *(Fair enough.)*

And she proceeded to pull out an org chart and pointed to it. At the top was Wayne. And she said, "See that guy right underneath him, Powell? He works for Angus McQueen." *(Uh, not true.)*

In her mind, I worked for Angus McQueen and was in charge of all the Ackerman McQueen stuff. *(Getting colder.)* And that, in essence, Angus McQueen was running the NRA. *(Warmer, back to partly true.)*

Oh, and by the way, she said, pointing at Bill, you're Angus's son-in-law. *(Conspiracy, check and mate . . .)*

So all that happened . . . and to unpack it you have to figure: If Ackerman had been doing marketing and publicity for the NRA for thirty-five years, why, now, were their invoices being questioned?

Then someone leaked all of this information to the *Wall Street Journal.*

We knew we had some internal leaks. One of the reasons Wayne ran so much of his financial stuff through Ackerman was because we didn't trust his own accountants. Classic NRA protocol: Rather than fix the problem, Wayne came up with a somewhat paranoid and backasswards work-around.

Anyway, the whistleblowers came forward, claiming there were all these things wrong with our finances and payments. One of the things Wayne and Bill and I had to do was to chase all the claims down and make a report to the finance committee of the NRA board.

And now for a very telling moment...

Wayne got on the phone with Angus, telling him that Bill Brewer needed to look at his books and records. And Angus went batshit. He screamed that he wasn't giving them to us. He didn't trust Bill, his own son-in-law, and felt that Wayne, Bill, everybody was out for revenge and to pin everything on him. In truth, Angus had opposed Bill marrying his daughter Skye, and there was no love lost between them. "If you think I'm going to give you our records and books, you are crazy."

Instead, Angus, over time, convinced Wayne that if he used a different attorney, the NRA and the audit committee could get what they needed. It was a giant beatdown by Angus, and it worked; Wayne caved. He took Bill Brewer off the case.

I couldn't believe it.

In retrospect I should have walked out then.

So they brought in Chuck Cooper, a good friend and colleague of Steve Hart's, who had been doing business with the NRA for a long time, and was a very well-known attorney in Washington. But Chuck's firm wasn't really set up to do the kind of forensic audit that we needed.

So Chuck engaged Bill's team to help him out!

This circus went on for six weeks. Finally Chuck bowed out—he must have realized he was wading into the middle of a huge mess. And Bill got pulled back into this, trying to get the documents from Ackerman. And around we went...

★

Now, while all of this was happening, someone had been leaking documents and information to Mark Maremont at the *Wall Street Journal*, the Pulitzer Prize–winning reporter whose articles had helped bring down Tyco years before. Maremont rooted around everywhere, calling Wayne's high school friends, Susan's friends, my dad, for months. And then he ran his story on November 30.[4]

Here's in part what Maremont had: One of the leaked memos claimed that the NRA had made payments to the "significant other" of Woody Phillips, our recently retired CFO. Bill disputed that, replying that the money was paid to an IT consulting firm, and had been vetted and approved by the audit committee.

But the real killer from the whistleblowers were payments we made to Associated Television International, or ATI. From 1998 to 2014 they produced a show called *Crime Strike* that Wayne would host or introduce that reenacted an actual crime from police case files. These episodes often involved a gun being used in self-defense. It was a fairly good concept, one that has been copied by half a dozen true crime murder shows. But the older original shows had very low production values. And later on we were paying a ton of money for a much higher production quality.

But damned if I could find the show hardly anywhere online or on the air.

According to whistleblowers, the NRA paid ATI "$1.8 million for the rental of a house" that belonged to David McKenzie, ATI's president. Michael Donaldson, ATI's outside counsel, confirmed that the company sent us "seven invoices" referencing the house, which added up to roughly that amount. He claimed the invoices were for refurbishing the house after completing the original episodes of *Crime Strike.*[5]

Bill said we had a long relationship with ATI, and that the invoices were part of an ongoing review by the association.[6] Code for: This is a huge problem.

But this was a claim that might really hurt Wayne in the New York State investigation, even if it proved to be false, as he was a part of each show, and we had spent millions on that show. It gave Bill Brewer heartburn; he described it as "nitro in a bottle." We tried to get to the bottom of what the payments were for, but it was never resolved. It could have been entirely legitimate, but I never learned of a full explanation, if there was one.

☆

In addition, the whistleblowers' complaint named four executives who violated "accounts payable procedures" and HR policy—hiring staff without the knowledge of HR. The four executives they named were Doug Hamlin, executive director of publications, Eric Frohardt, director of education and training, Joe DeBergalis, executive director of General Operations, and me.[7] I'm assuming I was the guy that "hired staff" without the knowledge of HR. Now I'm the chief of staff (COO); the hires obviously had to be directed to HR so the guys could get paid, among other things. The point is some of these issues they brought out were absurd. It hurt their case. I also bought a computer outside of the "IT purchasing department."

The NRA concluded that the claims involving the other three executives had no merit.

As for me, it caused a real dust storm. Wayne asked me to be his chief of staff with a sizable goal in mind—find ways to modernize the organization. I reviewed the organization from top to bottom and found plenty of opportunities. Many were rooted in organizational or individual power grips. The effort needed a strategic plan and executive buy-in if we had a chance to move the dial . . . and an outside firm. McKenna & Associates, an advisory firm with an existing vendor relationship and good reputation from working with NRA executives for over six years, was under consideration for the work. Both Wayne and Woody were on board with the project, the hiring of McKenna & Associates, and that my wife, Colleen, was employed by the firm. We needed someone we could trust, and who did great work, and McKenna fit the bill. The whistleblowers' complaint involving me was that it had not been previously reported to the audit committee that my wife was working for McKenna.

Fine, so we provided a well-documented package with details of the contract, my wife's twenty-five-plus-year consulting career credentials that included stints at IBM and Ernst & Young, and the work products produced by the McKenna team. It was approved by the audit committee.

There was one other allegation laid at my feet—that I had hired my father, who was a professional photographer, to do work for the NRA. That was not true. As soon as I heard that, I called my dad—it was the first I had heard of it. It turned out that Joe DeBergalis had reached out to my father to hire him to do a job for his side of the business. He knew of my father because he had done some photography work previously for Ackerman McQueen. But I had known nothing about it, and I quickly put the kibosh on it.

What was a disappointment was how it was portrayed internally. And worse, that Wayne's first reaction to being told about the complaint against me was to fire me. Given his selective memory, Wayne tended to duck responsibility when things went south. It was easier to let others take the hit than to speak up and say, "Hold on a second, no one is hiding anything. Woody and I approved of it." But that is not how he rolled. Upshot: This became a classic example of the self-interest, based on fear, politics, and expediency, with which Wayne manages. Meanwhile it became a huge distraction and, for those whose worlds could possibly be changed by a modernization plan, a welcomed delay in anything happening.

This turned into a big deal, after the fact, because the accountants were like, *Oh, now we have something on Powell, and the "Royals."*

Wayne's reaction baffled me—hiring McKenna and Colleen was something he and I had discussed together before bringing her on board. It was Wayne who asked me if Colleen would be able to help us out with Carry Guard. "She's smart, we know what we'll get," he said.

Ultimately Mark Maremont at the *Wall Street Journal* wrote a story about it. I actually sat down with him to answer questions he had for me.

Maremont asked me straight out, "Do you think it's a problem that your wife, Colleen Gallagher, is working for the NRA?"

And I said, "No, I don't." And then, "I know you've looked up her résumé. You've talked to some people over at Ernst & Young, she's really good at what she does."

And he said, "That's right."

I told him honestly, "Mark, it's hard to get people to work here. People don't want to work for the NRA. I mean, I understand why you would raise a red flag. But there is really nothing here. She and her firm worked for us and delivered a great product."[8]

As Andrew Arulanandam told reporters, "The audit committee was aware of the relationship and approved the consulting arrangement with McKenna."[9] And in the end, Mark wrote a pretty fair article, infographics and all.

★

That fall, the NRA announced a new title for me, senior strategist and chief of staff for Wayne. And the press office put out an announcement along the lines of "Josh is uniquely positioned to defend the organization, to work with our outside legal teams, and to run this operation." Chris went bananas over that, according to Wayne, as he was constantly jockeying for position as successor to the throne.

Pete Brownell, the president of the NRA, had resigned in May as a result of the fallout from the trip he took with other NRA board members to Russia (see chapter 5 for that fun adventure). Carolyn Meadows, a vice president and fellow board member, served as interim president over the summer. In the fall, in response to behind-the-scenes maneuvering by Angus, Wayne met with Ollie North several times as a possible permanent replacement for NRA president.

So Ollie was Angus's big brainchild—he told Wayne that he needed a wartime president. Ollie, he said, could be the second coming of Charlton Heston while the association was under attack.

In my mind, there was an enormous and clear conflict of interest—Ollie was Ackerman's guy. He had been hired away from Fox News with a $2 million contract to create a show for NRATV. So he was under contract to Ackerman, although the show was never filmed. And now he was going to be the president of the NRA?

Meanwhile, tired of my questioning invoices, and concerns about the content and cost of NRATV, the Ackerman people found a way to push me aside. When I became the official designee on the new contract between the NRA and Ackerman McQueen, I was not only negotiating the agreement, but asking for all kinds of information to perform my due diligence.

Two weeks later, the NRA general counsel received a letter from an executive at Ackerman—a woman who had been there for decades whom I had worked with—who suddenly was claiming sexual harassment. She insisted that the NRA open up an investigation of me—and that I no longer be allowed to continue to negotiate the contract. The NRA hired an outside counsel and gave that person all my communications with this Ackerman executive.

Her claim in part was that had she sent me for approval an ad that Ackerman had created and were planning to run of a woman in a tight T-shirt, and I responded, "Was the shirt the wrong size?"

To which she responded, "No shit!"

My attorney looked at the documents and told me, in her opinion, it was nothing more than a negotiating tactic. There was nothing there. It was all very odd and I was shocked, to say the least. But I guess these were the tactics Ackerman was willing to take to protect the millions they had at stake.

This woman and her attorney never responded to our calls to provide more information.

But the claim served their purpose. I was removed from the Ackerman negotiations, and from any further oversight of Ackerman, and never spoke to Angus or any of the folks at Ackerman McQueen again. The following August, a story came out about how I'd sexually harassed two different women and paid them off.

On a Sunday morning my daughter pulled up Twitter and showed me the headline, "Josh Powell, Multiple-Time Sexual Harasser," with an accompanying gray-filtered "mug shot" photo of me.

And that's how you get smeared in Washington. As Angus had once said to me, "The smear is all about if you can make it stick."

CHAPTER 7

Game of Thrones

Oliver North, as I feared, was a nightmare from day one. I understand the popular conception of Ollie—that he was the inspiration for Jack Ryan and he came out of Iran-Contra as some sort of patriotic Boy Scout. But decades later, let me tell you that was much more myth than reality. A close friend of mine who served with the Reagan administration asked me, "Josh, what are you doing making Oliver North president? The guy is a consummate liar."

Very soon after Ollie was elected president of the board, a largely ceremonial position, we met briefly and Ollie took the time to tell me, "Things are going to change around here."

At this point, Ollie's boyish good looks had deepened with age lines—he was about seventy-five at the time. At over six feet tall, he still struck a commanding figure. Angus and Wayne had wanted a wartime president, a kind of reincarnation of Charlton Heston, and without question Ollie was an iconic figure in conservative circles. And like Heston, he was a media regular, hosting the television show *War Stories with Oliver North* on Fox for fifteen years, as well as appearing as a regular commentator on *Hannity*. He liked being in charge, and was experienced in navigating organizational bureaucracy. And to his credit, he brought a unique perspective to some of the difficult days and issues we confronted. He knew what it was like to go through hard times. At one point I complained to him about something that had happened that day. "Bad day for the NRA."

And he replied to this effect: "A bad day is when you leave a Marine on the battlefield."

I took that to heart. In other words, I was overreacting. And he was right. Whatever the issue was, it wasn't life or death. At times, I became so obsessed with the mission that it clouded my reaction. Later on that day, I called to express my thanks for him telling me that.

From day one, he expected to take over the organization. I was clear with him who I worked for, without having to say too much. Everyone at the NRA would call Ollie "Colonel North." It was a bit comical—we were the NRA, not a branch of the military. He'd been out of the military for almost three decades. To me he was just Ollie—he played the Boy Scout routine still, but that was combined with a blunt righteousness that was part of his huge self-regard. We always conducted our conversations with respect, but we both knew we weren't quite on the same team. He'd have gutted me, followed by Brewer and Wayne, if he could have. And he tried.

Did Ollie respect me? I doubt it. Look, I wasn't a military guy, and most of the folks around him wanted me out of the way—especially Ackerman McQueen, who had hired him.

Less Jack Ryan and more rogue operative, Ollie was loathed by many in the military community, especially by Reagan's people, because he lied, couldn't stay in his lane, and was always pushing for more territory. His attitude seemed to be, *I don't need to abide by the rules.* And he was arrogant enough to assume he should lead things. He warned me early on, "I'm going to be in the office every day."

Again, the position of president at the NRA is an unpaid, ceremonial title. He was not the head of the NRA. His only job was to preside over the board. He had an office in the building, but no president in our history came in on a regular basis. It was quite amusing watching all the division directors parade into his office to kiss his ass.

Within a few days of being appointed, Ollie told Wayne, "I'm going to have a staff meeting." Wayne told him he didn't think that was a good idea. But Wayne couldn't just come out and say that's not your place—and there's the rub. Wayne's conflict avoidance led directly to the insanity that gripped the place. Ollie and I clashed from day one, because I was Wayne's chief of staff, managing so many of our day-to-day operations. We were trying to keep Ackerman McQueen in check and he was motivated to do just the opposite (they were paying him a couple million dollars a year by then).

All of a sudden, Chris and his team were giving presentations to Ollie. And Joe DeBergalis, who now headed General Operations, which really meant education and training, would sit down for gab sessions with Ollie. They'd answer all his questions "yes sir" and "no sir."

We needed one leader of the organization, one CEO; now we had two.

Wayne did little to try and stop him. He talked to Ollie, sometimes for hours. And after several such conversations, Wayne told me, "I felt like I was being waterboarded." Ollie was determined to rein Wayne in and cut back on Brewer's legal expenses in the investigation. And he was relentless—he would talk to Wayne behind closed doors for hours, and he was a persuasive and convincing guy, despite my eye-rolling. "It's not about you, brother," he would constantly tell Wayne. "I'm trying to protect you." And Wayne took the easy way out, every time. Worse, if Ollie called a meeting with parts of the organization, Wayne would often attend. At some point you have to lay down the boundaries, plain and simple. The employees didn't know who they were working for.

Board members would swing by the NRA offices and take a meeting with Ollie. They were not on staff, they didn't run the NRA—they were board members—and they shouldn't be coming and going. Board members can't just call down to the head of tech and say, *I want to see you*. No organization in the world would put up with that. It's about corporate governance. No one and everyone was in charge. It was a nightmare.

My advice to Wayne was, "Tell Ollie to go do his TV show, that's what he's getting paid to do"—the TV show Ackerman had hired him to create. At one point, in exasperation, I grabbed a copy of the bylaws and highlighted with a yellow marker the words describing his position. "Why don't you give this to him so that you can explain what he actually does? Or I'd be more than happy to talk to him. He can call board meetings. That's about it."

If Ollie barely put up with me, he hated Bill Brewer. He hated Bill's suits, that he didn't wear a tie, that he was from New York, and that Bill was just as brash and arrogant as he was—there just wasn't enough oxygen in the room for the two of them. And Bill of course was a Democrat, and not a gun guy, and had no previous experience with Second Amendment law, which just gave Ollie more ammo to attack him with.

Ollie and Chris were convinced Bill was overstating the NRA's legal jeopardy in order to bill us more. Ollie was outraged that Bill was making so much money—almost $2 million a month, or

$24 million in one thirteen-month period.[1] In leaked documents to the board, Ollie and board member Richard Childress, the former NASCAR race driver and current team owner, wrote in an April 18, 2019, letter, "The Brewer invoices are draining NRA cash at mind-boggling speed. Invoices of this extraordinary magnitude deserve immediate attention, oversight, and a careful, competent and unbiased examination."[2]

It's hard to argue that $24 million a year isn't an immense amount of money. Especially considering not one case has gone to trial yet. And by the time this book is published those legal costs will have pushed north of $70 million. Put another way, one year of Brewer's legal fees was equal to about five hundred thousand NRA member dues.

But most of all, Ollie hated Bill because Bill was now involved in our effort to get documents and invoices from Ackerman to support their billings. Letitia James, in her campaign for attorney general in the fall of 2018 in New York, pledged to look into the NRA's tax-exempt status, given the reports of financial self-dealing and irregularities. To prepare for the investigation, Bill told us he needed to audit our spending practices, and our contracts with vendors, and deal with the whistleblowers' claims—including, of course, Ackerman.

Ollie, who was essentially an Ackerman Trojan horse, was determined to block those efforts. He claimed Bill was constantly straying out of his lane, getting into things Ollie didn't think he should be wading into.

There were also some darker claims against Bill by the NRA whistleblowers from the auditing department. Remember Emily Cummins, the managing director of tax and risk management? She claimed Bill tried to silence and intimidate NRA staffers who processed his bills; the whistleblowers became concerned by the exorbitant spending levels at the association, as well as "mismanagement" and conflicts of interest. She stated that Bill "threatened our professional livelihoods," and that he compiled "burn books" with personal information that he could use against opponents.[3]

Was there any truth to this? I don't know. I'm not sure what a "burn book" is, but I've seen many of the binders on folks within the NRA, including me.

Partners at Bill's firm denied it and defended his work, as did we. And while I know Bill would admit his fees were high, they were no higher than those of other top lawyers, and he felt his work was worth it. As reported by the *New York Times*, the NRA had an independent firm do a review of the bills, which concluded that they were high, but not unheard of in the context of high-stakes litigation. On a per-hour basis that is true. However, at that pace of billing it was like nearly a dozen lawyers were working on the NRA full-time. As Hal Marshall, a former partner at Bickel & Brewer, described it, "Bill's representation of the NRA is a classic example of 'servicing the client to death.' We tried to leave no stone unturned in our cases, and it often yielded great results. On the other hand, the bills were hefty."[4]

In other words, little strategic thought was given to how to curtail legal spending versus what the outcome would look like from the board or anyone else at the NRA. That is a simple question that at a minimum the legal affairs committee ought to ask, which by definition is their job.

During that time the NRA was subpoenaed by one of the congressional oversight committees about the Russia trip. It was a whole mini-saga (see chapter 5) in the press for four or five weeks—did Wayne authorize the Russia trip or not? At one point, Wayne told me, Ollie confronted Wayne, screaming, "Why are we throwing [former president] Pete Brownell under the bus? And why is Bill Brewer working on Russia?" He wanted Bill off the Russia investigation.

The point that Bill—and I—made was, "all roads lead to New York," and this stuff was going to come up in the New York investigation. That was the first time Ollie came out publicly saying we had to get rid of Bill. (And me, by the way.) Bill would say, "You need to help me sell this," on an array of topics. Which I would do daily with Wayne and others. Get the buy-in Brewer needed to proceed.

Ollie demanded to see Bill's invoices and made all sorts of other pleas and petitions. But at the heart of it was the fact that Bill was taking on Ackerman. We needed to get back to the audit committee on the questions that were raised by the whistleblowers. But this documentation also got to the core of our legal response to the New York State investigation—they were asking to see Ackerman's bills, questioning the expenses and the pass-alongs, things paid by Ackerman and later reimbursed by the NRA. We'd been pressing Ackerman for months for our books and records and the response was woefully inadequate. And despite Ackerman's claim that it was "simply false" that they hid any facts from the NRA, I didn't see us getting anywhere with them. Ackerman had already gotten me removed from oversight of the firm, so all of this was handled by Craig Spray, our new CFO, Wayne, or Bill. And now Ackerman and Ollie were doing their best to squeeze Bill out.

By late fall of 2018, Wayne himself seemed to be on board with concerns over Bill's fees. "We've got to get rid of Bill. I'm getting too much pressure from the board."

The board was concerned because Bill had a team of people working on a plethora of legal issues, and was getting paid a king's ransom in their eyes. And to some board members, he was gaining too much power in the organization. Bill had come aboard in February 2018 to handle the New York legal probes, and at this point his position within the NRA wasn't cemented yet. Most, on the other hand, thought that Bill was their best bet to beat back New York, and, as Wayne would later say, keep out him of jail for financial improprieties.[5]

This all came to a head when I heard "dump Bill" rumors swirling through the halls. So I called Ollie and said, "Clear your schedule. I'm coming over."

And I made it crystal clear to Ollie how critical Bill's work was to the NRA's success in the New York investigation. We needed Bill to drive to the finish line, to save our butts. We could not afford to start firing people for political reasons, or worse, to not continue the investigations and compliance work we had started.

"I'm not going to have any part of it," I told Wayne and Ollie. "If Bill goes, I go. Let me know in the next forty-five minutes." Wayne went on to say, "Well, maybe Bill can just handle New York." I responded, "Wayne, you're in charge, but if you go down this path it won't be with me. It's your call. Let me know."

That derailed Ollie's train for a while. As Bill said to me and others later, I had lain down on the tracks for him. And I had. But I believed in what he was doing. At the time we were fighting the right fight and cleaning up the mess and I was committed to my bones to seeing it through. I knew if Brewer was dismissed or his role reduced at this point, we had no chance. I'd make the same decision today.

Steve Hart, chairman of the Washington law firm Williams & Jensen and a longtime NRA counsel, who had worked with Bill Brewer previously and brought him into the NRA, ending up defecting to the Ollie camp. I was very surprised, as he represented the board and shouldn't be on anyone's side, but this is the NRA, after all. In addition, he started representing past president Pete Brownell against the NRA, claiming, as I mentioned in chapter 5, that the Russia trip was authorized by Wayne, and we should reimburse him for expenses. All of which pulled Bill further into the Russia inves-tigation, and further pissed off Ollie. Remember, there were some pretty serious allegations of Russian dark money flowing into the NRA, even though that wasn't true. We suspected Pete's PR firm then leaked a story to the *Daily Beast* that Wayne approved the Russia trip, which ultimately was a poorly played hand of cards.

In tandem, a Senate inquiry chaired by Senator Ron Wyden requested all sorts of documents relating to Russia. There was a ton of material to go through. Some of the members of the board were asking why Bill was involved in Russia at all. David Coy, a mem-ber of the board finance committee and audit committee, declared, "This was an ILA issue, not an issue for Brewer"; he claimed there was "scope creep" with Bill's engagement—that we were paying him exorbitantly for work he shouldn't be doing. In retrospect, the dire warnings Bill gave us—that we were going to be dragged up to the Hill to give testimony about Russia—never happened. On the other hand, we had to be ready for that.

In the new year, Steve Hart and Ollie shifted their tactics—they no longer wanted to get rid of Bill, they just wanted him to focus on the New York legal front. That was their pitch to the audit committee in January. They told Wayne, "We're just trying to protect you. We need to audit Bill's invoices."

Brewer was furious, and said, "No way, they will blow up the whole case, everything will no longer be privileged." In truth, that was a pretty silly argument. However, tearing into our lawyer's billing at this point would have been counterproductive, I thought.

By the new year, Ackerman claimed that Bill was going after them "to serve as a distraction from the failure of NRA executives and its board to properly fulfill its oversight duties." But what else where they going to say? Bill's office responded, "The NRA pursued documents from several major vendors, not just Ackerman. But Ackerman, singularly, resisted."[6]

There was a constant drumbeat from Ollie, Ackerman, and Hart to back off.

In February, Ollie and board vice presidents Richard Childress and Carolyn Meadows wrote a letter to Wayne claiming that Bill's retainer agreement wasn't properly executed, demanding that NRA payments to Bill's firm cease until they could discuss it with him. On top of that drama, Carolyn withdrew her name from the letter and basically stated, "They made me sign it, but I didn't want to." That pissed me off. Carolyn is an absolutely lovely person, and those two guys were badgering her into signing a dubious, gorilla dust complaint.

Bill cautioned Wayne about the legal threats that they faced, claiming he was uniquely positioned to defend him. As he stated in a *New York Times Magazine* article in a conversation with Wayne, "They believe that you guys are ripe to be taken," a reference to the expectations of New York attorney general Letitia James.[7] Steve Hart warned, in an internal memo leaked to the *Times*, that James was interested "in pursuing a dissolution case"—essentially prosecuting the NRA out of existence—and the association should contemplate reincorporating in Texas, Tennessee, or Delaware.

"LaPierre said he was advised that a safe-harbor provision in New York law gave nonprofits leeway to correct potential violations," reporter Danny Hakim wrote, "and Brewer began looking at anything that might attract the attention of a regulator."

That was exactly right. Brewer sold Wayne, myself, and the board on the idea that we could "self-correct," and still had one get-out-of-jail-free card left to play. We even gave ourselves a date by which we had to fix things. But it was not clear that this was in fact a silver bullet. A month later Ollie pushed us to hire an outside auditor to examine Bill's invoicing and billing. Wayne quashed that, telling Bill to ignore the request. "My office, not any member of the board, has the authority to hire and oversee legal counsel," he wrote. "Please keep up the good work, and disregard this and any similar missives you may receive."[8]

Moreover, Wayne warned Ollie to stop asking about legal bills, given his conflict of interest as an employee of Ackerman. It was one of the few instances of Wayne acting like a real CEO, which I welcomed.

But Ollie was determined to assert himself in this contest of wills. There was a flurry of letters between the NRA, Bill Brewer, and Ackerman McQueen that did nothing but fuel the hatred and insanity. Ollie started writing Wayne letters and having them hand-delivered to his house at night, just to get his attention—and to screw with his head. Wayne would have Susan send me a picture of the letter, which I'd send to Bill. And while we would shrug and say no big deal, it was effective to the extent that it became the next day's crisis, and took us off what we should be focused on. It was a clever bit of psy-ops, honestly.

By this point, it was clear Ollie was determined to take over the NRA and we were in for a proxy fight with the board over the vote for CEO and Wayne at the annual convention in late April. In another month, the fight would, as the *Washington Post* reported, "burst into the open."[9]

★

Because of the falling-out with Ackerman, that year we (Bill, Andrew Arulanandam, Travis Carter, and me) wrote Wayne's CPAC speech for him. Wayne gave me a sense of where he wanted to go, I took notes, talked with the guys, and we started writing. The team was not convinced that Wayne would follow through with our draft, because it didn't have any of the rants and tirades that he had become famous for. It wasn't *Ackermanesque.*

"Is he going to be okay with this?" I was asked.

"One hundred percent," I told them.

Because we wrote something much closer to who Wayne really is. He's not a firebrand—that was a cartoon character created by Ackerman. Wayne still took swipes at Bloomberg, and talked stridently about the lawsuit against Governor Cuomo and New York: "In real time, right before your very eyes, we, the National Rifle Association...are fighting perhaps the most important piece of First Amendment constitutional advocacy in the history of our country."[10] But there were none of the weird, paranoid political rants that made him come across as a crazy guy.

Normally, Wayne had coaching sessions before giving the speech, and it was a big production. He would ask me, "Do I sound crazy?" at various points.

This year that didn't happen. Andrew was concerned. "How do you think he'll do without the coaching?"

"Trust me. It's going to be fine. The reason he needed coaching with the Ackerman speeches is that he had to become an actor. In this speech, he is just being himself."

I mentioned the conversation later to Wayne, and he said, "That's right," and smiled.

I think we both thought that we could pull this off, turn the place around, and do the righteous thing. I certainly did.

★

The NRA's financial concerns once again moved to the front burner. Revenue from dues had fallen 21 percent since 2016, from $163 million to $128 million. And donations fell from $128 million to $98 million.[11]

In a famously reported gesture, Craig Spray decided to stop supplying employees with free coffee. That miserly decree was attributed to me in the media, but it was actually Craig, wanting to send a message that it was time to tighten our belts. As if cutting Dunkin' Donuts would fix the finances. The *Trace* and Rachel Maddow ran with the story, saying I had cut the coffee to the employees. Wayne asked me to fix this and restore office coffee, but the damage to morale had been done.

Soon after, Wayne sent out an alarming fund-raising letter, warning that Governor Cuomo and New York State's legal investigations could lead to the NRA being forced to "shut down." As he put it, "Right now we're facing an attack that's unprecedented not just in the history of the NRA, but in the entire history of our country."

He ended the pitch saying, "The NRA cannot survive without your help."[12]

And it worked. It was one of the highest-performing fund-raisers we had ever done. Selling the fear—real or imagined—never gets old.

Throughout the spring, Steve Hart seemed to use any excuse to involve himself in the NRA's decision making. He loved to play *Game of Thrones*, and saw himself as quite the Littlefinger.

He would tell head of operations Joe DeBergalis that he was going to be the guy, referring to who would head the NRA when Wayne left or was deposed. And then he would turn to me and say the same thing—"You're the guy. You're going to take over the NRA."

I told him, "Steve, seriously, give it a rest." As the annual convention approached, we got wind that Letitia James, who had won her election for attorney general of New York in the fall of 2018, was planning to come after the NRA more quickly than we were prepared for. So we looked for a way to put the brakes on any investigation, because we were nowhere near ready to deal with her. The problem was, if the attorney general closed down the NRA in New

York, through a process known as dissolution, it would effectively be closed down everywhere. This is exactly what she had done with the Trump Foundation, so it's not as if we were crying wolf. We couldn't unilaterally reincorporate in another state because all of the NRA's trademarks, branding, everything was domiciled in New York. We didn't own the name, the logo, anything. In a crazy twist of fate, the NRA is incorporated in the most regulated state in the country.

We had to leave the charter in New York because if we left, it would set off massive alarm bells, and allow them to initiate an in-depth forensic audit, which would be a disaster or we would have done it already. If everything at the NRA was squeaky clean, we would have left long ago. The fact that we couldn't is a little-known indictment of the NRA. In terms of corporate governance, we were set up like a mom-and-pop grocery store from 1950.

In 2018 I told Wayne, "We really need to look at how the association is structured and bring it into the twenty-first century. We'll leave the charter in New York, and we will create a substructure, just like every other corporation. McDonald's doesn't have one corporation in Delaware—they've got fifty thousand of them. If some part of the company wants to use the IP, they have an agreement with them, so if one piece goes bankrupt, you don't lose the corporation.

"We set it up on paper beautifully, the way it ought to be. We're not attempting to hide anything, we're just protecting the assets of the members, which now all sit in New York."

But after running through a litany of lawyers to put together a bulletproof corporate structure, I simply couldn't get it done. The gears of politics and bureaucracy at the NRA ground it to a halt. No one wanted to change, everyone was protecting their turf. Folks were living in the NRA of past glories and were just not able to adjust to the new political reality.

Bill advised us that if we could just clean up the place, it would make a huge difference—if there was any noncompliance in our past, but if we'd cleaned everything up, it would look much better for us.

Also, we believed that if James, newly minted in November as the attorney general for the state of New York, went after us so soon after the election, she would be adding evidence to our suit in federal court on viewpoint discrimination. (Or at least that's what Bill told me. As I came to believe, Bill tended to overpromise and underdeliver. We were now fighting legal battles on multiple fronts, and Bill was making a boatload of money from the NRA—over $2 million a month. And yet, as of the writing of this book, none of those suits have yet been settled or have reached a conclusion. He has taken the NRA into a litigation quagmire, rather than finding ways to end the association's disputes. And that is particularly true with Ackerman McQueen.)

In my opinion, Attorney General James has been taking her time investigating the NRA and building her case. But Bill kept telling me, "She's not that smart, and is scared to death of us."

Well, she now has a dozen or more attorneys working on this, and they're methodically gathering documents, interviewing the people involved, and trying to build a case against the association. I'm not sure she is on the right track, but to my mind there is no question that her goal is to bring down the NRA. Among gun control advocates on the left, she would be a hero. Dismantling the gun lobby would be huge within Democratic circles, and I've been told she has further political aspirations. Personally, I think Letitia James has been incredibly patient and played her cards masterfully, at a very steady pace. So far she's batting .1000 and has won every battle with Brewer. I'm not betting against her, that's for sure. What people don't understand is the pressure James is under to "get the NRA." She's in no rush and is compiling everything she needs for a complete field stripping of the association when the time is right. My hope is she doesn't overstep and try to actually destroy the place but rather removes the leadership and allows it to move forward.

And besides, Wayne and the NRA have done much to dismantle itself in the past two years, so James has followed the best political advice of all: "Never interfere with an enemy who is in the process of destroying himself."

★

Going into April, we began to prepare for a vicious proxy fight. Ollie was insistent that Wayne back off on investigating Ackerman, and Bill and Wayne refused to do so. So Ollie, goaded by his true employers, no doubt, took action. In a letter to NRA officials, he said that "allegations of financial improprieties could threaten our nonprofit status."

Now, Ollie had a point—we should have pumped the brakes and looked at how we were handling our litigation. At the time, we were hemorrhaging money, and we were paying Bill almost $100,000 a day. And Bill had a reputation for escalating disputes into expensive legal battles.

And it was clear that Ollie, after failing to stop Bill, was going after Wayne. Wayne and his "kitchen cabinet" on the board kicked into high gear, lobbying the rest of the board members for the upcoming fight. Wayne may have been a terrible manager, but he was a cagey, effective politician; he started making calls, telling members he had their backs. Nothing motivates you like the prospect of losing your job.

And that was the point—when it came to lobbying people, he was terrific, but when it came to managing people, he was a train wreck.

Wayne would do whatever he had to do to survive. And while I was there, I made sure nobody inside the NRA could get to him—that's how I came to define my job—which is not what I came to the NRA to do.

But the internecine conflict was constant, both minor skirmishes and full-blown battles. It was like one episode after another of *Game of Thrones*, as contenders vied for power, favor, and the crown. And I'll be honest with you, I felt a lot like Ned Stark—I was a trusted confidant of the king, but I walked into an onslaught of competing interests and weird secrets, and was unready for the treachery and realpolitik.

Let's hope I survive better than old Ned...

But what I discovered during that month leading up to the board battle in Indianapolis was that Wayne was not particularly loyal himself. In a scathing profile of Wayne and the NRA, written by Danny Hakim, Wayne was quoted as saying, "If I lose every friend, I'm prepared to do it."

I heard him say this once before—to me directly. It's a big window into his moral compass, and a stunning admission. Fundamentally he really didn't care about the people around him, or he is so scared that fear is driving this mindset. Either way he's taken zero ownership of what's gone on. It's truly bizarre, and just as bizarre that the board buys all this. He was all about survival and political expediency. He constantly fell back on plausible deniability, claiming he didn't know anything, sidestepping accountability, like half of Washington. He had been there for thirty-five years for a reason. Loyalty to Wayne LaPierre was a one-way street.

Wayne feels he has sacrificed everything to the NRA. That he *is* the NRA. That he is owed something, somehow. That he is the Jesus Christ of the Second Amendment, hands nailed to the cross. And that is how he justifies his actions in his mind. Why do I think that? Because I heard it from him for years.

No one is arguing the guy didn't get beaten up in the press. But that isn't the point. If you don't want the heat, if you don't want the stress on you, no one will fault you for that. Quit. Leave. But you don't get to claim after thirty-five years that you had nothing to do with this financial debacle. Don't take the $2 million-plus annual salary—plus expenses well north of that (see chapter 9). The members, the association employees, the entire gun-owning population of America deserve much better.

★

On Tuesday, April 17, less than a week before the start of the annual convention, Bill, on the NRA's behalf, filed a lawsuit against Ackerman, alleging that they had held back access to information and records that they were obligated to give us, amid "bloated deals, lavish payments and opaque financial arrangements."[13] Ackerman was incensed—from their perspective, the NRA was trying to blame everything on Ackerman for thirty years of work together, despite the fact that the way the NRA and Ackerman had done business had been blessed by Wayne and the board. And the NRA was taking no responsibility for that. And with that, the thirty-plus-year relationship with our longtime marketing and PR firm ended, and the behind-the-scenes skirmishes broke out into open warfare.

Wayne and Bill Brewer and I decided we had to relieve Steve Hart of his duties as outside counsel and counsel to the board. Steve had left the reservation and aligned himself with Ollie's attempt to stage a proxy fight and toss Wayne out.

You might ask how the CEO has the power to fire the counsel to the board, which would be a fair question. It is another example of messy NRA governance that isn't covered in the bylaws as it should be. Regardless, it was a really big deal—Steve was the first person to go down. We wrote a letter to Steve, terminating his employment, which John Frazer, as general counsel, was supposed to send. I was in Michigan during this crucial period, and I heard that John wanted to adjust this and change that, and this went on interminably.

I was pretty exhausted at this point—I'd spent so much energy trying to address the issues within the NRA, respond to the lawsuits, and manage the internal fighting that I hardly had a minute to do my actual job. Now Wayne was days from a major proxy fight and I was dealing with this current circus. I was pulling my hair out, and this all seemed like legal dithering.

And sure enough, just minutes before Frazer hit the send button to fire Hart, he received an email from Hart that Hart had addressed to a number of board members, alleging that he had information about Wayne that could be damaging, both to Wayne and to the NRA, about Wayne's personal expenditures on the NRA dime.

Clearly it was a move that had been choreographed by Ollie and Ackerman weeks in advance. The leaked information about Wayne's expenses could *only* logically come from Ackerman, since that was the whole point—that Wayne had funneled these invoices for personal expenses to Ackerman, to be reimbursed by the NRA, rather billing the NRA itself.

Ollie and Ackerman and their camp had made their play to bring Wayne down, minutes before Hart was let go himself.

Bill called me up, furious. "Why can't we get this fucking letter out? This is what we get when we don't execute. Come on, man. Primacy is key. Who leaked this? What the fuck?"

He was pissed—rightfully so—and all I could do was shake my

head and say, "I know, I hear you. But you know who I'm dealing with."

Hmm, I thought. *Things like this don't happen by coincidence.* To this day I have questions about Frazer's motives during this period. John was far from the stereotype of the general counsel for a big, bad lobbying association like the NRA. He wasn't this aggressive, take-charge kind of guy at all, which is one of the reasons Bill Brewer was able to take over the reins of all of the NRA's litigation. Frazer and Chris were close, and Wayne and I suspected he sometimes funneled information down to him. And we thought Chris and Ollie could push him around. I couldn't help but notice that North would call him into his office on the fifth floor all the time.

Frazer eventually sent the letter, and Steve Hart became the first casualty in the war inside the NRA.

A story quickly blew up on *The Daily Beast* by my favorite NRA beat reporter, Betsy Swan. The headline read, "NRA Suspends Top Lawyer."[14] And Ollie, in retaliation, fired off his own version of Hart's memo about Wayne's expenses to key board members, to gain an edge in the proxy fight ahead.

Ollie and his allies were infuriated by the firing of Hart, and were determined to strike back. And he didn't wait long.

CHAPTER 8

Shootout in Indy

The 2019 convention of the NRA started on Tuesday, April 23. It ran through Sunday, culminating in the NRA board meeting, which was to be held the following Monday. On Wednesday, April 24, Millie, Wayne's longtime executive assistant, called me on my cell phone and said, "Get your ass up here." Something was very wrong. I could hear the concern in her voice. It was around three o'clock. I went upstairs, where we had a big suite at our hotel in Indianapolis, and found Wayne, Carolyn Meadows, a longtime board member and our second vice president, and Millie. They were looking incredibly agitated. Now, Carolyn is a wonderful lady—she had been like a mother to me, and was always very encouraging to me in an incredibly pressure-packed position.

"What's up?" I asked.

"Ollie called me," Millie said.

"Okay," I said, waiting for the other shoe to drop.

"He told me that either Wayne resigns as executive vice president tomorrow or Ackerman will smear Wayne in the press."

Wayne chimed in, saying, "Yeah, he talked about you and the bullshit sexual harassment stuff. Can you believe this? They go into this whole Beverly Hills $275,000 suit thing, and the house in Dallas, it's crazy."

I couldn't believe it. On the call, Millie recounted, Ollie went on to say that Wayne needed to support North. The conflict of interest was off the charts. Ollie, remember, was getting paid $2 million to produce an NRATV show for Ackerman. Meanwhile, despite Wayne being aware of the basic terms of the deal, he hadn't given a copy of his full contract to the audit committee per the bylaws, despite a hundred requests. And he promised to negotiate a generous retirement package for Wayne, Millie went on. He had ended the call by saying that Wayne needed to withdraw the NRA lawsuit against Ackerman as well.

Great—of course he said all that.

Millie, Carolyn, and Wayne, being the veteran political animals that they are, just saw it as dirty politics. There was almost a kind of *holy shit, can you believe this?* look on Wayne's face. We were expecting a power play by Ollie, but none of us imagined him going after Wayne this way, threatening him. We thought that there would be a raucous board meeting, sure. Honestly, I think that no one in the Ollie/Ackerman camp believed that Wayne would see all this through—I'm positive of it. They didn't think he could hang on. For decades, everyone had seemed to be able to beat him into submission and get what they wanted. With enough pressure, they thought he was sure to cave, because that is what he had done in the past.

I looked around at everyone in the room and said, "Guys, this is called extortion, not political shenanigans."

I immediately called up Bill Brewer and told him, "You're not gonna believe this." And I walked him through it.

"Oh my God," he said, listening to me. "Wow, this *is* extortion."

Bill and I immediately decided that we had to send a letter to the board. *Let's blow this up*, we thought. *Let's just throw it straight back at Ollie*. And so I said to Bill, "Look, call up Wayne, talk to him, tell him we've got our plan." At this point I was sitting in the bathroom of the hotel suite talking to Bill. I told him, "Just give me five minutes, let me tell him I talked to you, and then you call. Because Wayne is gonna say, 'Okay, great,' when I advise him, and then ask, 'What does Bill say?'"

Bill had to weigh in. Did Wayne trust me? Of course. But Bill had become the go-to legal adviser for Wayne and me at this point.

Bill then asked if we had any of this conversation written down. "No," I said. "But Carolyn Meadows was standing right there during the call. And Ollie didn't know it—Millie had him on speaker. So two people heard the call." Carolyn didn't announce herself, so Ollie didn't know that she was on the call. I had already told Millie to sit and write down notes on everything that happened, so that she and Carolyn could corroborate this. So she did. And I took pictures of all her notes with my phone. Later, in one of Ackerman's recent lawsuit amendments, they stated that I coerced Millie into writing down statements that Ackerman McQueen was responsible for Oliver North's actions. But that's total nonsense.

So we all agreed to write a letter to the board about Ollie's demand. The original draft was written by Travis Carter, Brewer's PR guy, and Andrew Arulanandam, our PR point guy, and Sarah Rogers, who also worked for Brewer. Sarah was a pistol—she constantly argued with the entire office, including Bill. I think she saw that as her way of operating. Ultimately, when I left, she did everything but twist a dagger in my back, but hey, that's just what we do at the NRA.

So we got this letter drafted, while Millie corralled a number of board members—probably thirteen to fifteen—whom Wayne considered to be his "kitchen cabinet." It was a big kitchen.

Sandy Froman ran that operation and worked hard to whip the necessary votes to make sure Wayne survived a board vote. Sandy was a fixture at the NRA—she was our second female president, after Marion Hammer.

Sandy was somebody the board really respected—a total take-charge, I'm-gonna-get-shit-done kind of person, and a lawyer in her own right. So she organized the whole group of people, the kitchen cabinet. At four o'clock, Wayne decided he had to talk to Chris. "He's been calling me to set up a meeting."

And I tried to dissuade him, telling him, no way, Chris was aligned with Ollie. Brewer almost had a heart attack over the idea. "What's the upside?" I pleaded.

But Wayne was determined. So I said, "Okay, look, if you go talk to him, could you please take Carolyn with you so your conversation can be corroborated?" He did, and the two of them headed to another hotel suite for a lecture from our chief lobbyist on how things were.

The whole time, Bill was constantly calling me from New York, in his very neurotic fashion, obsessed about making sure everything was all right, and he was asking me: "What the fuck is going on? What's happening? Is the letter done? We have to get this out."

So Wayne went over to talk to Chris, and when he came back, he told us in essence that Chris delivered the same message: "Wayne, you've got to resign. These guys are gonna kill you. You've got to get rid of Josh. They're going to talk about the sexual harassment thing. It's gonna be awful for you. We can work this out, but you've got to resign. You've got to get rid of Powell, and you've got to get rid of

Brewer. Back off the lawsuit against Ackerman McQueen and we'll get this calmed down."

Chris didn't threaten Wayne, just said Ackerman was going to smear him. Soon after the Annual Meeting, I learned that Chris had offered to take my job, and said he would sort everything out. It didn't happen, but that gave me some insight into the guy's thinking.

So we were incredibly anxious about getting this letter out to the board members right away. We had been writing letters for months to Ollie, and to Ackerman, asking for financial records and receipts. I still had Bill on the phone—he was constantly calling me now. We had to get this letter out, because in Bill's mind, we had to get out in front of this. I knew he was right, but we'd turned a process that was already taking forever into a group project!

"I understand," I told him. "I'm trying to manage everyone." We were fighting as hard as we could. And we were all saying to each other, can you believe this? At this point we had ten people in the room trying to finish this letter, and I was flipping out. It was six o'clock and then it was seven o'clock and then it was eight. And poor Andrew, our PR guy, was sitting with his laptop, surrounded by all these people, telling him let's use this word, and let's add this. It was insane. I was beyond frustrated. Brewer had fully lost his mind by this point. Finally I said, you guys have five minutes, that's it. Andrew was frazzled beyond belief, so I looked at him and asked, how is it? And he said, I don't know—I didn't put half the shit that they told me to put in. And he showed it to me. "This is what I got." And I told him, "Just write the truth, finish it, then send it to Bill." None of us could put a coherent sentence together at this point, but Andrew was able to pull it off.

And then I realized we also needed to send it to John Frazer, our general counsel. And once again we waited, and waited. Frazer was the one who had to actually send the letter as an email. Frazer can be a classic bureaucrat, the epitome of Washington, a guy who has zero urgency. In the words of Wayne: "I wouldn't use him for my parking tickets." He was one who always played politics. Decision making was not in his wheelhouse. Nice guy, but in my opinion, in the wrong position. Brewer would spend hours getting Frazer to agree to a decision we needed to move ahead. In an exasperated moment Bill once told me, "Every fucking thing is like getting an act of Congress." I had a "we need to move now" mindset, and Frazer was stuck in this vortex of NRA politics with Chris, Ollie, the board, and our team.

At some point I met with him in the middle of this mess, frustrated with his approach of running everything through a committee, and asked him point-blank, "John, look, I know you're close to Chris and Ollie, I get that, but I've got to ask you straight out if you are comfortable working with Wayne. If not, that's totally fine, we can figure that out, but you work for him, just like I do. Not for Chris or Ollie North."

He replied, "No, I like Wayne."

I said, "John, everyone likes Wayne. That's not the point. The question is, are you going to be able to work for and answer only to him?"

His answer was, "Yes, I can do that." I'd described the conversation to Wayne, and he seemed to appreciate in an odd way the value in just being straight with folks. At least at that moment.

Many within the NRA described my approach as that of a business guy, not a politician. And I would always laugh. "I guess you can call it being direct." As chief of staff, my job was to get stuff done. Nevertheless, it rubbed some people the wrong way. In truth they were all incredibly undermanaged, and were not comfortable with my directness. Frazer was the epitome of this.

Somehow, some way, we finally got this letter out. Andrew and I went back to our rooms and collapsed. We had sent out a link to the board members, but as far as we could tell, no one had read it. It was incredibly quiet. Crickets.

And the next day we realized that the ideal thing would be for someone like Mark Maremont at the *Wall Street Journal* to get the letter and write about it. It would really authenticate what had gone on, because our fear at this point was that no one on the board would actually read the letter.

Friday morning, President Trump was scheduled to speak—it was his third year in a row giving the keynote at the NRA conference—and the vice president was going to speak too. Chris was on the docket, of course, because this was his show.

Would it surprise you at this point to learn that Wayne would always have to jockey for position as to when Chris would let him go on? It was another insight into the incredible dysfunction and politics within the NRA. Wayne would tell me, "I got a deal with Chris," and I would say, "Just tell him, you're the CEO. You're going introduce the president. Period."

"No, no, no," he told me, "I don't want to upset Chris." It was a never-ending dance with those two, and now we were in an internal war, with Ollie and Chris clearly on the other team.

Chris had become enamored with Trump going back to the 2016 election and saw introducing him at the convention as good politics for him personally. In the end, the two of them—Wayne and Chris—brought out POTUS. It reminded me of something Angus said back in a meeting in 2016, just after the election. Angus went on a rant, saying, "Wayne, I'm telling you, I just watched this video with Chris, it's gone viral; he's close to Don Jr. and has real power, I'm telling you—you got to be careful."

And Tony Makris and I rolled our eyes, thinking, *Who cares? Are you kidding me? The NRA just got the president of the United States elected. And Wayne was the guy leading the NRA. What are you talking about?* Angus loved stirring things up like that—he ate up the drama. It was all part of his *Game of Thrones* routine, setting factions against one another. But it gives a glimpse into the constant bickering, back-stabbing, and self-aggrandizing that went on there, with folks like Chris and Angus believing they were a whole lot more important than they really were.

I remember saying to Wayne at lunch after I was there for a few months, "You know, I totally have it figured out."

He asked, "What do you mean?"

I said, "Nobody here in Washington does anything and all they do is trade information, and then figure out how they're gonna screw you with that."

Wayne laughed. "Yep, you got it."

I was walking over to the convention floor with my wife, Colleen, and our two PR guys, Andrew and Travis, when Bill Brewer called. Bill wasn't in town yet; he was still in New York. And we talked about the fact that if we could get this letter out to the media, if we could make this public somehow, we could bury Ollie. Now the two of us were getting neurotic. How could it be this quiet? My God, we just accused Oliver North of extortion.

Our team never leaked documents, even as our adversaries became adept at it. We just didn't do that. Of course we would spin our stories with reporters as much as we could, but we weren't in the business of leaking documents. So Travis, Andrew, and I were talking to Bill, and I said, "God, if we could just get this out there."

As if God himself heard us, within minutes of that conversation, Mark Maremont of the *Wall Street Journal* phoned Travis. So Travis got up and dashed off to talk to him, and came back a few minutes later with his eyes as big as saucers, with the news: "He's gonna print the letter in the *Journal* right now; he's basically just verifying it. He's got the letter." Within minutes the story published, and all hell broke loose.

Someone on the board must have leaked it to him. With seventy-six people on the board, it's hard to contain something like that. The headline in the *Journal* that morning was, "NRA's Wayne LaPierre Says He's Being Extorted, Pressured to Resign. Group's Longtime Leader Says Ollie North, President of the NRA, Wants Him Out."

To this day, I don't know who leaked it. But it wasn't something we maneuvered. Of course everybody thought we did, but the truth is, we didn't. We can't really take credit for it. We certainly took credit for going straight back at Ollie, though.

So these leaks became the headlines Thursday morning just as all of the speeches were about to be given up on the podium—and just before the president's keynote. There were thousands of people in the auditorium for the ILA forum. You can picture what was going on behind all the curtains—mayhem, as the various NRA people tried to get POTUS's attention and push their agenda. And one of the things the Ollie camp was clearly pushing was getting rid of Bill Brewer. I'm sure they told the president that Brewer was spending a ton of the NRA's money, and he was a Democrat, and he needed to go. So I think Trump got caught in the middle of that. I hated going backstage during the forum, and frankly Chris didn't want me there. It was a mutual feeling. Truthfully, I really enjoyed sitting among the crowd with the rest of the members, so I could gauge the reaction. I don't need to shake hands with the president and the vice president. Cool, but not necessary. The energy in those crowds was palpable, and I preferred to pace along the edges and watch from that viewpoint.

Meanwhile, backstage, the president of the United States and Don Jr. continued to chat with Wayne and Chuck Cooper, our former NRA counsel to Chris. And suddenly the president was telling Wayne, "You've got to get rid of Bill Brewer. This guy has cost you too much money, you need to get a good Republican attorney in there, you've got to get rid of this guy. You're spending yourself to death."

Wayne told me this afterward. I'm sure Trump only knew who Bill Brewer was because Chuck Cooper and others told him.

Here is what Danny Hakim at the *New York Times* said about Trump's conversation. "At the National Rifle Association's annual meeting in Indianapolis in late April, President Trump stood backstage and...pointedly told Cox and LaPierre that they need to get themselves better lawyers. One of the sources...who was present at the time, said Trump referred to the NRA's legal team as lousy. The second source said, the remark rattled LaPierre."

Hakim was right. It did rattle Wayne.

Shortly after that, the president took the stage and the crowd went nuts. Trump bragged to the audience about what a big supporter he was of the Second Amendment. He was literally onstage as this extortion story broke, saying, "They want to take away your guns. So you'd better get out there and vote."[1] And then the vice president (he's a former Indiana governor, remember) spoke, and they both blew out of town as fast as they came in. After the president left, Wayne gave his speech.

Later in the day Trump tweeted out, "The NRA is under siege by Cuomo and the New York State AG, who are illegally using the state's legal apparatus to take down and destroy this very important organization.

"It must get its act together quickly, stop the internal fighting, & get back to GREATNESS—FAST!"

In another tweet he added, "So much litigation. The NRA should leave and fight from the outside of this very difficult to deal with (unfair) State!"

It was clear to us that Ollie, Chris, or Chuck Cooper had gotten to POTUS and had set this up. The whole day was surreal. I kept thinking, *This thing goes all the way to the president of the United States? Are you kidding me?* But Trump was right: We needed new counsel and needed to get our act together.

★

It became the biggest news story in the world that day. After the speeches, I went down to the restaurant bar at the Hyatt where we were staying, and there were a bunch of TV screens tuned to different channels. It was wall-to-wall NRA. "Chaos in Indianapolis!" "NRA Infighting Takes over Its Convention." CNN talked about Ollie's coup for ten minutes. "Ollie North Tries to Oust Wayne LaPierre, Internal Fighting in Indianapolis." We couldn't have scripted it better.

While I was sitting there, my dad called me up.

"What the hell is going on?"

And I told him the story, acknowledging that a lot of what he was hearing about was true.

"You know this doesn't make you guys all look very good?" my dad replied.

Boy was he right. And I knew it—we all looked like village idiots. Nobody came out of it looking good. People had to be wondering, *Who's in charge?* I was embarrassed for us. It was truly a sad day for the members and the association. But at this point, my job was to do everything I could to ensure they did not throw Wayne out. I was determined to save the pope—as were his college of cardinals, a.k.a. our kitchen cabinet of Millie, Carolyn, Andrew, trusted veteran board members, and Brewer's team. We were all in to win this fight. Wayne had been at the forefront of gun rights for decades, and we had no intention of ending his term now. We viewed it as an existential threat. If Wayne went, so went the NRA, a view that I propagated as much as anyone. In retrospect, that isn't true, and I should have known better. The NRA is about the membership, it isn't about one guy. It's about the NRA's mission to advocate for gun rights and promote gun safety—to be the voice, the spearhead for the tens of millions of Americans who believe in the right to bear arms, and to do so in a lawful manner. It should never be about the guy at the top. Because sooner or later the person at the top is going to retire, or die, or move on. Or do something stupid that will result in his resignation. And Wayne had been doing plenty of stupid things. But worse, he just hadn't been around that much. He was supposed to be the NRA's spokesman, on all the cable shows, explaining our position. But he had mostly been absent.

Andrew, Bill, and I spent our time over the next day and a half talking to board members, building support. The board members, oddly enough, weren't entirely clear what was going on. But we were clear: We had to get rid of Ollie. He had to go. This internecine fighting had to stop. But there were real reservations. Inside the kitchen cabinet, one of our vets argued, "Look, I agree North needs to go. But you're talking about removing one of the conservative icons. This won't be easy. But I'm not saying we shouldn't do it."

The members meeting took place on the Saturday of the annual convention. Picture a sort of shareholders meeting with a couple thousand card-carrying NRA members. All the members with voting credentials vote on certain ballot issues; they each have the ability to bring complaints or motions to the floor. It was mostly nonsense, but it also illustrated the completely antiquated structure of the NRA, which was nearly 150 years old at this point. Usually, nothing of any consequence got done. Wayne gave a speech, which was typically the highlight of the meeting. But the members could get out of hand, firing off all sorts of crazy requests. One member wanted to vote on taking away the memberships of Maria Butina and Alexander Torshin. Another wanted to vote on making Alaska the site of the next NRA Annual Meeting. If it wasn't handled right, who knew what could happen. It was another part of the NRA that needed to be retooled and modernized. Basically, during the meeting, anyone could put something to a vote as long as they handed in their request on a card fifteen minutes before the meeting started. And then our buddy John Frazer, the general counsel, got this stack of things to vote on.

On Friday before the members meeting, everybody was wondering whether or not Ollie was going to show up the next day and sit up on the stage, after having been flogged across the media as an extortionist. Was he going to stay in Indianapolis or was he going to go? The president of the NRA was primarily a figurehead, a ceremonial position, but one of Ollie's few real tasks was to run the members meeting and the board meeting on Monday. If Ollie was sitting up on the podium running the meeting, he could totally screw it up for Wayne.

I was pretty sure that Ollie had flown in on board member Richard Childress's plane. So I called up a friend of mine and asked him if he could tell me where Childress's plane was right now. I was trying to figure out if Ollie had left Indianapolis. My friend talked to his pal at the FBI, and he called me back a few minutes later saying the plane was sitting in Indianapolis.

Damn.

Then, later Friday evening, we got confirmation that Ollie had fled town. His aide, Nick, told me he took Ollie to the airport and that he got on a plane, that he got a one-way ticket. I was relieved, but the kitchen cabinet was still on high alert and completely paranoid.

"I know, I know," Bill said, still in New York. "I'm gonna get there. I'm just buried with all this..." Bill is always notoriously overbooked—he's got too much stuff going on. On any given day he'd have five different planes booked for four different days, along with his own jet sitting in New York.

Anyway, the next day at the members meeting, Ollie was not there. I got word that Childress, who at the time was a second vice president, was going to run the meeting. Which was okay—Richard didn't have the balls or capacity to make a run at Wayne. We could deal with him. Wayne walked onstage to a standing ovation, taking a seat next to several of the other executives on one side of the podium, while an empty seat on the other side marked where Ollie was supposed to be sitting.

Childress started off by reading a letter Ollie had written to the members at the meeting. There was a vote on a resolution to ask for Wayne's resignation, and to express "the lack of confidence and ability to guide the association out of the dangerous mess he has created," but that was batted aside. As Tim Mak at NPR reported, it "failed to garner enough support from NRA members after an impassioned defense by a member from Jay Prince, a former law enforcement officer, who is on the board of directors."

Jay didn't go up there by accident. The "kitchen cabinet" had him ready to go at a moment's notice. So Prince got up there and said, "I'm the sheriff. I may be retired...but you ain't dragging Wayne LaPierre anywhere." We weren't really worried about the members vote, but any outbreak of mutiny could sway the votes of a few of the board members on Monday. Fortunately, the kitchen cabinet had wired the meeting to direct the debate if it got out of hand. Jay went on and said, "I'm in from Montana, you know. I've had enough of this shit." And he closed his remarks with, "We're shutting this down." The whole crowd went crazy.

Remember, Wayne has been the head of the NRA longer than some members have been alive. And when Prince walked off, I said to myself, *That will do it.*

Earlier, when Childress read Ollie's letter, he told the audience that Ollie had written, "I'm informed that I won't be asked to run again. But of course, I will if I'm asked." Or words to that effect. Within minutes, Danny Hakim from the *New York Times* ran up to me with his laptop open, typing frantically as he ran around the floor, writing in real time, and asked if I could confirm that Ollie had resigned.

Well, I couldn't, that wasn't what he said, so I replied, "What did you hear?"

He said the *Washington Post* was going out with that.

"Well," I said, "that's your call." The *Washington Post* had just put up online that Ollie had resigned as president. But he didn't actually resign. If you parsed the letter that Richard read—I suspect that someone at Ackerman wrote that thing—Ollie basically said, "I'm being targeted, poor me. But if you want me to come back, I'll come back." I can imagine the conversation: *Look, we will tell them Ollie is a soldier and if asked to do his duty he will. I'm a Marine, and I'll go through fire for you!*

I'm sure the thinking was, *Once we offer this, the crowd will go nuts and he'll be dealt back in the game.* But honestly, I don't think anyone in the audience even understood what Childress said. Richard did a lousy job delivering Ollie's message.

But everybody interpreted it as Ollie's resignation. And of course Ollie was not there, which was the big thing. So everybody went with the story that Ollie resigned.

I mean, come on, if you're going to beg for your job back, at least show up for the fight.

We were almost home free, but we still had Monday's board meeting and a potential vote of no confidence. The board had received a letter from Steve Hart, our outside counsel, listing all the financial improprieties that Wayne had run through Ackerman and billed back to the NRA. Meanwhile, the *New Yorker* had just run a story with the headline "Secrecy, Self-Dealing and Greed at the NRA" that had caught on like wildfire. Not exactly a ringing endorsement to kick off a board meeting. The article was scathing, exposing a lot of Ackerman's influence on everything within the NRA.

Wayne's kitchen cabinet met on Sunday night before the Monday board. I had been working with Bill to prep Wayne on what his presentation to the board should look like, what the talking points were, and so on. It was always a tussle and always last-minute, but Wayne knew how to put on a show and deliver his message with confidence. He viewed it as theater, more of a propaganda speech than anything else. Bill also had to give a presentation to the board, as part of a fiduciary obligation to let the board know what we were doing (that is, spending obscene amounts of money). The irony was the board had little appetite to sit through Brewer's presentations, and constantly complained about how long they ran.

The NRA board is made up for the most part of old conservative white guys who saw Bill as a slick lawyer with pinstripe suits from Oxford, custom shirts, pink ties, and fancy cuff links. And he was a Democrat no less, who donated to Hillary, and Beto O'Rourke, as well as a number of other Democrats. They didn't trust him. On the other hand, they believed he could win for them, and that's all they really cared about.

So we were getting ready for this meeting, and for a proxy fight we knew might be coming. Once I left my position as executive director of General Operations, I generally didn't really participate a lot in prep on those big board meetings—I was focused solely on the legal fight with the state of New York. So I just sat and listened and scanned the room for the reactions from the board.

During one of the prep sessions with the kitchen cabinet, Jay Prince suddenly said, "I don't think Josh should go to the meeting tomorrow. He's a lightning rod and Wayne is under fire."

I was completely taken aback. I glanced across the room at Wayne. He just looked at his shoes, didn't say peep. I thought, *You have got to be kidding me. After all I've gone through for you? You don't have the balls to say, Jay, I get it, but he's my guy and has been in this fight every day.* It was another moment when I saw the real Wayne. Once you are no longer valuable, you get tossed aside like yesterday's newspaper.

I took it hard—this was personal—but they were adamant about not wanting me there this time. I was not a happy camper.

But when it came down to it, Wayne only cared about Wayne. But I still didn't see that yet; I chose to ignore the signals.

Bill knew I was pretty upset about it, and frankly I was ready to roll out of town, but he took me aside afterward and said, "Wayne shouldn't have done that. It's not right. But you have to stay. You're part of the team. You gotta stay, man."

Bill and I had gone through a lot together. I laid myself on the tracks for him any number of times, because I really believed in what he was doing. And I believed he was a principled guy.

Was I taken advantage of? Was I naïve? Did my relationship with

Bill blind me from questioning the $2 million a month the NRA was spending on the firm's legal bills?

It's possible. Look, that's a ton of money. What I did know is that Bill was a brilliant attorney. And to this day I don't regret a minute of our time together, because I learned so much. In fact, Bill would talk to me about coming to work in his firm. "When this is done, you gotta come in. There are all sorts of things we can do together. You can help me strategize on this, this, and this."

We talked about it all the time. I believe he was being honest, and when the politics changed later I guess he didn't have much choice but to roll that way. But I'll never understand that.

Wayne was another story. All that mattered to him was survival.

One thing is for sure—when Bill came on board a year earlier, he didn't realize the much bigger fight he was getting into. He didn't really understand the politics within and against the NRA and the pure hatred the Democrats would bring to the fight against us. And certainly he couldn't have fathomed we'd spend a year fighting with Ackerman McQueen and Ollie North.

At any rate, Monday morning came, and I told Wayne good luck, go get 'em. The meeting lasted a long time, which was not a great sign. They broke at lunch, at which point I was able to get the scoop. It was pretty wild. At some point during the meeting, Bill told me, some of the board members, Richard Childress in particular, were questioning whether Ollie had actually said the things he'd said in terms of extorting Wayne. It was unbelievable. Millie was on the call, Wayne offered, but somebody countered with, "Well, we cannot trust Millie," which is total bullshit.

As I was told, Carolyn Meadows got up, quivering, and told everyone she was there too, she heard it word for word.

Everyone respected Carolyn; she's like your grandma. "I was there, and Millie is telling the truth; he extorted Wayne."

Apparently all the air left the room at that point. Childress responded, "I didn't know that."

And I have no doubt that's what Ollie told Childress: *I didn't extort him. We want him to resign. I told Wayne, you know it's time to go.* What Ollie didn't realize was that Carolyn was on the phone call. So Childress shut up and sat down.

There was certainly some impassioned debate during the meeting. Brewer and Wayne told me that Chris got up during the meeting and completely surprised Wayne by talking about how Ollie was like a father to him, and what a great guy he was. Chris refused to make eye contact with Wayne as he attempted to throw Wayne under the bus. Wayne was blown away by Chris's betrayal.

But at the end of the day, it was over. People raised questions and asked Wayne about this and that, and in the afternoon they voted on whether or not to have him continue as CEO. The vote wasn't close. Wayne carried the day—it was a majority vote, and he was given another year, by acclamation. There was talk before the board meeting that Allen West (remember him? Florida congressman?) was going to throw his hat in the ring for Wayne's job, but that didn't happen. Once the attempted coup by Chris and Ollie had been beaten back, there was no more fight left in the board.

And with that, the war was over. Or so we thought.

In fact, it was just the beginning of a battle for survival.

CHAPTER 9

"The NRA Is a Criminal Organization"

T he attempted coup at the Annual Meeting opened the flood-gates to a deluge of negative publicity about the NRA over the next four months. There seemed to be another scandal or revelation every week. The attacks from inside and outside the association, combined with a smorgasbord of smear campaigns from Ackerman McQueen, kicked into high gear, and it was effective. As Angus McQueen famously said again and again, "The truth doesn't matter if the smear sticks."

First, a number of Wayne's personal expenditures, billed to Ackerman and then later reimbursed by the NRA, came to light. Wayne, ostensibly worried about his security after the Parkland shootings, explored having Ackerman, and the NRA, buy him a French country-style $6 million "safe house" in a gated community on a golf course outside of Dallas. Wayne tried to dismiss it, saying the purchase never went through, that he "killed it," but he and Susan toured the place around Easter of 2018, and Susan complained about the lack of closet space. It was a ten-thousand-square-foot, four-bedroom, nine-bath McMansion with lakefront and golf course views in Westlake, Texas.

Mark Maremont of the *Wall Street Journal* reported, "Mr. La-Pierre shut down the transaction after discovering that the ad agency intended to use NRA funds for the deal."

"Not a cent of NRA money was ultimately spent," Bill Brewer responded.

However, the *Journal* noted that the NRA sent a $70,000 check to a company called WBB Investments LLC. WBB Investments was a shell company set up in Delaware by an Ackerman attorney to buy the house. They returned the money the following month, after the deal was exposed.

This was a really bad look. An Ackerman employee had a punchlist of all the things Susan wanted to resolve before closing, so they were pretty far down the road. They planned to close on the house in July so they could move in in August.

Our team, including Travis Carter, who handled PR for Bill, Andrew Arulanandam, our PR guy, Bill, and me, twisted ourselves into pretzels trying to figure out how to spin this. Andrew and I were especially pissed. As Andrew said in response to the "closet memo" from Susan, "If I'm going to put myself out there and defend this shit I'd sure like to know what else there is."

Any way you cut it, looking to buy a mansion in Dallas with NRA money was an especially stupid idea. As Maremont reported, "The newly revealed document reviewed by the *Journal* was dated at the time of WBB Investments' formation in May 2018, and was signed by Wilson H. Phillips Jr., the NRA's then-chief financial officer and treasurer. In it, he agreed that the NRA would contribute $6.5 million for 99% ownership of WBB Investments, while an Ackerman entity would contribute $10 for 1% ownership. In a statement, Andrew Arulanandam said: 'As we have said repeatedly, neither Mr.

LaPierre nor the Board ever formally considered, much less approved, an investment in the house in question or the other properties shown by Ackerman McQueen's real estate agent.'"

In other words, our defense was, *Hey, never mind that there was an LLC in place with ownership spelled out in writing, and that the NRA cut a check as a deposit. Forget all that, it was never "formally considered or approved." So no harm, no foul!*

Folks, it's called intent.

It was also reported in the *Washington Post* that Angus was furious at Wayne's claim that he needed the property for security reasons. "[Angus] said 'The scales fell from my eyes,'" said one person familiar with the discussions. "They were buying a Taj Mahal on a golf course with a social membership."[1]

Andrew tried to throw it back on Ackerman. "Frankly, this is yet another example of Ackerman twisting the truth to promote a false narrative.... These accusations...are just the latest installment of a smear campaign." But the only false narrative, unfortunately, was the one Wayne had created. And presumably this is all now part of the New York State investigation into the NRA's tax-exempt status.

And, oh, by the way, how come Wayne never mentioned the safe house until it blew up internally? *Wayne* didn't kill anything.

"Well, it wasn't my idea," Wayne told me when I asked him about it. He would never take responsibility for anything, and took zero ownership of his actions this time. It was one of the few times I became visibly angry with him. "Well, clearly you participated," I told him. "You went to look at it. Susan was bitching about the size of the closets. There was already an LLC set up for it. What were you thinking? Come on, man, you've got to be kidding me."

I was shocked by his denials. He refused to take ownership of what he'd done. This was the person I was going to bat for? I was furious. And it was at this moment I first accepted that I had to get out of there.

The only other time I lost it with Wayne was about his willingness to let people go around me behind his back. And of course he would cave. And I would find out about the end run after the fact. I told him, "I don't think that you want a chief of staff. And that's okay, if that is the way you want to operate. But just tell me that. What I can't put up with is this dysfunction, with people going around me and me feeling like I'm holding the short end of the stick. Deal with me straight."

Wayne, I heard afterward, was freaked out about my conversations with him both times. And the folks around him—Brewer, Andrew—would close ranks to protect him, telling me I couldn't upset Wayne that way. They were enabling the very dysfunction I was trying to beat down.

Bill Brewer and I had many discussions on the topic, and our conversations exposed the differences in our jobs and attitude. He was hired to defend the NRA, and that was his job, regardless of the facts. In truth, he was defending Wayne, not really the NRA or its members. Also, lawyers have a term for when their clients get into deeper and deeper trouble. It's called billable hours.

I was not an attorney, with the ability or obligation to reconstruct the moral ground into something I could stand on. Defending Wayne was sucking the soul out of me. I came into the NRA to protect the Second Amendment, not save our feckless leader at all costs. But here I was signing off on statements to the *New York Times*. And I began asking myself: Who was more corrupt, me or Wayne? The spinmeister or the master?

★

There was more. Ackerman leaked documents showing that the NRA, through Ackerman, had paid $542,000 for private jets for

Wayne, including a trip to a resort in Eleuthera in the Bahamas with Susan right after his Sandy Hook speech, and over $270,000 in suits that he bought for himself at Zegna's in Beverly Hills. The bills would flow directly to Ackerman, who would get reimbursed by the NRA. (Wayne would later claim there was nothing improper about the suits—he needed to look good since he "was the face of the brand.") I guess that was Wayne's work-around to avoid the folks conducting the NRA audit.

The CPAs out there reading this might ask the question, "Well, okay, but you have a team of CPAs tying expenses against invoicing, right? And didn't those same CPAs sign off on the accounts previously, for the same things, in their management rep letters to the auditors?"

Bingo. We had accounting failures at many levels. With Wayne and the NRA leadership for invoicing the way we did. With Ackerman McQueen for invoicing us the way they did. With the board for exercising little to no oversight. The way we had done things in the past was a mess. The irony was that some of the same CPAs who were "whistleblowers" had signed off on management rep letters for Ackerman for years, and were now paraded around as this righteous group of auditors saving the NRA from itself. The same CPAs who are still there today watching over members' money.

Now, could Wayne justify the suits and the trips? I'm sure he could rationalize it. To him, he was the NRA. He led the battle, whatever the cost. And the suits and the private planes were necessary, in his mind, to protect him. Despite credible safety concerns, however, he was acting like a corporate fat cat. And it looked even worse when he was trying to cover his tracks. Everything he did was a means to hide or work around the internal accounting system.

In 2018, when a lot of this was taking place, the NRA was

running a deficit for the third year in a row. The association had to cut back budgets for gun safety and legislative work, as well as many other departments. We had to freeze the employee pension (something that should have been revamped years before). Bottom line: Times were tough, and it was not the time for Wayne to treat the association like a personal piggy bank.[2]

★

Hours after Ollie North resigned from the NRA at the Annual Meeting, Letitia James, the attorney general for the state of New York, announced that she had launched an investigation into the NRA's tax-exempt status. And every day, in the weeks that followed the attempted coup, Bill Brewer would call to tell me the latest bad news, or vice versa, depending on who had the source. Bill was trying to get documentation from the NRA—emails, subpoenaed texts, memos, and other paper trails—to piece certain things together in the lawsuit against Ackerman. It was a colossal job. And that summer, Wayne began to repeat what became a constant refrain for the rest of the year:

"Do you think we can get a deal from Letitia James?"

One day Bill called me up in a frenzy—"You are not going to believe this," and went on to tell me that Frazer, our general counsel, called him up to tell him he'd gotten invoices that were "inadvertently" sent to him. The invoices showed that Chris Cox had been strategizing with Chuck Cooper, the prominent outside attorney who worked with Chris (and also for Wayne years ago), on "The Brewer Matter," all the while invoicing the NRA.

In other words, the NRA was footing the bill for Bill Brewer and his firm's legal battle with Ollie North, Ackerman McQueen, Letitia James et al., as well as paying for Chuck Cooper and his team's legal fight against Brewer and Wayne.

Just to step back for a second: The membership dues of the NRA were paying for a lawyer to defend us against our own president and his $2 million salary, our $50 million marketing firm, the New York attorney general, and another lawyer on the other team who was part of a failed coup (which we were still billed for).

Lord help us.

Shortly after that, Bill asked for any texts and emails from Chuck Cooper and Dan Boren, a former congressman, who was on the NRA board of directors. Cooper turned over a fair amount of material, including emails during the week of the annual convention between Steve Hart and Chuck that suggested a clearer picture of the attempted coup.

Bill called me up to New York. When I sat down with him, he showed me a series of emails among Steve Hart, Chuck Cooper, and David Lehman, Chris's in-house counsel, provided evidence of the whole scheme to rid the NRA of Brewer, me, and ultimately Wayne. They would base their argument against Brewer on what they claimed were the exorbitant fees that he was charging. (As I've detailed, he wasn't cheap.) Steve sent an email to Chuck Cooper saying that Brewer was either a "Manchurian candidate or a fucking idiot." Cooper answered with an email in response: "Well, he's kicking our ass because we're not leaking the documents yet."

In other words, these guys were up to their necks in the plot to take down Wayne. It's one thing to *say* they were all conspiring against us, but another to see it in black and white. It was chilling, to use Bill's words.

And Chris Cox was in the middle of it—and authorizing the NRA to pay for it.

As we sat there, Bill received a call from Wayne—Chris refused to turn over his information. He literally told Wayne, his boss and

CEO of the NRA, "I won't give you my emails." Brewer and I were dumbfounded, especially now that we had the text stream making it clear Chris was in the middle of the coup. "Give me 5 minutes," Chris wrote in one text. "I really need to talk to you. I don't think Millie got the message [about Wayne resigning, or else Ollie would go public]." Still, Cox would later deny that he sought to oust Wayne, calling the claim "offensive and patently false."

At this point, there was so much litigation going on, I'd begun to lose track of all the cases. I desperately needed a spreadsheet from Brewer's team laying everything out and indicating the status of each case. Bill was running the whole show, with very little oversight on costs. (Again, I know, he wasn't cheap.) I helped with strategy and information and holding Wayne's hand, but the general counsel John Frazer and Craig Spray, the CFO, were in charge of Bill's retainer and fees and they let it roll. In fairness, they had little to no choice. Bill had Wayne's backing, and everyone was cleared out of the way.

★

In May, Ackerman McQueen launched a countersuit against the NRA, claiming that the association was responsible for the April coup, and that Bill had leaked documents to the *New York Times*.

Meanwhile, Ollie North wanted to be indemnified by the NRA. A letter from his attorney said in essence, *Hey, I want to know, are you guys are going to pay for my legal fees?*

"Screw that," I told Bill. So it was back to New York, again, to file a case against Ollie, as a sort of preemptive strike. And in our affidavit we dropped in Chris's texts with Boren so we could make it public, hoping some reporter would pick that up and Chris's role would come to light.

Then Bill asked me, "What do you think we should do about

Chris?" And I said, "Look, Chris has got to go. You're accusing Ollie of extortion. And Chris was in on it. What are we talking about?"

Bill agreed. "Yeah, you're right. Do you think Wayne is willing to let Chris go?"

I said, "Probably not yet, but we'll get him there. How can he not? The guy tried to cut his throat."

It was now late June, and I offered to talk to Wayne back in Washington. Wayne stalled. "I hear you. What's Bill's take?"

After a number of conversations together, some more hemming and hawing by Wayne, we made the decision to fire Chris Cox.

I called John Frazer in the morning. I told him, "I know that you and Chris are close. If you can't do this, I'll have somebody else do it. I totally understand. It's a tough job." John said, "No, no, no, I can do it." I had assumed that we would let Chris's number two, his chief of staff, Scott Christman, go as well, but I realized I had never talked to Wayne about him. As I told Wayne on the drive out in the morning, "If you don't clear him out now and get rid of these people who are loyal to Chris, this is never going to end."

Wayne agreed to let him go.

Later that day—June 26—Chris was let go. The story exploded in the media. Chris had been at the NRA for twenty-five years, and had long been seen as the heir apparent to Wayne. His resignation (termination) was a big deal, and it rattled the whole building. Chris tried desperately to reach Wayne to present his side of the story—he called repeatedly over the next few days. But Wayne never took his call.

There was a general housecleaning after the attempted coup in Indianapolis. Dan Boren, former congressman and board member—as well as a top executive for the Chickasaw Nation, a major client of Ackerman—resigned, given his role in "choreographing the ultimatum" the usurpers presented to Wayne.[3]

Richard Childress, former NASCAR driver and the owner of a NASCAR team, resigned. He too had been a supporter of Ollie.

And Craig Morgan, a country music star, would resign by the end of the summer, as would Sean Maloney, Tim Knight, and Esther Schneider, all of whom authored a letter demanding an outside investigation into financial misconduct at the NRA, and who claimed their confidence in the association's leadership had been "shattered."[4] Julie Golob, another prominent board member, would resign in August as well.

In our initial discussions about who would replace Chris as the head of ILA, Wayne plaintively said, "You know nobody wants this job, nobody's gonna take it. It's so awful here now."

Wayne had this constant *poor me* attitude, which was exhausting. I said, "You've got to be kidding me. You're right in the heart of it, politically, with a big budget, and access to everyone. If you are into politics, lobbying, and guns, it's the best job in town." What I didn't point out was that you also had to put up with all of Wayne's bullshit.

With Wayne's approval, I started talking to one, the premier lobbyist in Washington, who worked for the big drug companies, as someone who could take over Chris's job. He was in charge of a massive budget, had been super successful, and was incredibly bright. And he was interested, and on top of it.

Shortly after Chris was fired, Wayne swung into my office with a big smile. "Hey, I just talked with Mitch McConnell and he was pitching that guy you were pitching for the job." I told him, "Honest to God, I'm not out there campaigning for the guy!" It was a funny moment and I know Wayne didn't believe a word I said, but at least I was in good company. McConnell and I both thought he was good, independently of each other. And he was and is one of the top lobbyists in the country.

We spent a lot of time talking about how we could bridge the gap with Democrats. He viewed it pretty simply—we needed to start engaging them in discussions. Even if we can't get a yes vote on an issue, if we can take them from being haters to highly resistant, that was progress. We both wanted to see the debate get back on a more bipartisan footing. It was ground he had to constantly cover, and he was very adept at it. Next to guns, drugs are the most difficult thing to lobby for. It's not like Republicans are supportive of higher drug prices.

But ultimately, I told him, there was a lot going on at the association, and I really didn't think he ought to come on until the mess was sorted out.

In the end Wayne asked Jason Ouimet to serve as interim chief lobbyist in place of Chris. Jason had run the NRA's Federal Affairs—the piece of ILA that lobbied Congress, under Chris, had contacts with Mike Pence and the White House staff, and dealt with all the heavy lifting on Capitol Hill. Jason didn't understand exactly what had happened to Chris, and asked us for the unabridged version, so Bill and I met with him to explain. He couldn't believe the behind-the-scenes jockeying for power. Chris played it very close to the vest in terms of what he communicated to his staff.

Jason is a great guy, a committed family man, someone I have a lot of respect for. He's been trying to fix a lot of the dysfunction on the ILA side since his appointment, and I think he's doing a good job and has turned into a heck of a leader.

Jason's only drawback was he didn't like to go on TV, he didn't like to be in the limelight. He didn't want to spar with Chuck Todd on *Meet the Press* on Sunday, which is a bit of a problem for that position. On the other hand, Chris rarely went on TV either.

★

We formally shut down NRATV in May—long overdue in my mind—with a letter from Bill that I helped to write, which we sent to

Ackerman. And with that, one of the saddest and most painful and expensive chapters in recent years was finally behind us. That one move alone would save us $25 million a year.

And yet the bad news surrounding the self-dealing and financial revelations at the NRA kept coming that summer, in one wave after another. In April, just before the Annual Meeting, Mike Spies at The Trace, writing for the *New Yorker*, raised a number of dubious financial dealings and conflicts of interest, such as Susan LaPierre's ties to Ackerman through her support for the NRA's Leadership Forum, which she co-chaired, and which she promoted through Ackerman, where she kept her email address.

Spies brought up Tyler Schropp's work in the NRA's advancement team, a fund-raising group that went after wealthy members. Tyler had been an executive at the Mercury Group, the Ackerman subsidiary that Tony Makris had run. In return, Tyler seemed to steer more business to Ackerman, including the production of a beautiful, glossy high-end magazine, *Ring of Freedom*, focusing on the lifestyles of the wealthy. According to Spies source Aaron Davis, who worked at the NRA's fund-raising department for ten years, we only printed about twenty-five hundred copies, but Schropp was getting over $600,000 a year, had about thirty people under him, and the department was bleeding money.

And of course, the audit committee memo came to light, listing all the ways the NRA was spending money, with little oversight and dubious billing procedures.

It was a full-on shit show.

Former NRA employees were getting paid hundreds of thousands of dollars in consulting fees, without, according to the CPAs, "documentation."

All of this rattled the board and kept the plotting and factionalizing and infighting going strong.

But that was only the first salvo. In June, Spies ran another article revealing that Woody Phillips, our former CFO for over twenty-five years, who had retired in 2018, had been caught embezzling money at his previous company, Wyatt, in 1991, reportedly taking at least a million dollars. According to the article, he was "quietly fired" and ultimately paid the money back over a period of years, but it was just one more scandal linked to a senior executive at the NRA that made us look bad.

There were also claims in the article of a "questionable business arrangement." While serving as the CFO of the NRA in 2001, Woody was also CFO of a company called Memberdrive, a marketing start-up. Memberdrive's top client—the NRA.

Wayne's wife, Susan, was also an executive at Memberdrive, as was the wife of the NRA's director of membership at the time. All in all, a huge conflict of interest, at least on the surface.[5] (Ironically, none of this did anything to drive membership.)

And the Washington, D.C., attorney general began to look into the NRA Foundation, a charity arm that had been established decades ago. Both the foundation and the NRA itself are tax-exempt, but only donations to the foundation are tax-deductible; NRA lobbying efforts are not. And the NRA had shifted a bunch of money given to the foundation to the NRA—some $36 million the previous year, more than it ever had before.

As one of our former lobbyists said, given our red ink, the lawsuits, and the New York inquiry, "the NRA is now in grave danger."[6] People were starting to wonder if we would have the resources and firepower to survive. And Wayne, privately to me, began a second refrain about quitting, throwing out names of potential candidates who could take over the NRA, including former congressman Jason Chaffetz and former governor Mike Huckabee.

★

We were getting desperate. That summer, Bill Brewer reached out to Lanny Davis for help. Yes, that Lanny Davis, the Clintons' veteran fixer—he has known Hillary since college and was Bill's personal attorney from 1996 to 1998—and Beltway spinmeister, who had also represented Martha Stewart and Alex Rodriguez. Lanny had a great talent for framing the narrative and selling it. "People don't come to me with great news," he says. "They come to me with troubles."[7]

He was a fixture in Washington politics, and Bill thought he could help. I was skeptical about hiring him—how would the Trump administration react knowing that we were thinking about hiring a lifelong Clintonite as a consultant?—but I agreed with Bill's thinking about reaching across the aisle. Bill told me that if we went ahead, he would hire Lanny to be part of his team, so that the NRA was not directly linked to him.

So I agreed to a meeting. We met downstairs in the restaurant at the Four Seasons in D.C. over a pot of coffee. We walked him through everything, and he was blown away by all that had gone on, most notably the Ollie North extortion response. Lanny was an absolutely charming guy, and I enjoyed the meeting immensely. I also felt we could use another set of eyes on what we were doing. We had a lively meeting and Lanny agreed with our approach in New York—countersuing the state over their viewpoint discrimination. The plan would be that Lanny was going to help Bill on the PR side of things, because he knew everyone—he was regularly on Rachel Maddow's show, for example.

Wayne was fully supportive of having Lanny Davis on the team. And I thought it was interesting that we were thinking about trying to make some inroads with key Democrats. But I was so afraid that all this would blow back on Wayne and that Trump would go crazy that nothing actually came of it.

Just imagine the tweet on a Friday morning: *Are you kidding me? Lanny Davis, the Clinton fixer who represented liar Michael Cohen, is representing the NRA!! LaPierre has lost his mind!! Time for new leadership!! I'll always support your Second Amendment.*

Not good. Lanny was retained by Bill and helped on a couple things, but we never really let him loose. I agreed with Brewer on trying to focus some of our messaging to Dems—thus hiring the super-connected Lanny Davis—but then we risked upsetting the president and blowing up Wayne. Doing the "right" thing wasn't always possible. It also pointed to a truism of Washington—everyone's contacts were up for sale. Connections are a source of revenue. And we all knew that—that is what power is.

But it is disheartening, as well, knowing that everyone is for sale. Trump had talked about draining the swamp, to position himself as someone from outside the Beltway, which is great for campaign speeches. But lobbying and connections are a part of politics, and unfortunately I don't see that changing.

All that said, I felt stuck, unable to push ahead on the changes I knew the NRA needed to make. I had gotten far away from addressing the real issues of the members.

★

On August 4, I was with my wife and kids on Gibson Island, on the Chesapeake Bay, about to go out to dinner, when I heard there had been a mass shooting outside a bar in Dayton, Ohio. Nine people plus the shooter himself were killed and a score of others were wounded.

I texted Bill Brewer, Travis, and Andrew. Coming back from dinner, the news got dramatically worse. There had been a shooting in El Paso as well, at a Walmart, where twenty-three people were killed.

It was obvious that this was going to be a major gun rights battle, involving everyone from the president on down. Four days later, on August 7, as I was driving in to work, Steve Bannon called me and said, "Josh, what the fuck!! You guys have allowed people around the president to feed him highly selective misinformation—and he could come out in favor of all these fucked-up background checks. You need to get Wayne and get over to the White House ASAP and make sure he gets *all* the information. Do that and good things will happen. Don't do that and be prepared to live with something that won't work for anybody."

As we've all discovered, you never know what you're going to get with the president. One minute, he's 100 percent behind the Second Amendment, and the next he wants to raise the age that you can buy guns, or propose universal background checks, or pass red flag laws.

Why did Bannon care enough to forewarn me? He knew our membership was a big voter bloc for Trump, the NRA was in a weakened state, and that this was a chance to reassert its strength going into an election year. His number one goal was to get Trump reelected. Hardstop.

I told Steve, "No question, Wayne needs to lay down the law here."

I'm not opposed to universal background checks personally— I think the NRA has to offer that concession to move forward on the issue of gun violence. But I also knew the timing was terrible for Wayne.

At this point, I was the loyal number two, the guy who was supposed to protect Wayne. And I knew that after the attempted coup in Indianapolis, and the resignations of so many board members and senior executives in May and June, this wasn't a time when Wayne could offer a major concession. The members would crucify him. Game over.

Steve asked, "What do you think the move is?"

I told him, "Well, what if we put out a statement on Twitter written by Wayne himself? He's never done that, and never responds this quickly. It could be very powerful. You know, lay down the gauntlet, speak softly but directly."

Steve loved that. With our relationship with Ackerman severed, this would be our first PR statement without them in response to a shooting in thirty-five years. Angus usually made Wayne wait a week or two before reacting. I suggested, "How about, 'The NRA is not in favor of any laws that would impede the freedom of our members'— something like that, but pointed."

Steve and I brainstormed together on the phone. Andrew Arulanandam made my word salad into something comprehensible and twice as good.

I called Wayne up after the conversation to bounce it around with him, and he liked the idea. So I read him the statement we had come up with. And Wayne asked, "What do you think?"

I said, "Well, I think we need to push back on the president, because this is going to get crazy if it turns into a free-for-all on background checks. We cannot survive if you look weak to the members right now. We lose Ted Nugent and they will throw your ass out."

So politics drove a good part of my decision. Steve hopped on the line with Wayne to help convince him.

"You cannot waffle on this," I told Wayne. "The board will revolt."

Steve added, "Look, you've got to let the president know there is no equivocation from the NRA. He only knows one thing. Power. Show him that and you'll get a big victory for the NRA. Victory begets victory."

Steve was all in on helping us with the media, and Wayne loved the support. At the same time, another part of me knew: This was *the* opportunity to get a background check bill out of the way and get on to the real fight over gun violence.

It's pretty hard to make a solid argument that I need to get a background check when I go to Bass Pro Shops, but not when I go to the gun show, or when I buy a gun online from another individual. It makes no sense, and has impeded the NRA politically for nearly a decade.

I can't find one person I know who's bought a gun without having a background check. We're talking about adding an incredibly small percentage of checks to the system.

I had always envisioned a much more widespread crimefighting bill that put more money into the ATF's prosecuting and convicting those who failed a background check, pushed for much more prosecution in large cities, and closed the loophole for gun shows and online purchases.

But reality was really sinking in for me—that my job was just about saving the pope. It wasn't about what I thought was in the best interests of the membership anymore, or the hundred million gun owners in the country. Of the eighty thousand in 2017 that committed a felony through their background check, less than one hundred were prosecuted. It's basic law and order.

I was just another soldier in Wayne's army. Or as others might have said, a sellout.

★

Wayne's statement got tweeted out at about eleven o'clock that morning, something to the effect of, "The National Rifle Association does not support any legislation that would impact the constitutional rights and liberties of its members." It was not specifically directed at the president, per se, but it was pretty clear who we were talking to.

Within fifteen minutes of our putting out the statement, Steve called me up and told me, "Dude, you're mac daddy on Drudge." Meaning that Wayne was the headline item.

RED FLAG: NRA WARNS TRUMP

I was in my office and Wayne came in, asking what reaction we were getting to the tweet. I had a couple of TVs on, and all of a sudden CNN came up, and I just pointed at it.

National Rifle Association draws a red line.

Wayne LaPierre tells the president no.

Wayne LaPierre puts down a marker for the president.

You know how obsessed the media is with Trump. Every network and cable news show reported it: *The NRA told the president no.*

That afternoon, the president called Wayne and had a thirty-minute call with him. The president told Wayne, *Look, we're gonna do this background check bill. Everyone's gonna love it.* And if any of the NRA membership or Trump's base didn't like it, Trump told him, "I'll give you cover."

I wasn't on the call, but I knew Trump was on the phone and I could hear Wayne talking to the president.

After the call, Wayne gave me the gist of the conversation. Trump told him he was going to support legislation for universal background checks, and red flag laws, which allowed courts to temporarily take a person's guns away under certain situations. "This is going to be great," Trump told him. "We'll have a signing in the Rose Garden." When Wayne told me the bit about Trump providing air cover, I told him he should have told the president, " 'I'm *your* air cover. The NRA.' That's what you should have said."

Wayne put out a press release, in which he said, in part, "I'm not inclined to discuss private conversations with President Trump or other key leaders on this issue. But I can confirm that the NRA opposes any legislation that unfairly infringes upon the rights of law-abiding citizens. The inconvenient truth is this: the proposals being discussed by many would not have prevented the horrific tragedies in El Paso and Dayton."

In later conversations with the president and his circle, Wayne pushed back, and afterward, Trump seemed to back down. People on the left were pissed, because they thought they were going to finally get some movement or concession out of Trump on gun rights. And after consulting with us, he started waffling. We would go on to work the administration—Vice President Pence, high-level staffers, and others—and Congress with calls underscoring our position. And Trump backed down, just as he did after Parkland, after promising to support legislation banning assault rifles.

It wasn't an example of the power of the NRA. It was about all the voters we could bring to the election around the issue.

Trump called back about a week later. The call was scheduled, and I helped to prep Wayne in advance—we had half a dozen legal pads spread out in front of him on his conference table, so that he would have all his talking points handy. He told the president, "Look, I'm not going to support background check legislation. The membership would go wild. That happened in the Bush years, and our people just didn't come out in the same way."

When Trump tried to talk over him, Wayne spelled it out more clearly. In essence he told the president, "We don't control the voters. Gun owners are single-minded—they are single-issue voters, whether they work in an office or in a manufacturing plant. If they become angry at you, they simply won't vote. There is nothing I can do."

And after the second call, the president acknowledged to the press that background checks were off the table. Instead, he agreed to increase funding for mental health issues and prosecuting gun crime, taking his cues from Wayne.

Within minutes of the second phone call, Elaina Plott at the *Atlantic* called me asking for details. I had to laugh at how leaky the White House was. I went to Andrew to get the talking points down and gave her a ring back. I confirmed that the president tried to sell Wayne on a "celebration" of the background check agreement with a ceremony in the Rose Garden.

Elaina replied, "God, that's so Ivanka."

She was right. We both knew Ivanka and Jared had been pushing the president to come out more forcefully in favor of gun control. Interestingly, it's not something the gun community talks about much.

But I told Elaina she had to find another source at the White House to confirm it. So she found someone else, an unnamed White House staffer who confirmed the story, and she wrote it up with a kind of human interest angle as a lead-in.

"Ivanka has her Dad dreaming of the Rose Garden....Trump's phone call reveals the NRA's influence," she wrote. "Three days after a pair of mass shootings in Ohio and Texas that left 31 people dead, President Donald Trump was preoccupied with visions of a Rose Garden ceremony."

Elaina went on to describe the phone call with Wayne. "Trump reportedly said, I'll give you cover....Wayne's listening to that and thinking, *Uh, no, Mr. President, we give you cover.*"

I had given Elaina the quote, but told her that she had to find someone else in that room to attribute it to. It couldn't come from me.

I got in trouble for it anyway, but it was fun.

"With that, 'the Rose Garden fantasy'...was scrapped as quickly as it had been dreamed up." As Bannon put it, "It was epic." And we won that round.

★

But that was the thing with Trump. After a shooting, in the face of public outcry he would get sucked into this gun debate, and start promising background checks and so on, and sometimes we would have to remind him of that when he got too far over his skis. As Elaina subtitled her article, "Days after considering implementation of universal background checks, President Donald Trump has side-lined the issue."[8] It's called walking it back.

Several weeks later, Wayne had a call with Attorney General William Barr to talk about Project Gotham, the federal program that had been started in Richmond, Virginia, in 1997, under the name of Project Exile, to prosecute gun crime. This is a program I personally cared about, and I was eager to help Wayne prepare for the call, but in truth he knew it cold.

Barr was excited about Project Gotham, once Wayne walked him through it. He seemed committed to trying it out in more cities. It seemed like a genuine step forward, and for a moment I relished hav-ing a small part in moving the ball forward.

But that was a candle against the night, and nothing had changed in terms of the NRA's response to shootings and gun violence. Wayne was able to flex the NRA's muscles in calls with Trump, but there was no change in terms of offering solutions. Just saying no was still our general modus operandi.

In August, Wayne put out a statement, something to the effect that the NRA "opposes any legislation that unfairly infringes upon the rights of law-abiding citizens." Willes Lee, the second vice president of the board, and a key ally of Wayne's, went even further, tweeting, "Nothing short of disarming America satisfies @democrats. Give them NOTHING," and adding the hashtag "allguncontrolisracist." Hardly an olive branch that would help make the NRA part of the solution.

Two gun control bills passed the House in 2019—one to close the loophole on gun shows and internet background checks, and a second aimed at closing lapses in the FBI's background security sys-tem, which enabled Dylann Roof, the guy who shot nine people in a church in Charleston, South Carolina, in 2015, to buy an AR-15.

But both bills died an instant death in the Senate. Honestly, these measures would have done little to curtail gun violence. But a lot of people and politicians were desperate for any effort to reduce mass shootings, however ineffective.[9] The public was fed up with the NRA's stonewalling these mass shootings. There was so much anger and resentment against us that the San Francisco Board of Supervisors passed a resolution declaring the NRA a "domestic terrorist organization." In part the wording read, "The National Rifle Association spreads propaganda that misinforms and aims to deceive the public about the dangers of gun violence."[10]

The resolution had no force of law, and we countersued the board immediately, but it shows how out of whack the NRA's stance had become in a world that was tired of mass shootings and was looking for answers.

Wayne and Jason Ouimet went to the White House a month later to hash out the president's position on gun control legislation. It was Jason's first meeting at the White House, and their first meeting without Chris Cox. As the *Times* reported, Wayne asked the president to "stop the games" over gun control.[11]

But when they got there, Trump was upset about his latest scandal, the phone call about Ukraine, and it was all he could talk about. They never really got around to talking about gun rights, as Trump grilled them on their impression of the Ukraine scandal and whether or not that would lead to impeachment. At one point, Trump turned to Jason and asked him, "What do you think? Is this good for me, or bad?" It was probably a question he was asking everyone around him.

Jason replied, "I think it's good for you."

And Trump responded, "So do I. I think the Democrats have totally overplayed their hand."

Side note: What was odd was that Bill Brewer was furious when he heard that Wayne and Jason were going to the White House. "Trump is going to kill you guys."

I was flummoxed—Bill was way out of his lane. When the president of the United States summons you to the Oval Office, you go, come hell or high water.

As Wayne told him, "We're not going to refuse a meeting with the president." It was a sign that Bill, like Angus before him, seemed to think *he* was the puppet master now, and no NRA issue was out of his purview.

Privately, Trump questioned whether the NRA would be able to support him the way we had in 2016, when we put $30 million behind his election. Given all the defections, and the scandals, investigations, and lawsuits, as well as the failed coup at the Annual Meeting in April, he "voiced concerns that the group looks like it is going bankrupt and may lack the political clout it had last election cycle."[12] Public filings showed that the NRA had "exhausted" its $25 million line of credit on the deed to our headquarters in Fairfax, and had borrowed against insurance policies taken out on NRA executives.

And we were paying Bill Brewer $2 million a month to handle all the lawsuits.[13] Despite our best efforts and intents, Bill and Wayne and I had done little to resolve our noncompliance issues as a nonprofit. And the only difference was that Bill now, with Craig Spray, were the Svengalis behind Wayne. And I had helped hire both of them. I knew that I was spinning my wheels, and was doing little to advance the concerns of the NRA members.

So what was I doing?

☆

When I wasn't dealing with attacks from outside the NRA, I found myself confronting more insidious attacks from inside. In October, the CPA folks came to Wayne and Craig Spray claiming I had misled the NRA on my expenses. They said I owed the NRA money. I was taken aback—I knew that while I wasn't the most organized person in the world in terms of my expenses, given my hectic travel schedule, that couldn't be true. I'd regularly reimbursed the association all along the way. So I told them, fine—you show me the itemized invoices, so that we can go through them together.

This turned into a monthlong fishing expedition, and proved to me one thing: It was getting time to go. Wayne was upset at the third degree I was getting, and said, "This is all Craig. You know he's just out to get you. I'm really sorry." Which was kind of a push or a deflection by Wayne, but at least he acknowledged the forces at hand—the very same people who approved and paid the expenses—were now going back in a concerted effort to prove I had not expensed certain items properly. And again, I had many months where I would reimburse the NRA for expenses like any other corporate exec would do.

Craig Spray and I had never gotten along, so of course he was eager to give me the boot and become Wayne's chief of staff—essentially his COO—which is really what I was hired to do. What Wayne and Bill should have said to Craig is, "If there are any expense issues with Powell, let's look at it, and then we'll deal with it and get it cleared up." But they were afraid to cross him at this point. As Bill would say to Wayne, "You can't have an adversarial CFO when we get to the attorney general."

Instead, Wayne and Bill took the position that we were going to let the process play out. Both of them told me they couldn't look like they were favoring me, but in the meantime, I was left twisting in the wind.

In any normal world this could have been dealt with overnight. But that wasn't the game being played here. It had nothing to do with expenses and everything to do with finding a way to get rid of Powell in the Game of Thrones.

They came back after looking into my expenses and reported that I owed the NRA $28,000 for personal expenses billed to the NRA in the years 2016 and 2017. So I asked to see the invoices and went over everything with them to get them cleared up. A lot of the charges were genuine, but after reviewing them, I think we agreed that I owed the NRA $22,000. And I admitted it—hey, you're totally right, there are some expenses in there that I should have paid for personally. And I wrote them a check for the outstanding expenses.

Steve Bannon and I talked a lot in the fall of 2019. I would complain to him about this and that, and he would offer support. Contrary to the Prince of Darkness media perception of Steve, he was generous with his advice and was loyal to me. Steve really wanted me to hang on, at least through the 2020 elections, to help get Trump reelected.

But he knew it was killing me too.

I couldn't do it. It was time to go and I'd prepared my exit. Steve and I had some heated debates about it. I remember Steve telling me at one point this was a war we had to finish. That one stung.

There is a scene from the classic movie *Twelve O'Clock High* where Gregory Peck, a World War II general, says to his pilots, "We've got to fight. And some of us have to die. But stop worrying about it. Consider yourselves already dead."

That was Steve's sense of humor and sense of duty. He was committed more than anyone I know, and that's one of the main reasons he wins.

I started thinking more deeply about what I was doing at the NRA. We'd gotten a long way from the mission, from concerns about the members and Second Amendment rights. Now everything we did was to prop up our czar, to help Wayne survive, despite the scandals, the $6 million house, the incompetence and waste, the red ink. And it was frustrating that Wayne never copped to anything—he never owned his mistakes. It reminded me of a certain other chief executive who never admitted fault and always found someone else to blame.

Wayne hounded me for months, call after call, day after day:

What is going on with Bill's legal strategy?

What is the latest with Letitia James?

Do you think we can get a deal with New York?

Wayne was terrified, and self-preservation was all that he could focus on.

I realized we weren't doing our jobs anymore. And I came to the conclusion that what I'd been brought in to do—to help fix the procedures and processes, to modernize the organization—just wasn't going to get done. Everything was focused on the legal attacks and counterpunches, and with saving King Wayne.

I had come into the NRA to make a difference. Over time, I watched how our angry rhetoric and attacks had painted us into a corner. Wayne continued to preach to the most extreme faction of the membership, and no one was willing to change our approach and work to be part of the solution.

Maybe, I realized, the NRA, as it was currently set up, didn't deserve to continue. Maybe gun owners needed a more compassionate defender, an organization that would try to work for the rights of all Americans.

Instead, Wayne, with and without Angus and Chris, had continued to escalate things, to add to the toxicity of the debate, to make the NRA the lobbying organization no one wanted to invite to the political table.

People at the NRA would say, if we lost Wayne, "The world is over." And I thought to myself, *What the fuck? The guy is seventy years old, and doesn't even want to be there. He doesn't want to go on TV, and hates the whole fight.*

There was this mythology that had built up at the NRA that we couldn't survive without Wayne. Which at first I had completely bought into, promoted, and sold. Lock, stock, and barrel. I poured the Kool-Aid, stirred it, and drank it along with everyone else.

But the truth was, if we were really running the place correctly, with a proper board, they would see that Wayne was a drag on the association. We really needed to retool, to bring in new leadership. And on that point Bill Brewer and I disagreed. The political intrigue and endless lawsuits were good for him. His billings went through the roof, and gave him unprecedented power within the NRA. It was in his lucrative interest to play a never-ending game of stalemating the king.

I remember walking out of Steve's house, the infamous "Breitbart Embassy," late one evening that fall after talking through my many concerns. I stepped into drenching rain, and realized, *I'm done. I'm not going to fight for this anymore. They won, they can have it.*

I needed to save my soul. And I wasn't going to do that by continuing to save Wayne. I was on my own, and so was Wayne, whether he realized it or not.

Brewer said the same thing to me in a late-night dinner in New York City: "The sooner you realize you're alone the better."

Prophetic words.

CHAPTER 10

Searching for Answers

I wrote this book because I wanted to move the discussion of gun control toward sanity and offer a different path forward. Ironically, I spent very little time thinking about the Second Amendment while I was at the NRA; instead, I was sucked into the vortex of Washington politics, and found myself becoming exactly what I despised before I joined, part of the Establishment. This book has been my attempt to shed some light on what the inside of the NRA is like, and point out its failings to society, to gun owners, and to its members.

I'm not the hero of this story—in fact, I was part of the problem.

So I want to offer real solutions to the problem of gun violence, not empty words or hyperbole. As I've said repeatedly, too often the debate devolves into "solutions" that do not really solve the problem. And the NRA, the organization that knows the most about guns, self-protection, crime statistics, and the issues, has pandered shamelessly to the most extreme faction of its membership. In the aftermath of every mass shooting, every school tragedy, Wayne's answer, and the NRA's answer, has been "No." No to any proposal that could be construed as a restriction on gun rights.

There has been little attempt to come up with solutions. The NRA never exercised its power to shift this debate. And, contrary to popular belief, there *are* solutions, and they don't necessarily involve banning guns. Instead, the NRA has poured gasoline on the fire and fanned the flames, claiming that any infringement on any gun right is an attack on freedom and the Second Amendment; that if we give an inch, we are on a slippery slope to firearm confiscation and the complete overthrow of the Second Amendment. Wayne, and the rest of the NRA executives, have consistently invoked that old bogeyman—that any regulation is tantamount to the overthrow of American life, liberty, and the pursuit of happiness. That Democrats or people in favor of gun control, however modest, are trampling the Constitution.

Do I believe Mike Bloomberg would like to trash the Second Amendment as it pertains to the individual right to bear arms? Yes, I do. But that does not preclude the rest of us from coming up with solutions that would save lives.

It does require a commitment from both sides, based on the gun crime data. When it comes to gun violence, we have reams of data to work with, incredible law enforcement officials across the country, and an eager majority of Americans who want to stop the violence in our largest cities and, most of all, stop these mass murders.

Mike Bloomberg's Everytown for Gun Safety teams are the most data-driven in the world. These are smart people. I do not doubt that Bloomberg, Dianne Feinstein, and other gun control proponents want to save lives. I also know that gun owners and NRA members are disgusted with the lack of action in addressing mass shootings.

This is our country, whatever our political persuasion. We are better than this. Let's temper the politics on the gun debate and pull back from the dark rhetoric and this toxic standoff.

★

In order to form a more perfect union on this issue, let me address this first: The Second Amendment is going nowhere.

The Second Amendment has been enshrined in our Constitution for 240 years. There has not been a new or repealed amendment to the Constitution since 1992, and that amendment took 202 years to be ratified—it was first proposed in 1789. Amending the Constitution of the United States requires the approval of two-thirds of the House and two-thirds of the Senate, or a constitutional convention called by two-thirds of the state legislatures, and then ratified by three-fourths of the states.

To be clear, no president, Republican or Democrat, can magically erase the Constitution. I know the NRA has implied that's not the case. With the country split pretty evenly between Democrats and Republicans, where even getting sixty votes from the Senate to override a filibuster requires an act of God, the chances of the Second Amendment being repealed are zero. Not happening.

Moreover, the voters aren't in favor of it. The *Washington Post* did a poll in February 2020 to ask how many Americans are in favor of repealing the Second Amendment. The answer—21 percent. Even among Democrats the percentage was only 39 percent.[1] In other words, almost 80 percent of the American people are in favor of the Second Amendment. And that should be reassuring to any citizen, whether they are a gun owner or not. Eight out of ten Americans believe in the Second Amendment.

I start with this only to be clear about what we are talking about when someone raises the specter of gun control and its impact on gun owners. Yes, the *D.C. v. Heller* interpretation of the Second Amendment, conferring the right for individuals to keep and bear arms, is only twelve years old. But given stare decisis—precedent—and the current makeup of the Supreme Court, it is highly unlikely that interpretation will be altered or overturned in any foreseeable future. Our right to bear arms, our heritage as Americans, is secure.

All that said, what can we do to address the very real problem of gun violence (which exists primarily in large cities)? And more specifically, what can we do about mass shootings?

As someone who worked inside the NRA, who believes fervently in the Second Amendment, and who has seen the ways the NRA has been successful and has failed in addressing America's concerns, I have a number of solutions to offer. And some will surprise you.

★

First: I think we need a regime change at the NRA.

Wayne LaPierre and most of the top executives at the NRA should resign or be forced out as a result of the investigation by Attorney General Letitia James in New York into the organization's tax-exempt status.

We need to start over again. Rebuild from the bottom up. Wayne has got to go. He has lost his way. And while he made critical gains a decade or two ago, today he is only focused on his own survival, and is holding gun owners and members hostage while he defends himself.

Half of the NRA senior staff has resigned or been escorted out in the last year. It's time to clean house completely and start over. The board of directors will be faced with a very large challenge to find the next CEO. I would encourage them to look beyond their own political beliefs, outside of the gun community, and focus on someone who has the gravitas to mend decades of division. A leader who can look across the aisle and talk about real solutions, not just reflexively say "No." Someone who understands that the NRA is the most knowledgeable organization in the world when it comes to guns, who understands that gun owners have not only a right to bear arms, but a civic responsibility to offer and promote solutions.

To fix the association will require a CEO who is willing to dive into the serious business of untangling its business practices and increasing oversight, and who can get the place back to the basics of promoting gun safety and training.

And, of course, protect the Second Amendment from those who wish to dilute or delete it. There are one hundred million gun owners, and more than a third of them are Democrats. The NRA must expand its ranks and get back to being a bipartisan association focused on gun rights and gun training. If you are a political figure who can support that, we will support you, whatever your party affiliation. It wasn't long ago that a third of the NRA's political contributions went to Democrats.

Gun rights, and organizations that represent gun owners, are not going away. But that doesn't mean the NRA will necessarily go on— or that it deserves to. Hundreds of millions of dollars of members' money has been wasted on exorbitant marketing, on hyper-political TV ranting and raving, on self-dealing and greed, on a bloated organization with endless consulting and legal fees. This is a complete misuse of members' money.

And in the meantime, the NRA has done nothing to address gun violence, or enlarge its tent. The NRA, if it is to continue, must serve all gun owners, not just cater to the most extreme. It must be an organization that is sensitive as well to society at large—to Americans who are fearful for the lives of their children and their families, whether they own guns or not. As so many commercials are messaging today, we are all in this together.

So the first step is to clean house.

★

Second: We need to pass universal background checks and be done with this.

Yep, the former number two at the NRA is calling for background checks.

Most gun owners are in favor of universal background checks. You read that right—the NRA is not in step with the majority of *gun owners*. However, background checks should be part of a bigger legislative package that includes increased funding for enforcing existing laws—including violations by convicted felons in attempting to purchase a gun—and closing loopholes like the gun show loophole. And that would fund the ATF to make sure that we prosecute people when they break the laws. That they will be punished. That there are consequences—strong ones—if you try to purchase a gun illegally.

What's the point of having background checks if you are not going to prosecute those who break the law? Last year eighty-eight thousand people failed to pass background checks because they already had committed a felony. And we prosecuted a handful. That is sending the wrong message.

We need to prosecute those guys, as well as "straw purchases," meaning when someone buys a gun and turns around and sells it to a "friend" who can't pass a background check.

We talk very little about prosecuting those folks who break the laws that are already on the books, focusing instead on closing loopholes. Closing loopholes is fine, but it will do little good if people breaking the existing laws are not held accountable.

Will passing comprehensive universal background checks really solve anything? Not really. What it would do is take the issue off the table, so that we can move forward with other things that actually *will* help to reduce gun violence.

Over 80 percent of guns used in a crime are stolen or trafficked. Background checks will not fix that. Now, some guns used in crimes are purchased legally. Background checks are not going to impact that. And only 1 percent of all the guns used in crimes come from gun shows.

But I think we should pass universal background checks, and close the gun show loopholes, just so that we can move forward. In the immediate aftermath of a mass shooting, politicians and gun control people jump up and down about comprehensive universal background checks. And again, even gun owners are overwhelmingly in favor of them.

So let's take it off the table, but let's do it with comprehensive legislation that adds additional funding to go after the bad guys.

Wayne and the NRA have opposed universal background checks because internal polling of the membership has found that 50 percent are against them. But the membership is not representative of the entire nation—it makes up just 5 percent of the hundred million gun owners.

The NRA claims the government will turn this into a gun registry. And that message frenzies the most extreme faction of gun owners, who see any encroachment as an effort to take away their liberty. But most of us have no problem with background checks, and would in fact welcome the day ex-felons were completely unable to purchase a weapon.

★

Third: Implement the School Shield safety program.

As I wrote earlier, I am a huge fan of this program, and I helped to advance it when I first came on board at the NRA. Nothing is more important than protecting our kids. The horrific rise of school shootings is an indictment of our entire society. We have to stop it. And the answer is not merely banning a specific gun, or limiting magazine capacity. Banning assault rifles is not going to solve the problem—less than 30 percent of the mass shootings we've seen have involved those kinds of rifles. Furthermore, guns are a part of the American landscape—they are not going away.

So what do we do?

After Wayne LaPierre's speech in response to Sandy Hook, the media and the public came away with the false impression that the NRA wanted to arm teachers. That is not what he said. But he did suggest that we should harden our schools with the most prudent and advanced security protocols available. And schools should consider having armed security guards watching over our children. I personally have yet to find a mother who thinks that's a bad idea. We protect our politicians, our athletes, our celebrities—why don't we spend the money to protect what we value most in our lives, our kids?

But that is only one step in a program designed to safeguard our schools. After extensive interviews and study by hundreds of experts, we came up with a list of hundreds of ways that schools could be better protected, which can be customized to each school and district. First, the NRA offers a free vulnerability assessment to determine your school's current state of preparedness and security. Based on that assessment, the program suggests a number of possible ways forward, including more secure facilities—hardened doors, full-time security, visitors being buzzed in and checked in, protective glass, metal detectors—as well as increased partnerships between local law enforcement and the schools, additional training for school staff, and specialized training in the case that a potential active shooter situation should arise. Based on the initial assessment, each school can receive a customized approach to next steps, depending on their budget. Based on tactics and methods developed by the Israeli security forces, the program is a way to ensure that every child in every school is safer, in a world where mentally unstable individuals with access to weapons exist.

Is there a cost? Yes, there is. But aren't our children worth it?

After 9/11, we had no problem adding hardened doors to airplane cockpits, and U.S. marshals to every flight, as well as rigorous security measures that passengers have to go through before we can even get on an airplane. Those same precautions should be implemented at every school across America.

School Shield got off to a slower start than it should have because of bureaucracy with the NRA. Announced in 2013, by 2016 it had only surveyed a handful of schools. But since then it has amped up significantly. In 2018, the NRA awarded $600,000 to schools in twenty-three states to help fund better security in schools. Now, that is a drop in the bucket, compared to the $24 million the NRA is paying Bill Brewer in legal fees each year to fight against the NRA's nonprofit compliance issues. Should the NRA increase those grants, by, say, ten times? Yes, it should. Or even offer more. That would help to make a real difference at any number of schools across the country. The NRA would be seen as part of the solution.

Some communities hesitate to reach out to the School Shield program and toolkit because it was developed by the NRA. Thanks to decades of "No," the NRA's "brand" in many circles is toxic, or at the very least viewed with suspicion.

I get it. So why not make it a free *federal* program, promoted by the Department of Justice in conjunction with the Department of Education? And put some matching federal money behind it for states to give to local school districts to fund the changes that will better protect our schools. It's a small price to pay to better safeguard our schools against active shooters, and save our kids. And it's a program that works. Will it stop every shooter? No. But if it stops 50 percent, isn't that a huge win?

★

Fourth: Implement Project Gotham and prosecute gun crime.

The days of hundreds of people a year being murdered in Chicago or other major cities must come to an end.

I wrote briefly about this earlier in these pages, but in 1997, Richmond, Virginia, was a city with one of the highest homicide rates per capita in the country. It was murder central. The attorney general for the state of Virginia decided to prosecute all the gang members who were committing crimes with guns to the fullest extent of the federal law. And he told the bad guys in advance. He met with all the gang leaders and told them there was a new game in town—he wasn't going to prosecute under Virginia laws, where the Richmond jails acted more like detention centers, with people going in and out, because the jails were overflowing. He then went to work with federal prosecutors, and the ATF and the FBI, and coordinated this effort with local prosecutors, judges, the mayor, and local law enforcement.

Using a gun to commit a crime under federal laws has a mandatory minimum sentence of five years, and results in convicted criminals being sent to federal penitentiaries.

Originally called Project Exile, Project Gotham resulted in hard sentences and hard time. Prosecutors and local politicians advertised the program in the media, and met with community leaders, church leaders, and parents to let them know about the new policy. Given the level of gang violence in Richmond, there was strong community support for the program.

Billboards with the slogan "An Illegal Gun Gets You Five Years in Federal Prison" popped up throughout the city. In 1998, the first year after Project Exile was launched, homicides were down 33 percent, and armed robberies were down 30 percent. And the rates dropped another 21 percent the next year. In 2007, Richmond had 57 murders, compared with 122 the year before implementing Project Exile.[2]

The great thing about the program is that it doesn't require passing new laws, but merely prosecuting criminals under the existing laws. The program has been duplicated in a few cities, but has never become a nationwide movement.

What a difference it could make in Chicago, where I lived for over fifteen years. The number of shootings and homicides that go on there is absurd. There were 2,948 shooting victims in Chicago in 2018, and 561 people were killed.[3]

To give you a point of comparison, Kabul, Afghanistan, has a fraction of that number shot and killed. It's insanity.

And here is the kicker. There are ninety-two federal districts in the country. Chicago ranks *near the bottom* among those districts in prosecuting federal gun crimes. Meanwhile, Cook County jail is like a revolving door.

New York City prosecutes a lot of people using the federal system. If you shoot somebody using an illegal gun, commit a burglary with a gun, or steal a car with a gun you're going to go to prison. There is a mandatory sentence. And not somewhere local—you serve time in a federal prison in another part of the country, doing hard time. What federal law enforcement makes clear is that there are consequences for using a gun to commit a crime.

Why is that so important? Three-quarters of all the guns used in a gun crime are stolen and trafficked. And the prosecution rate of gun traffickers in Chicago's Cook County is close to zero.

If we really want to clamp down on gun violence and gun-related homicides, we should be prosecuting to the full extent of the law the criminals who use guns in committing a crime.

That would truly make a difference. People in favor of gun control have looked at me in amazement—would gun owners, would the NRA, support that?

Absolutely. The NRA are law-and-order people. What do you think we stand for? Gun owners are among the most law-abiding citizens in the country. They would fully support prosecuting gun crime. When I tell people this—folks who would never in their wildest dream vote for Donald Trump—they're amazed.

There are two fusion crime centers in Chicago that house all the law enforcement from different branches together in one building. This is a collaboration between local police, the FBI, and the ATF to monitor what is going on in the city in terms of crime and share information and analysis. There are video screens everywhere, monitoring camera feeds from throughout the city, and they've got Facebook and Twitter they are tracking. They're following all the gangbangers closely.

Again, there are three thousand shootings a year in Chicago—and the police know the people who are doing it, by and large.

I guarantee if you visit the South Side of Chicago and stop the mothers who walk by and ask them if the gang members shooting up the city should go to jail, you will not find one who wouldn't turn the jail cell key herself. I know, because I've had those conversations. So let's apply the federal gun laws against those the bad guys, and put them in jail. That kind of action, like security at an airport, also works as an effective deterrent.

I was hopeful when Barack Obama was elected that he would be the one who could solve this. As a guy who is from Chicago, he could walk into the South Side and say enough is enough. Unfortunately, that didn't happen. It was a lost opportunity.

The issue that arises is that a lot of the trafficked guns are in poorer, inner-city neighborhoods, which are predominantly black. And the concern is that there would be more black convictions than white. And that incarceration rates for black men are incredibly high. And that the police will racially profile, or will implement martial-law-like strictures on minority communities, like stop-and-frisk.

Part of the challenge with all this is having a police force that is trusted by the public. And the fact is that many people, as we've seen this summer following the homicide of George Floyd at the hands of four officers in Minneapolis, especially those in metropolitan areas, don't trust the police. I get that too. I am aware that police shootings are statistically much higher for black men in this country. But if the issue is stopping gun violence and genuinely making a difference, what are the measures of enforcement we would be able to tolerate in order to save lives? Are cameras and a 24/7 security presence in a public housing block invasions of privacy and civil liberties, or are they good policing and protection?

Rather than argue with me about it, why don't we ask the people who live there? At the very least, I believe it is something for us as a society to discuss and debate. In 2013, the U.S. Court of Appeals for the 7th Circuit ruled that laws that banned concealed weapons were unconstitutional, given the Supreme Court's ruling in *D.C. v. Heller*. Since then, every state in the union has passed some form of legislation allowing citizens to obtain concealed weapons permits, with the proper training. In Illinois, the law that was originally proposed only benefited the well-to-do. It left poor people who lived in the inner city—those in most need of protection—with little recourse. So I worked with inner-city parents in the South Side of Chicago to help pass a concealed weapons law that gave them an equal right to carry a weapon, so that people in poorer neighborhoods could carry a gun on them as they walked around in their neighborhoods, or to and from work, to protect themselves. I found that almost without exception, those moms and dads were eager for concrete solutions to gun crime that would protect their kids and save lives.

So if protecting our kids and families is our goal, let's have that discussion, rather than grasping at politically correct "solutions" that don't really address the problem.

In September 2019, I prepped Wayne for a call he had with Attorney General William Barr about Project Gotham. And Barr was excited about it. Two months later he unveiled it as a new Justice Department initiative, rechristened Project Guardian. With the impeachment hearings and the coronavirus pandemic, I don't know how much progress Project Guardian has made yet, but it has enormous potential to genuinely deter gun violence, by putting the bad guys who use guns to commit a crime in jail.

★

Fifth: Identify the people who are at risk, and keep guns out of their hands.

I say this with some trepidation. For the NRA, the problem with "red flag" laws—state statutes that allow law enforcement or family members to identify people who are mentally unstable and petition a state court to issue an order to temporarily take away their guns—is that without due process, this can become a means by which government can take gun ownership away from any citizen it chooses. This is a prime example of a slippery slope that could deprive any number of citizens of their Second Amendment rights, and it is dependent upon the subjective rulings of individual judges. That said, seventeen states now have some version of red flag laws on the books, including New York, Florida, California, Oregon, Connecticut, Illinois, Indiana, Hawaii, and Nevada. Many of these are recent. Before Parkland, only five states had red flag laws.

The NRA is not opposed to red flag laws in theory, but the association never condoned a single red flag law in practice. It's tricky, but the basis of a fair law would guarantee due process to any citizen who came under the purview of such laws.

On the other hand, we do know something in advance about the people who are likely to attack a school or a church or a nightclub and just open fire. These people (and I know, it won't stop every shooter, but it could stop a lot of them) usually have a long list of altercations, have often been in and out of psychiatric facilities, and have a history of interactions with law enforcement and the courts. Can't we stop these clearly unstable individuals from inflicting harm on others and on themselves?

Personally, I am in favor of red flag laws, as long as there is a process involved in taking away their right to own or purchase a gun that involves both medical doctors and psychiatrists, and some sort of bipartisan oversight, so that this is used sparingly and appropriately.

Early research suggests that the people who benefit the most from such temporary confiscation orders are those prone to suicide. And given that roughly 60 percent of gun deaths are suicides, red flag laws may well save lives. In one study, people subject to confiscation orders were thirty times more likely to commit suicide. But these laws are so new, there haven't been a lot of studies yet.

When I was at the NRA, we talked a lot about the role of mental health—it's not guns that kill people, people kill people. But once we have identified a person at risk of hurting himself or others, we need to do something about it. So this is the one instance in which a body of professionals, including but not limited to a judge, can head off a school shooting and save lives.[4] But let's be aware, red flag laws can easily be abused if there are not strong safeguards in place.

★

Sixth: We should consider applying the same law enforcement tactics we use for terrorists in this country to tracking potential mass murderers.

This is what Israel does. And you don't hear of school shootings in Israel, because they take the protection of their citizens and children very seriously.

We're not going to stop every one of these mass murders. You can't ban every weapon in this country—Americans own over three hundred million handguns and rifles.

But that said, as mothers, fathers, citizens, and politicians, are you okay with your kid's social media being tracked by law enforcement agencies? If there was an algorithm at Facebook to monitor and identify troubled individuals, should Mark Zuckerberg let the government use it? And how do we square that with the Constitution?

And the thing we have to decide is, when we identify a disturbed individual like Adam Lanza, what steps can we take? The FBI visited that kid's house in Newtown on four separate occasions. So what are we going to do when we do identify someone at extreme risk? How do we ensure that we get them the help they need, and don't hurt others? Red flag laws are a good start. What other things can we put into place? Is there a way to flag with law enforcement the medical records of those who are suffering mental health issues? It seems like a huge violation of individual rights. But are there times when such actions might be to the benefit of society? I don't pretend to be a health care professional, but I think these are at least reasonable questions to raise.

The other issue around gun violence is that, as pointed out previously, of the nearly forty thousand gun deaths each year in America in 2017, nearly twenty-four thousand were suicides. Less than fifteen thousand gun deaths were homicides. We need to separate those numbers to avoid a false impression of what's really going on.

The NRA has always steered away from talking about gun deaths as a result of suicide, claiming it is not their job. But again, if our goal is to reduce gun violence, if our goal is to save lives, then as an organization we should be involved in the search for solutions.

★

Seventh: We need to look at real data. We need a bipartisan commission to gather the facts about gun violence.

The NRA fought research into gun crime for twenty-five years, through the Dickey Amendment to the 1996 omnibus spending bill that Congress passed. They stopped it at every corner.

Why? Because Wayne felt a lot of the federal agencies have a liberal bias.

Okay, fine. But that doesn't mean we shouldn't get the facts and argue the merits. At least we'd be moving forward. I believe the solution is to create a bipartisan commission to gather accurate data about gun violence, rather than keeping us, the government, and law enforcement in the dark.

I can hear the howling now inside the NRA, but the fact is the only way to move our country forward on this issue is to agree on what the facts are. That would be a giant step forward.

★

Lastly, let's do a quick FAQ with the hope of dispelling some myths and advancing the conversation.

Why shouldn't assault rifles be banned?

As I wrote earlier, the problem with banning the purchase or owner-ship of a particular gun is the question: What are we trying to solve?

An assault rifle has become the notorious inflection point of the gun debate in America. But assault rifles are used in only 25 to 30 percent of mass shootings. And if they didn't exist, there are a lot of other guns, from semiautomatic rifles to shotguns to semiautomatic pistols like the Glock, that a crazed individual can resort to which are equally deadly.

Assault rifles are the bane of gun control advocates because they look scary, have military origins (although the military versions are far more serious weapons, with larger-caliber bullets, and are fully automatic), and because they are relatively new and their purchase was banned for ten years. The fact that they are used by some of the crazies in mass shootings speaks more to their popularity than their effectiveness.

I'm fine with solutions that will solve the problem of gun vio-lence. But that, rather than political expediency, should be our guide. Yes, we could ban future sales of assault rifles, and if enough voters and politicians get behind that, it will happen. But it's not going to solve the real issue—saving lives, protecting our kids, and reducing gun violence.

It might make some people feel like they've accomplished some-thing meaningful, but it's not going to change the equation. Poli-ticians should resist the urge to "just do something" to look good to their constituents, knowing it will have little to no impact and will not lead to real solutions. "Fixes" that restrict gun owners' rights without solving the problem play to the deep distrust of the NRA membership.

Can we limit the size of the magazines used in semiautomatic pistols and rifles?

Look, this is a question that a lot of gun owners raise. Why does an AR-15 come with a thirty-bullet magazine? Who needs that much capacity to target shoot, to hunt, or for protection?

We can we limit the size of a magazine to ten bullets or fifteen bullets. Of course we can.

But I come back to the question of what are we trying to solve.

That should be our true north. The crazies who undertake these mass shootings don't do so on the spur of the moment—they are planners, who bring extra weapons, extra magazines, a virtual arsenal. So, sure, we could limit the magazine capacity to, say, fifteen bullets. But their response would be to carry an extra magazine or two (which these shooters already do) to make up the difference.

The amount of time it takes to swap out a magazine is a matter of seconds. So, sure, we can limit the magazine capacity, but what have we really solved? Will the number of shootings, or the number of casualties in a mass shooting, go down? We will have expended a lot of political capital limiting the size of the magazine—and upset a lot of gun rights people—but it will have almost no impact on mass shootings.

Again, if enough voters and politicians get behind such a move, it could happen, although it would be challenged in the courts. But have we really addressed the issue?

Can we limit the number of guns a person can own?

I think this is a reaction to reading about mass shooters like Stephen Paddock, the shooter in Las Vegas, who brought an entire arsenal of weapons up to his hotel room over three days before opening fire on the crowd below attending a concert.

Is there a way to limit the number of guns one can have? What would it achieve?

There is no data to suggest that having more guns in a household equals more crime. And remember, such a restriction would only apply to people who buy their guns legally. Criminals illegally obtain however many firearms they want to commit their crimes.

The problem is that people have guns for different purposes—a pistol or two for protection, several hunting rifles for deer season, a shotgun for birds, and other guns for target shooting and competitions. And often more than one member of the family is a gun owner, so you have multiple weapons.

Others are gun collectors—they collect fine guns of different makes and models the way some people collect cars, or antique furniture, or paintings.

So how do you take all those uses into account? What would an "acceptable" number of guns be? You see the problem. That said, when someone who goes off the rails, like Stephen Paddock, is able to legally acquire and cart dozens of rifles and handguns to his hotel room in Las Vegas, it is alarming to everyone. He may be an anomaly, and a horrifying one. But I just can't imagine the Supreme Court would sign off on a restriction like that on the number or kinds of models of guns that individuals can own, given the Second Amendment.

✮

The bottom line is that if the NRA is going to continue as a success-ful political and gun rights group, it has to offer solutions to the issue of gun violence. And I believe it has a duty to reengage its core mis-sion, which traditionally has been focused on gun safety and educa-tion. To the extent the association does that, it will be seen, I believe, as a positive force for gun rights in America, and can begin the long road back from the extremism that it has become synonymous with in the minds of so many.

With a hundred million gun owners in America, I would encour-age new leadership to make its goal attracting a quarter to one-half of all gun owners in the country, and to more broadly represent their concerns and issues, without compromising their right to keep and bear arms. The NRA, or a more modern version of the association that represents gun owners, has the potential to rival the size of the AARP, if it moderates its messaging and becomes a proactive think tank for solutions to gun violence, and if it stays squarely in the lane of gun ownership and firearms training, rather than venturing into other, often extremist political issues.

As I've tried to make plain several times, gun owners are among the most responsible and law-abiding citizens in our great country. Almost all of them would love to be a part of the solution to gun vio-lence in America.

CHAPTER 11

Cleaning House

In December 2019, I got a call from Wayne. I was out of the NRA at this point. He wanted to talk about the interview he did with Danny Hakim for the cover of the *New York Times Magazine*. It was something Bill Brewer had been trying to set up since the summer. He said, "I think it went well, but I don't know." He sounded exasperated.

"How long was he in there with you?" I asked.

"Three or four hours?" Wayne replied.

I thought, *Oh, shit, he's in real trouble...*

I was in sheer disbelief that he would be put in that position. Wayne, alone in a room for hours with a hard-nosed *New York Times* reporter who knows the NRA and is famous for getting the goods. Who knows what Wayne might have said over the course of three or four hours, as he meandered past his talking points? So I called Andrew, my old PR buddy, and asked him how it went. He told me it went okay, in a pinched sort of way.

The article came out just before Christmas. I found it absolutely devastating. My phone was blowing up and it wasn't good. *WTF were you guys thinking?* was what everyone seemed to be asking me.

The piece spotlit Wayne with all his foibles and idiosyncrasies. Hakim's depiction of Wayne was right on: self-involved, self-pitying, filibustering. Someone who deflected blame and somehow, despite being the EVP of one of the most powerful lobbies in America, saw himself as a victim. Part of me wished I'd have protected Wayne from it, and part of me acknowledged that it was a pretty truthful portrait. Hakim and his editors at the *Times* were probably doing cartwheels.

Then Wayne called and asked, what did I think? He said that Susan was crying. "She thinks it makes me look terrible. Bill tells me it was great. He's telling everyone it's great."

I said to him, "You know, it's probably best that I don't say anything, given where we are."

He went on to say he hadn't read the article yet, "but you know I told [Hakim] everything he asked."

As I hung up the phone, I knew that would be the last conversation I'd have with Wayne. It was over.

For me, I couldn't forget the part in the article where Wayne said, "If I lose every friend, I'm prepared to do it." I can't remember the actual context of the first time he said it, but that really hit home. And for the first time I accepted that my relationship with Wayne, and with the NRA, was really over.

Wayne was holding on for dear life and the whole place was falling apart. I was shocked that he agreed to do the interview. This was not the piece that Brewer had been pitching to everyone. It was supposed to be a great article about how Wayne and Bill and I were turning the NRA around. I wondered exactly what Bill was doing here. Either he was oblivious to how damaging this was, or he was trying to cover his ass while Hakim field-stripped Wayne in front of the entire country on the cover of the *New York Times*. Brewer couldn't acknowledge when a case or an article was not going well, an arrogance that is a huge problem if you're involved in business strategy. He apparently skipped the chapter in *The Art of War* that sat on his coffee table about understanding the reality of the facts at hand and applying them. He blindly allowed Wayne to walk straight into a firefight, and as a result his client had been torched.

And instead, I was on the outside looking in, and saw a desperate man hanging on by his fingernails, with the curtains coming down around him, like the end of a Eugene O'Neill tragedy.

★

For over three years, I was closer to Wayne than anybody in the world, apart from his wife, Susan. And the way our relationship ended breaks my heart. I don't blame him for that—I blame myself. I'd compromised my own principles, and my reasons for joining the NRA. Ultimately I'd spent the vast majority of my time defending an administration that needed to be replaced. My days were filled with infighting, politics, mismanagement, paranoia, and dysfunction. I'd failed at reforming and modernizing the place the way I'd hoped, and done nothing to expand the association's footprint with the other ninety-five million gun owners who were not members. It felt awful, but I also knew I had lost my soul working for Wayne.

And my relationship with Bill Brewer ended at the same time. But what I learned at the NRA was, *That's politics. That's Washington. Anybody can roll on anybody, at any moment, for any reason.* Bill Brewer said over and over that loyalty is what matters. At one point, earlier in the year, we were in a meeting, the three of us, Wayne, Bill, and me. Bill said to Wayne, pointing at me, "That guy is the only guy in the building who is loyal to you. Who else is going to get up and testify on your behalf?"

I realized the hard way, though, that with Wayne, and with Bill too, loyalty was a one-way street. I'd spent every day working with Bill for nearly two years, went to bat for him, and poured everything into achieving success. Despite being warned, I was drawn into his orbit and made the professional mistake of becoming too close to our attorney. It led to miscalculations on his value to the association, and allowed him, with Wayne's acquiescence, to run roughshod and unfettered all over the place. Looking back, that may be my largest failure in my time there, leading to astronomical legal billings. At some point you have to weigh the monthly expenses versus settling, which we should have done long ago with Ackerman McQueen. (Angus McQueen had died of cancer in July of 2019, but the lawsuits dragged on.) If Letitia James has a problem with Ackerman's billings, that's her issue, not the NRA's. The financial damage was significant. And the fight has gone on too long.

Bill knew that if Wayne left, he would be gone as well. So he had every reason to do whatever was necessary to support Wayne. And there you have it. Saving the pope was simply too profitable a business to get out of. And I'd cleared the way. Although there is plenty of blame to go around. The board will need to step in and act like a genuine board of directors, and provide real oversight.

★

The NRA today is a mess. I assume that is clear from reading these pages. But it's only gotten worse since I left. I seriously question whether it can survive in its present form. It will require a full turnaround and overhaul at this point.

I believe deeply in the mission of the NRA—in supporting the rights and responsibilities of the Second Amendment. That was why I joined. The right to keep and bear arms, on a most basic level, affords every individual an opportunity to protect himself or herself, and offers a safeguard against tyranny. And gun owners need an organization that will stand up for their rights.

But the problems with the NRA, as it currently exists, are considerable. It wastes too much of the membership's money on programs that should have been stopped thirty years ago, with no measurement of return on investment whatsoever, a bloated bureaucracy that could operate with a third of the people, and tens of millions of dollars in legal fees all spent to protect a corrupt pope, not save the institution. As one NRA official who spoke with *Guardian* reporter Peter Stone said (requesting anonymity): "The widespread COVID layoffs and furloughs have further harmed both the NRA's legal capacity and political influence beyond what was already a troubling deterioration." The official added, the outlook this election year for NRA spending was "deeply concerning."[1]

At the root of this was the devil's bargain the NRA made with Ackerman McQueen. Ackerman, as I've said, did some good early work, but there was little oversight on their invoices, their prices were way out of line with the market, and most egregious of all, they were the firm that helped to brand the NRA into an organization that focused on the most extreme factions of gun owners, and pushed NRATV. Because fear campaigns work, they pushed Wayne into constantly pouring gasoline on the flames, turning the National Rifle Association into one that many Americans view with distrust—a "terrorist organization" in the minds of some.

Ackerman made a fortune off the NRA, spent millions on the lost cause of NRATV and other boondoggles, and are a primary reason why the NRA is an organization that could only say "No" in the face of school shootings and mass murder.

So much has to change. It will be a tall task for a board not structurally built for such a feat. They will really need to come together, acknowledge the situation, and make some big changes. Either they will do it or Letitia James in New York will do it herself.

★

Change is coming. In December of last year, the *New York Times* reported that Letitia James, the New York attorney general, was "deepening" her investigation of the NRA, with fresh subpoenas covering campaign finance, payments to board members, and tax compliance. This is the same office that closed down President Trump's foundation.

One of the new things James is looking into are transfers from the NRA Foundation to other NRA entities. The foundation sent $36 million to the NRA, tax filings showed; an earlier analysis by the *Times* suggested that the foundation had transferred more than $200 million to the NRA between 2010 and 2017. Some experts claim the foundation became a back door for tax-deductible donations to the NRA itself (only donations to the foundation are tax-deductible).[2] And now Karl Racine, the attorney general of the District of Columbia, where the NRA Foundation is chartered, is investigating.[3] Mark Owens, who for ten years was the head of the IRS division that oversees tax-exempt organizations, said, "The litany of red flags is just extraordinary.... There is a tremendous range of what appears to be the misuse of assets for the benefit of certain venders and people in control. Those facts, if confirmed, could lead to the revocation of the NRA's tax-exempt status." And without that, in the words of the *Times*, the NRA could likely not survive.[4]

At the same time that the association is under attack from the offices of attorneys general, it was outspent by gun control groups in the 2018 midterms. And given the NRA's current finances, it doesn't look like it will be able to come close to matching the level of support it provided Trump and Republicans in 2016.

Perhaps that is why the NRA only kicked a measly $300,000 into the November 2019 Virginia state elections to preserve the Republican majority. Outspent by gun control groups, the NRA lost, and both houses of the legislature, and the governor's office, are now in Democratic control for the first time in over twenty years. And those in power in Richmond have already begun calling for new gun regulations. Tens of thousands of gun owners, carrying handguns, rifles, and tactical gear, have protested—nonviolently. But it has cast the NRA's future ability to influence elections gravely into question.

There is blood in the water, and even the gun control groups see that the NRA "is weaker than they've ever been."[5]

At a board meeting in January, Wayne LaPierre was secretly recorded saying that the NRA had lost over $100 million over the previous two years between its legal bills and declining revenue opportunities. He slashed the budget by $80 million, "down to the studs."[6]

And then came the coronavirus. In response, Wayne laid off sixty employees, cut back the workweek to four days, and reduced everyone's salary by 20 percent for the foreseeable future. (No need to worry about Wayne paying the rent—in 2018, he received a 57 percent salary increase, to $2.18 million.)

I'm convinced the pandemic was a godsend for Wayne. He'll use the fear and confusion to explain away many of the NRA's financial troubles and mismanagement. It's almost biblical, and apologies to Charlton Heston and Moses, but a plague year will give the pharaoh political cover for all the association's financial woes.

★

Meanwhile, the lawsuits drag on, and there is a drumbeat of media coverage every time there is a new filing by Ackerman McQueen or the NRA—a couple of lawsuits that should have been settled long ago, and have done considerable damage financially and from a PR standpoint.

But the feud goes on, and I would guess a third of the members' dues are going to legal fees at this point.

And the fierce political tug-of-war rages between gun owners and the folks who believe in more gun control. While campaigning in Michigan in March 2020, Democratic front-runner Joe Biden almost came to fisticuffs with a UAW worker who confronted Biden saying, "You are actively trying to infringe on our Second Amendment rights and take away our guns."

Surrounded by a phalanx of UAW workers, Biden responded, "Wait wait wait wait . . . I did not say that, I did not say that. I support the Second Amendment."

But the UAW gun owner refused to back down. "You work for me . . . You will never, I mean ever, touch our guns." (Biden had previously come out in favor of a universal background check, and a ban on AR-15s.)

Biden responded, "I don't work for you. Give me a break, man. Don't be such a horse's ass."

The exchange shows how far apart gun owners and gun control activists are. And I think it underscores how effective the NRA has been in framing the gun rights issue in terms of liberty, where any attempt at gun regulation is seen as a full-scale assault on the Second Amendment, and a first step toward gun confiscation.

Nor has the NRA changed its polarizing messaging. Country music legend Charlie Daniels, in a promotional video he recorded for the NRA from quarantine at his home in Tennessee, had a stark message in May 2020, just two months before his death: "They want your guns. They want 'em all."[7]

So can the NRA survive as it exists today? Will it rebuff the investigation into its tax-exempt status? Will Wayne, preoccupied with "staying out of jail," according to allegations in court documents filed in the NRA's battle against Ackerman, abdicate the throne and bring about the regime change the organization so desperately needs?[8] Can the NRA be restructured in a way that brings genuine oversight to the organization, rather than allowing the association through mismanagement and lack of leadership to run amok?

I hope so. I hope that the NRA can become that organization. The hundred million gun owners and supporters of the Second Amendment need a strong organization that will stand up for their rights. And that shouldn't be hard—the vast majority of Americans support the Second Amendment. But to do so, it needs to be part of the solution to gun violence and school shootings, and lead. It needs to be less extreme and inflammatory, and more focused on gun safety, education, and responsible gun ownership.

And the association needs to begin the effort to reach across the aisle and once again embrace the 41 percent of Democrats who own guns and believe in the Second Amendment. Nonprofit organizations, by law, are legally required to be nonpartisan. Interestingly, as I write this book during the COVID-19 pandemic, it's estimated that over two million *new* gun owners purchased their first weapon in the last several months. That may be the biggest jump in new gun ownership ever. But as Aaron Davis, a former NRA fund-raiser interviewed for the *Frontline* documentary "NRA Under Fire," acknowledged, the "NRA is part of a political movement that is, through and through, Republican in every part of the word." It needs to reach out to the 80 percent of gun owners who are in favor of background checks, not just the very vocal minority who see any regulation as an attempt to take away their guns.

The right to carry a gun for protection has been part of our nation's history since its founding, almost 250 years ago. It helped to secure our independence from the British. It provided the tools to enable us to conquer the West and achieve our manifest destiny. The colonists' courage and the pioneers' rugged individualism and belief in individual freedom are baked into our cultural DNA. If the NRA doesn't survive in its current form—and I hope and believe that it will—I am confident that another organization will spring up in its place, an organization more willing to reach across the political aisle and join hands to ensure our safety, and that will represent the positions and rights of all gun owners. The strength of the NRA was, has, and will be the gun-owning voters. Even if the NRA goes, those voters will remain, eager to embrace another group willing to advance their interests.

★

As for me, after I left the NRA, my phone, which would ring a thousand times a day, went quiet. I found the sudden silence allowed me the space to look back on and acknowledge my failures, the failures of the people who hijacked the NRA, including me, who were more focused on pouring gas on the fire and sowing discord than on grappling with finding ways to prevent mass shootings and save lives, and training citizens in firearms safety, and protecting the Second Amendment.

I have tried to describe the events that took place at the NRA as honestly and truthfully as possible. For three and a half years, I had become a part of the great Washington political swamp—a part of everything I despised before enlisting in Wayne's army. Now it is time to wash away the residue of the swamp and rejoin the rest of humanity.

In the end, I find I'm neither the villain nor the hero of this story. Instead, I feel like I'm a kind of pilgrim who lost his way, who abandoned his principles and lost his footing, for a time. But I'll leave that up to the readers to decide.

I had hoped to accomplish so much more in those heady times when I helped to run one of the most powerful lobbies in America. Now, not on the front lines, I am no longer on call 24/7, flying up to New York to meet with Bill Brewer to discuss legal strategies, talking daily with Wayne, managing the next crises, fighting internecine battles inside the building, sitting at the top of the NRA in silence as the next mass shooting plays out, or worrying about what the president tweeted out the previous night. I'd landed in D.C. with idealistic goals and visions to make the NRA a better place, and left as someone who had become the Establishment, morally bankrupt. It is time to change that.

I had ignored the toll the constant battles had taken on my family and my personal life. When the mission was *everything*—until it wasn't.

Today, I once again have the space to breathe freely and find my way. I'm back in Michigan, back home at the lake, a perfect backdrop to rethink the sense of purpose I had when I joined the NRA.

To make a difference. To save lives.

My plan is to do that once again, on my own terms, from outside. To be an informed voice in helping to tamp down the fear and anger in the gun debate, and work with an open mind, across the political aisles. To bridge the divide between the people who advocate for gun rights and those who would impose more gun regulation. And to address the real issues when it comes to reducing gun violence and making our country a safer, and freer, place.

As I was writing this book, my father challenged me, asking, "Son, what is your plan to make a difference?" Which got me thinking... out of the box. We need a breakthrough to eradicate senseless acts of gun violence. To task our best minds in a nonpartisan way to move the dialogue on gun violence forward based on data. That is...someone needs to form a foundation with an unwavering mission to gather, develop, and analyze the facts behind gun violence, unencumbered by an agenda, and devoid of propaganda. To focus on mass murders, suicide, and gun violence in inner cities. To be a consolidator of information, as well as a sponsor of research where information is lacking, and facilitate healthy debates, and brainstorm to generate new workable ideas.

As this book is printing, I am working to bring together a group of directors from both sides of the political aisle to research gun violence without bias, using the best available tools and approaches. People who have a passion for the truth, and believe that a heartfelt, intelligent discussion is possible on arguably the most controversial issue we face. To achieve this audacious set of goals will require the input of data scientists, crime scientists, and researchers. A top-tier team that understands the urgency to gather the facts, analyze them, and come up with new suggestions based on those facts. Filling the gap on what the NRA helped to shut down—government-funded research into gun violence. I believe that regardless of one's beliefs about gun rights and gun regulations, any effective ability to reduce gun violence, particularly in large urban areas, should be explored seriously and with vigor. It is a tall order, but one that I believe holds tremendous promise. Without having a true baseline of established facts, it's hard to have a fruitful discussion.

★

When I left the NRA, my daughters told me, "We're really glad we have our dad back. You're a lot more fun now."

They were more right than I knew at the time. I'll be making that up to my wife and kids for years to come.

Acknowledgments

First, a quick note about the writing of this book. The heart of the book is based on my personal recollections with the people I describe, based on my three and a half years working side by side with Wayne LaPierre at the NRA headquarters, and the two years serving on the board of directors.

This book was challenging—even painful—to write, and I took no joy in taking it on. But at the end of the day I had no choice but to write *Inside the NRA*. The five million NRA members have a right to the facts, as do the other one hundred million gun owners in America who aren't NRA members. They deserve nothing less. The NRA— or an organization like the NRA—that supports gun safety, training, and our Second Amendment rights is essential to our heritage as Americans and necessary to save lives. As a reader, you yourself will have to make your own judgment about the NRA and its place in the life of our nation. I have nothing to hide and everything to lose.

First and foremost, I want to thank my wife for her unwavering support of me. Period. You are amazing. I cannot imagine a life without you. You push me to the edges and support me more than anyone deserves.

To my mother, I hope you would be proud; I miss you. You had an idea about raising children and allowing them to find their own way. It is the biggest gift you could have given me. To my father, the same. I love you very much. Thank you for sharing with me your love of water, trout, the chase, and for sticking with me. Without you both I wouldn't be who I am. To my brother Noah—I hope this shows you my desire for truth.

To Elijah, Naomi, Eva, Miriam—I love you all so very much. I hope this book gives you some insight into me and my absence. I have much to give back to you all. With all my heart. Life isn't a straight line for any of us.

To my lawyers, Mark MacDouall and Abbey McNaughton—my thanks to you and your colleagues for your friendship, good counsel, and clear perspectives on life in America these days.

Steve Bannon, I couldn't have asked for a better sounding board.

To Roger Scholl, my collaborator and co-author. Nothing happens without you. You have been an amazing writer, partner, and truth seeker. Thank you for taking the journey with me.

To Michael Carlisle, my literary agent—you're the best. Thank you for believing in me and constantly pushing me. I'll never forget walking with you on that cold winter morning when we first discussed the book.

To Sean Desmond, the publisher of Twelve, and my editor. How can I express my gratitude for your belief in me, and in the truth? Thank you. I'm more grateful than you know. All of which speaks volumes about my imprint, Twelve, and my publishing house, Hachette Book Group, in this day and age, to stand in the line of fire and be a beacon of light.

To Marlo, Ingmar, Manu, Brian, Tracy, Mark, Jeff, Mike, Leann, Kina, Nellie—thank you for challenging me and talking me off the ledge! You are my rocks.

And last but not least, to my high school English teacher Mrs. Bishop—somehow you pulled it out of me, and all of us in class, despite my efforts to do the opposite!

Notes

Prologue

1. Danny Hakim, "Inside Wayne LaPierre's Battle for the NRA," *New York Times Magazine*, December 22, 2019.
2. Lydia Saad, "What Percentage of Americans Own Guns?," Gallup, August 14, 2019, https://news.gallup.com/poll/264932/percentage -americans-own-guns.aspx.
3. Asher Stockler, "The National Rifle Association Is Laying Off Staff," *Newsweek*, March 23, 2020.

Chapter 2: The Wizard of Oz

1. Hakim, "Inside Wayne LaPierre's Battle for the NRA."
2. Ibid.
3. David Cole, *Engines of Liberty: The Power of Citizen Activists to Make Constitutional Change* (New York: Basic Books, 2016), chapter 11, "People Power."
4. Robert Maguire, "Audit Shows NRA Spending Surged $100 Million Amidst Pro-Trump Push in 2016," OpenSecrets.org, November 15, 2017.
5. Nick Corasaniti and Maggie Haberman, "Donald Trump Suggests 'Second Amendment People' Could Act Against Hillary Clinton," *New York Times*, August 9, 2016.
6. Sam Frizell, "NRA Releases New Ad Calling Hillary Clinton a Hypocrite," *Time*, August 9, 2016.

7. Mike Spies and Ashley Balcerzak, "The NRA Placed Big Bets on the 2016 Election, and Won Almost All of Them," OpenSecrets.org, November 9, 2016.

8. "Percentage of Population in the United States Owning at Least One Gun in 2017, by Political Party Affiliation," Statista, December 5, 2019, https://www.statista.com/statistics/249775.

9. Cole, *Engines of Liberty*, chapter 7, "One State at a Time."

10. Tim Dickinson, "The NRA vs. America," *Rolling Stone*, February 14, 2013.

11. Bill Clinton, *My Life* (New York: Knopf, 2004).

12. Dickinson, "The NRA vs. America."

13. Ibid.

Chapter 3: The Puppet Master

1. https://www.esquire.com/news-politics/a18663982/who-is-dana-loesch-nra-spokesperson/.

Chapter 4: The Hammer

1. Ali Vitali, "Trump to NRA: 'Eight-Year Assault on Gun Rights Is Over,'" NBC News, April 28, 2017, https://www.nbcnews.com/politics/white-house/trump-nra-eight-year-assault-gun-rights-over-n752446.

2. Ibid.

3. Ibid.

4. Tara Golshan, "Trump's Madcap, Unscripted Gun Control Meeting with Lawmakers, Explained," *Vox*, February 28, 2018, https://www.vox.com/2018/2/28/17064120/trump-gun-control-meeting-congress-explained.

5. Michael Suede, "What Percentage of the US Adult Population Has a Felony Conviction?," *Libertarian News*, June 5, 2014.

6. Mike Spies, "The Arms Dealer," *New Yorker*, March 5, 2018.

7. Michael C. Bender, "Pistol-Packing Grandma Helps NRA Push Pro-Gun Laws," Bloomberg, May 11, 2012.

8. Cole, *Engines of Liberty*, chapter 7, "One State at the Time," p. 120.

9. Spies, "The Arms Dealer."

10. Ibid.

11. Ibid.

12. Ibid.

13. Ibid.

14. Ibid.

15. Ibid.

16. Cole, *Engines of Liberty*, chapter 7, "One State at a Time."

17. Ibid.

18. Cole, *Engines of Liberty*, chapter 10.

19. Megan Henney, "The NRA Lost $55M in Income in 2017," FoxBusiness, November 30, 2018.

20. Jacey Fortin, "NRA Suit Claims Cuomo's 'Blacklist' Has Cost It Millions," *New York Times*, August 4, 2018.

21. "Weapon Types Used in Mass Shooting in the United States Between 1982 and February 2020," Statista, May 4, 2020, https://www.statista.com /statistics/476409/mass-shootings-in-the-us-by-weapon-types-used/.

22. Torie Bosch, "Thirty-Two Victims, Two Guns?," *Slate*, April 17, 2007, https://slate.com/news-and-politics/2007/04/how-did-cho-seung-hui -kill-so-many-people-with-just-a-pair-of-handguns.html.

23. Awr Hawkins, "Johns Hopkins Study: No Evidence 'Assault Weapon' Bans Reduce Mass Shootings," Breitbart, February 18, 2020.

24. Hilary Brueck, "Switzerland Has a Stunningly High Rate of Gun Ownership," *Independent*, February 27, 2018.

25. Robert Farley, "Gillibrand Misleads on Trump's Bump Stock Ban," Factcheck.org, June 5, 2019.

Chapter 5: From Russia with Love

1. "Russian Who Infiltrated NRA Linked to Putin's Sanctioned Biker Gang Leader Caught Invading Ukraine," The Stern Facts, August 24, 2018, https://thesternfacts.com/russian-who-infiltrated-nra-linked-to-putins -sanctioned-biker-gang-leader-caught-invading-ukraine-dc4483eb3791.

2. Wikipedia, "Aleksandr Torshin," section "Allegations in Spain," https:// en.wikipedia.org/wiki/Aleksandr_Torshin#Allegations_in_Spain.

3. Anita Wadhwani and Joel Ebert, "Nashville Lawyer Who Introduced Russian Operative to the NRA Has Ties to Blackburn," *Tennessean*, March, 20, 2018.

4. Tim Dickinson, "Inside the Decade-Long Russian Campaign to Infiltrate the NRA and Help Elect Trump," *Rolling Stone*, April 20, 2018.

5. Ibid.

6. Tim Mak, "Depth of Russian Politician's Cultivation of NRA Ties Revealed," *Morning Edition*, NPR, March 1, 2018.

7. Dickinson, "Inside the Decade-Long Russian Campaign to Infiltrate the NRA and Help Elect Trump."

8. Ibid.

9. Ibid.

10. Ibid.

11. Danny Hakim, "N.R.A. Seeks Distance from Russia as Investigations Heat Up," *New York Times*, January 28, 2019, https://www.nytimes.com/2019/01/28/us/nra-russia-maria-butina-investigations.html.

12. Ibid.

13. Ibid.

14. Peter Stone and Greg Gordon, "FBI Investigating Whether Russian Money Went to NRA to Help Trump," Impact2020, January 18, 2018.

15. Ibid.

16. Matthew Rosenberg, "Maria Butina Pleads Guilty to Role in a Russian Effort to Influence Conservatives," *New York Times*, December 13, 2018.

17. Matt Apuzzo, Katie Benner, and Sharon LaFraniere, "Maria Butina, Who Sought 'Back Channel' Meeting for Trump and Putin, Is Charged as Russian Agent," *New York Times*, July 16, 2018.

18. Ibid.

19. Rosenberg, "Maria Butina Pleads Guilty to Role in a Russian Effort to Influence Conservatives."

Chapter 6: Under Attack

1. Clark Mintock, "Trump Promises Parkland Survivors," *Independent*, February 21, 2018.

2. Carol D. Leonnig and Tom Hamburger, "How a Hard-Charging Lawyer Helped Fuel a Civil War Inside the NRA," *Washington Post*, September 18, 2019.

3. Ibid.

4. Mark Maremont, "NRA Awarded Contracts to Firms with Ties to Top Officials," *Wall Street Journal*, November 30, 2018.
5. Mike Spies, "An Internal Memo Raises New Questions about Self-Dealing at the NRA," *New Yorker*, May 7, 2019.
6. Ibid.
7. Ibid.
8. Mark Maremont, "NRA Awarded Contracts to Firms with Ties to Top Officials." *Wall Street Journal*, November 30, 2018.
9. Ibid.

Chapter 7: Game of Thrones

1. Leonnig and Hamburger, "How a Hard-Charging Lawyer Helped Fuel a Civil War Inside the NRA."
2. Betsy Swan, "Leaked Documents," *Daily Beast*, May 11, 2019.
3. Mike Spies, "New Documents Raise Ethical and Billing Concerns About the NRA's Outside Counsel," *New Yorker*, July 30, 2019.
4. Ibid.
5. Igor Derysh, "Court Filings Show the NRA Is in Shambles," *Salon*, May 1, 2020.
6. Leonnig and Hamburger, "How a Hard-Charging Lawyer Helped Fuel a Civil War Inside the NRA."
7. Danny Hakim, "Inside Wayne LaPierre's Battle for the NRA," *New York Times Magazine*, December 22, 2019.
8. Ibid.
9. Ibid.
10. Spies, "New Documents Raise Ethical and Billing Concerns About the NRA's Outside Counsel."
11. Jane Coaston, "Why the NRA Is Struggling," *Vox*, January 17, 2019, https://www.vox.com/policy-and-politics/2019/1/17/18167430/nra-2018-midterms-trump.
12. Kristin Myers, "NRA 'Could Shut Down Forever,' Group Warns in Fundraising Letter," Yahoo Finance, March 29, 2019, https://finance.yahoo.com/news/nra-could-shut-down-forever-group-warns-in-fundraising-letter-194322998.html.

13. Mike Spies, "An Internal Memo Raises New Questions About Self-Dealing at the NRA," *New Yorker*, May 7, 2019.

14. Betsy Swan, "NRA Suspends Top Lawyer While Oliver North Warns Group," *Daily Beast*, April 27, 2019.

Chapter 8: Shootout in Indy

1. Tim Mak, "NRA Infighting During Convention," NPR, April 28, 2019, https://www.npr.org/2019/04/28/717970505/nra-infighting -during-convention.

Chapter 9: "The NRA Is a Criminal Organization"

1. Carol D. Leonnig and Beth Reinhard, "NRA Chief Sought Purchase of $6 Million Mansion in the Wake of Parkland Shooting," *Washington Post*, August 7, 2019.

2. Ibid.

3. Polly Mosendz, Neil Weinberg, and David Voreacos, "NRA Suspends Two Leaders Amid Accusations of Coup Attempt," Bloomberg, June 20, 2019.

4. Will Van Sant and Daniel Nass, "The NRA Exodus," The Trace, March 5, 2020.

5. Mike Spies, "The NRA's Longtime CFO Was Caught Embezzling Before Joining the Organization," *New Yorker*, June 19, 2019.

6. Peter Stone, "The NRA Is in Grave Danger: Group's Troubles Are Blow to Trump's 2020 Bid," *Guardian*, May 9, 2019.

7. Manuel Roig-Franzia, "Lanny Davis, the Ultimate Clinton Loyalist, Is Now Michael Cohen's Lawyer. But Don't Call It Revenge," *Washington Post*, August 23, 2018.

8. Elaina Plott, "Trump's Phone Calls with Wayne LaPierre Reveal NRA's Influence," *Atlantic*, August 20, 2019, https://www.theatlantic.com/ politics/archive/2019/08/trump-background-checks-nra/596413/.

9. Maggie Haberman, Annie Karni, and Danny Hakim, "NRA Gets Results on Gun Laws in One Phone Call with Trump," *New York Times*, August 20, 2019.

10. Joel Shannon, "San Francisco Declares NRA a 'Domestic Terrorist Organization,'" *USA Today*, September 4, 2019.
11. Maggie Haberman and Annie Karni, "NRA's LaPierre Asks Trump to 'Stop the Games' over Gun Legislation in Discussion About Its Support," *New York Times*, September 27, 2019.
12. Ibid.
13. Ibid.

Chapter 10: Searching for Answers

1. Christopher Ingraham, "One in Five Americans Wants the Second Amendment to Be Repealed," *Washington Post*, March 27, 2020.
2. "Project Exile," Wikipedia, https://en.wikipedia.org/wiki/Project_Exile.
3. Sun Times Wire, "Police Release 2018 Shooting Numbers," *Chicago Sun Times*, January 1, 2019.
4. Timothy Williams, "What Are 'Red Flag' Laws and How Do They Work?" *New York Times*, August 6, 2019.

Chapter 11: Cleaning House

1. Peter Stone, "Exclusive: NRA has shed 200 staffers this year as group faced financial crisis," *The Guardian,* June 29, 2020.
2. Danny Hakim, "New York Deepens Its Investigation into the NRA," *New York Times*, December 9, 2019.
3. Ibid.
4. Mike Spies, "Secrecy, Self-Dealing and Greed at the NRA," *New Yorker*, April 17, 2019.
5. Joe Heim, "The NRA Is Weaker Than They've Ever Been," *Washington Post*, November 5, 2019.
6. Tim Mak, "Secret Recording Reveal's NRA's Legal Troubles Have Cost the Organization $100 Million," NPR, April 21, 2020.
7. Jeremy W. Peters, "How Abortion, Guns and Church Closings Made Coronavirus a Culture War," *New York Times*, April 20, 2020.
8. Igor Derysh, "Court Filings Show the NRA Is in Shambles—and Wayne LaPierre Hopes His Lawyer Can 'Keep Him out of Jail,'" *Salon*, May 1, 2020.